MAKING THE

CLIENT

CONNECTION

MAXIMIZING THE POWER OF YOUR
PERSONALITY | PRESENTATIONS | PRESENCE

GARY DeMOSS AND MITCH ANTHONY

Dearborn™
Trade Publishing
A **Kaplan Professional** Company

Vice President and Publisher: Cynthia A. Zigmund
Acquisitions Editor: Mary B. Good
Senior Managing Editor: Jack Kiburz
Interior Design: Lucy Jenkins
Cover Design: Billert Communications
Typesetting: the dotted i

Published by Dearborn Trade Publishing
A Kaplan Professional Company

Printed in the United States of America

04   05   06   10   9   8   7   6   5   4   3   2   1

Library of Congress Cataloging-in-Publication Data

Anthony, Mitch.
    Making the client connection : maximizing the power of your personality, presentations, and presence / Mitch Anthony and Gary DeMoss.
        p.   cm.
    Includes bibliographical references and index.
    ISBN 0-7931-8696-X (7.25x9 hardcover)
    1. Financial planners—Marketing. 2. Investment advisors—Marketing. 3. Relationship marketing. 4. Customer relations—Management. I. DeMoss, Gary. II. Title.
HG179.5.A578 2004
332.024′0068′8—dc22

                                                                    2003024692

Dearborn Trade books are available at special quantity discounts to use for sales promotions, employee premiums, or educational purposes. Please call our Special Sales Department to order or for more information at 800-245-2665, e-mail trade@dearborn.com, or write to Dearborn Trade Publishing, 30 South Wacker Drive, Suite 2500, Chicago, IL 60606-7481.

Contents

Preface   v

PART ONE | Making Personal Connections

1. How Sales Professionals Make the World Go Round: "From a Box of Soap to a Soapbox"   3
2. How to Meet, Greet, and Treat Your Clients: Understanding the Dynamics of Charisma   13
3. The Emotionally Intelligent Financial Professional   23
4. Moving from Me to We   37
5. Understanding Personality DNA   53

PART TWO | Making the Personality Connection

6. You Have to Read Them before You Can Lead Them: Understanding Personality Signals   67
7. Keys to Connecting with Personalities   79
8. Pushing the Right Buttons   93
9. Turning Conflict into Opportunity   99
10. Connecting in Conflict   109

PART THREE | Connecting with the Individual

11. The Human Drama: Act I—Revealing the Characters and Dramas   123
12. The Human Drama: Act II—Addressing the Dramas   133
13. Act III—Resolving the Conflicts: Moving from Agreement to Action   143
14. The Power of a Story   151

PART FOUR | **Connecting with Dynamic Presentations**

15. Cornerstone #1 of Dynamic Presenting: Convicted and Convincing   167
16. Cornerstone #2 of Dynamic Presenting: Prepared for Battle   177
17. Cornerstone #3 of Dynamic Presenting: Having a Flight Plan   189
18. Cornerstone #4 of Dynamic Presenting: Deliver with Style   199

PART FIVE | **Connecting with the Crowd**

19. Know Thy Audience   211
20. Mistakes Speakers Make and How to Avoid Them   217
21. Setting the Hook   227
22. In the Palm of Your Hand: The Dynamics of Connecting with the Masses and Moving Past Fear   235

Bibliography   243
Index   244

Preface

Over the past 20 years, I have spent virtually every day of my business life observing or participating in the art of connecting with people. The past 10 years, I have focused with great fascination on what makes some individuals more successful than others in making those connections. I have been exposed to several sales training programs, and as professional trainer, I have studied about every sales system on the market. When asked my opinion on what I feel the best system is, I have a hard time stating with conviction that any one system is the best. As anyone who has been involved seriously in making a connection with people has discovered, no simple system deals fully with the complexity of human beings.

My evolution of thinking regarding what made people successful in the art of making personal connections began with thinking that what was most important was *process*. I had a firm conviction that a disciplined process must be involved to make people in our business successful. This process can be crystallized into three components: discovery, presentation, and advancing the case. You must first discover who your client is. You must present your products and services in a way that ties into the needs and values exposed in the discovery process. Finally, you must help the client to act by advancing the decision or closing the proposals you are making.

Next, I was exposed to a simple concept that values are critical to understand when connecting with people. The work of Russ Alan Prince involving a study of 911 affluent investors revealed to me the different values of this highly prized market segment and how important they are to connecting with this group. Also supporting the role values play is Bill Bachrach's excellent book, *Value Based Selling*. Bill has been a strong proponent of instilling this concept to financial professionals.

Acknowledging that both having a disciplined process and understanding a client's values are very important, my coauthor of this book, Mitch Anthony, introduced me to the critical necessity to understand the personality of the person being dealt with. I became convinced that this third factor was one of the most important for individuals who desired to improve their connectivity skills. This topic is covered extensively in Chapters 3 and 10 and illustrates how a person's personality impacts how he or she receives communication.

This book is an attempt to make what can be considered a complex topic—connecting with people and helping them act in their own behalf—simple by sharing the processes, values, and personality approaches used by the masters.

—Gary DeMoss

Ted Benna, father of the 401(k), was recently asked what he thought was the most underrated force in the financial services industry today. His answer, the "personal relational dynamic." This is precisely where wise financial professionals and firms are adjusting their focus—on making better human connections.

You may think, My practice is very sophisticated with a very technical approach to my clients' investment needs. Yet, the element of the human connection is more critical today than it has ever been. Today's investor faces many more decisions regarding investment choices. Events like 9/11, the bear market, and corporate corruption have caused great emotional turmoil for clients. If the truth be known, people want and need someone to connect with them on what is the best way to approach their financial future. Our business is and always will be one where success hinges on connecting with "who" our client is.

My neighbor came to me recently and informed me that he had just fired his financial advisor, because after years of doing business together he suddenly realized that this advisor had never asked one question about his personal life. He had failed to make a human connection.

I have stood and delivered speeches in front of millions of people in the last 20 years and have always felt like the art of making the human connection is a never-ending study. I can always get better. The quest of this topic has made a phenomenal difference in my life and career, and I have seen it make a difference in the lives of many other professionals.

Parts I and II, "Making Personal Connections" and "Making the Personality Connection," expose you to the fascinating role that our personalities play in the human connection process.

In Part III, "Connecting with the Individual," we give you some thought-provoking ideas on how to structure one-on-one presentations.

In Part IV, "Connecting with Dynamic Presentations," we discuss the four cornerstones of dynamic connection that people who are skilled in this art have. These cornerstones are conviction, preparation, structure, and delivery. This is a great place to start challenging yourself if you are just beginning or are relatively new in this business. They are also great reminders for the more experienced in our business to keep focusing on these qualities.

Finally, in Part V, "Connecting with the Crowd," we discuss some general ideas on how to deal most effectively with groups. Also included in this section is a specific focus on the top mistakes people make in front of audiences.

Our objective in writing this book was to provide a panoramic view of the human connection process. We recommend that you read this book one section at a time, in order to focus and meditate on those specific principles. This will help you digest the principles necessary for mastering the skills needed to connect with both individuals and crowds.

Our hope is that your career will see a quantum leap by expressing who you are and what you believe through the development of your connectivity skills.

—Mitch Anthony

ACKNOWLEDGMENTS

I would like to acknowledge the following people for the opportunities they afforded me and for assisting me in writing:

- My wife, Laurelyn, and children, Brandon, Matt, Jonathan, Leah, Lauren, and Tyler, for putting up with all my travel
- My parents, Robert and Janet, for their lifelong support
- Bill Molinari, former president of Van Kampen Funds, for believing in me for all the years at Van Kampen
- Jim Morel, President of J.A.M. Consulting, for encouraging me to move into the training and speaking field
- Steve Mikez, private consultant, for his ideas in the persuasion process
- Mitch Anthony, coauthor, for his inspiration to write this book

- My associates at Van Kampen Consulting who assisted in the editing process, Judy Wiegold, Karen Leparulo, Jack Tierney, and Kristan Mulley

—Gary DeMoss

Repeated and never-ending thanks to my wife, Debbie, who makes me better in every way she can. I would like to thank Cindy Zigmund who has been an unwavering source of caring critique and refinement in this and many other books. Thanks to my coauthor Gary DeMoss for his conviction and passionate pursuit toward meeting the needs of those we serve. Thanks to Sandy Thomas, Lucy Jenkins, Robin Bermel, Courtney Goethals, Trey Thoelcke, and Jack Kiburz and all those whose efforts and eagerness make projects like this successful. I owe you all a debt of thanks.

—Mitch Anthony

PART I

Making Personal Connections

How Sales Professionals Make the World Go Round

"From a Box of Soap to a Soapbox"

Persuasion, kind unassuming persuasion, should be adopted to influence the conduct of men.

—Abraham Lincoln

"I was standing in the aisle of the grocery store building an Ivory Soap display for the Procter & Gamble Company, who had been kind enough to hire me fresh out of college. I was 22 years old and, with my baby face, looked all of 16. One problem I occasionally had was being mistaken for one of the stock boys who worked for the grocery store. It happened again the morning that would forever change the way I looked at my job and career.

An elderly woman approached me and asked, 'Excuse me, can you direct me to the spices?'

'Oh,' I replied, 'I'm just a salesman.'

'You're just a what?' she asked.

'I'm just a soap salesman,' I replied. 'I'm just here to set up this display for Ivory Soap.'

'Well, young man, let me tell you something,' she began to lecture. 'There is no such thing as just a salesman. People who sell make the world go round. Just take a minute to think about it. This morning before I came here, I left my house, and the land where my house stands was sold by a farmer to a developer, who sold it to a builder, who sold the property to my husband and me, and we raised our family there. I got into my car that a good salesperson sold to me and drove down roads

3

built with materials that were sold. I think you're getting my idea here, young man. *There is no such thing as just a salesman. Salespeople sell products and services that make our lives better, and if they are not doing that, then they have no business selling them.* I'm sure that, somehow, the soap you're selling is somehow helping to improve people's quality of life. Remember, people need to be persuaded before they will improve their lives. You are in the business of connecting with people.'

I thanked the woman for her encouraging words, and with my raised esteem, directed her three rows down to the spices."

—Gary DeMoss

The above incident took place over 25 years ago, but fortuitously for Gary, it came early in his career. We have seen people in the world of sales, whose profession involves persuasion, who have never come to such a realization. They always seem to carry a tacit sense of imposing on other people's time and are, therefore, perceived that way—as an imposition, and as a burden. The little lecture Gary received next to the soap display started a necessary examination of how he viewed himself and his career. If, as a salesperson, he saw himself as an insignificant nobody with a "me too" product in an overcrowded marketplace, it would just be a matter of time before he would be swimming in the waters of mediocrity.

Gary had never before heard anyone articulate the perspective spoken by this wise woman. The sales professional is the energy that is spinning the globe on its axis. Change does not take place if somebody somewhere doesn't first persuade someone to make a change—someone has to *sell* it! Many think that, as sales professionals, they are somewhere between a carnival barker and a tax collector on society's totem pole. Even today, we try to cover up what we do daily—persuade people to take a course of action—by all the surnames we apply to salespeople. For example, a survey of different firms shows they describe their sales force as investment advisors, financial consultants, investment professionals, investment counselors, and so on. That was the sort of regard Gary, at the time, had suspected that the general public had for those who sold professionally. Selling was not the kind of job where you walked up to someone and proudly introduced yourself, saying, "Hi, I'm a salesperson!" Calling yourself a representative was more palatable, but that was simply a chocolate covering for salesperson. The lecture Gary received that morning, however, caused him to thoroughly examine what he was trying to persuade people to do. It caused him to pause and ask himself, "If they did what I was trying to persuade them to do, would it in any way improve their quality of life?" If, upon examination, Gary could not convince himself that what he was doing could make some sort of difference, then, in the words of the woman at the grocery store, he had no business selling.

Gary figured out some very good reasons to sell soap. For example, have you ever spent time around anyone who *doesn't* use soap? Gary arrived at good reasons to sell the other products that he was trained to sell. He also reasoned that this job was a great place to begin the process of becoming better at connecting with people.

Gary had walked into the store as a salesperson and walked out desiring to be a student of making human connections. His estimation of himself was raised in that short, chance conversation. Gary's focus about what he did for a living was transformed. It was no longer about the product—it was now about the customer and the value he could deliver. He wanted to learn everything he could, not about soap, but about people and how he could better persuade them to act in their own behalf. That conversation 25 years ago by that display of Ivory Soap eventually led Gary's career to the soapbox. The soapbox he stands on today is in teaching financial sales professionals how to better understand the value they can deliver in the lives of their clients.

It's not so important what a man is, but what he is becoming, for he
shall be what he is now becoming.

—Theodore Roosevelt

We know the short lecture that Gary received as a pup salesperson caused him to view his career path in a different way. His career was not going to be about climbing a ladder within a particular corporation; rather, it was going to be a quest of delivering the best value possible and to excel at communicating that value. That raising of sights has opened the doors to many persuasion opportunities in Gary's career in the sales realm. Some 20 years after persuading people to buy 19-cent boxes of soap—at a different company in the financial services world—he was given the job of helping to sell the company at a price tag of $1.2 billion. Gary came to the conclusion that we would like all our students and readers to come to: that the price tag of the product or service does not matter; selling all comes down to the same process—the process of helping people to act in their own best interests.

THE LONGEST YARD

During your next meeting, take a look at the distance between you and your client. If you're sitting across a desk or a table, about three feet lie between you and your client.

This distance represents not only physical separation but also possible separation of philosophy, motives, values, personality, and goals. The financial services business is all about the clients coming to a point to where they will trust you with both their hard-earned dollars and what they hope to accomplish with them. They have no reason to trust you until you give a convincing demonstration as to why they should trust you. This critical three feet of separation is what we call *the longest yard*. This distance is not bridged in a moment's time. Just because a client gives you assets to work with does not mean you have bridged this gap. The most observable gaps can be thought of in this way: gender (G), age (A), and personality (P). These three chief factors must be bridged to build a successful relationship. You cannot treat a 45-year-old female enterprising client the same way you would treat a 66-year-old analytical male. The fact that so many people leave their advisor relationships or do not entrust more assets to their financial professionals attests to the fact that they still feel degrees of separation.

It takes discipline to care where an ambulance is going.

—Anonymous

Your mission is to shrink the critical three feet of separation between you and your client. Relationships with clients are not static. That distance between financial professional and client is always in a dynamic, animated state, constantly expanding or contracting, depending on the temperature of the relationship at present. The distance in a good relationship could expand just a few inches by your not paying close enough attention when they talk. It could contract when you ask how their sick parent is recovering. This distance is always in flux, and you need to be cognizant of that fact because knowing how far your client or potential client perceives that separation is not always possible.

Great financial professionals are intuitively aware of the longest yard and how fickle that distance is, and they are constantly working toward closing down that gap. They take no relationship for granted, no matter how long it has been established. Great financial professionals understand that all relationships are dynamic in nature, and that the critical three feet of separation cannot be closed simply by telling their story. Many people mistakenly regard selling as a skill exclusive to speaking, communicating, or telling. Clear and brilliant speaking and communicating are certainly manifestations of a persuasive individual, but by no means constitute the whole formula. There is much more to the process of persuasion than dynamic telling.

Connecting with clients takes a combination of listening, positioning, speaking, solving, and acting. Excellent financial professionals do all of these things because they understand that their clients do not just care about what they know, but they also want to know that they care. The longest yard in business is fully bridged when clients understand that you are both competent and concerned regarding their financial welfare.

Build into your mind an awareness of these critical three feet that constitute the longest yard between you and your clients. Simply having this awareness will make you more cognitive of the impressions you give, the things you say, and the way you follow up on the promises you make. When you are fully conscious of this dynamic distance and its ever expanding or contracting nature, you will exercise more caution, concern, and follow-through. Every moment of every meeting with every client is an opportunity to connect. Clients are either being repelled further or drawn closer in. Your mission is to shrink that distance every opportunity you get.

WHAT BUSINESS ARE YOU IN?

If we are truly in the business of helping people, we must ask ourselves what we are attempting to persuade them to do. Are we trying to persuade them to agree with us, or are we trying to persuade them to act in their own best interest? All attempts at persuasion should be measured by our ability to positively influence behavior. If what we are saying or presenting does not add value, then it was nothing more than a song in the wind. The only reward we come away with is that we got to hear ourselves talk, and that reward will grow thin very quickly, as will our wallets, if we are not helping people help themselves. For your clients or prospective clients to nod their heads and say that they agree with you is one thing; it is wholly another matter for them to sign the dotted line and actually do something about their situation. What goes on in the heads of your clients between the time they nod and the time they sign the dotted line is something all great financial professionals understand and know how to influence. In Chapter 15 we will talk about what is going on in their thoughts at that moment and how you can become a master at helping people move first to agreement and, ultimately, to action.

SOME DISTURBING NEWS

We have witnessed many client presentations and public attempts at connecting and persuading delivered by financial professionals who seem to miss this point entirely. They throw seeds of knowledge on unbroken ground and wonder why people are reticent to sign the dotted line, or apply what they just heard. The seeds were poorly sown. There was nothing to disturb the hearers into believing that they needed to embrace the knowledge they were being offered. The seeds are quickly snatched away or blown away, and if potential clients do make a decision, the roots are quite shallow and the decision doesn't last for long. Persuasive skill is not judged by how charismatic and dynamic our delivery is, but rather by how decisive and lasting the client's action is. Do a good job of making human connections, and you will have clients bringing more assets to you for much longer periods of time—hopefully for a lifetime. This process of properly disturbing your audience, giving them the knowledge they need to change their situation, and implementing that change is what we call *the human drama* (which we will deal with later in Chapters 11 and 12).

OPPORTUNITY EVERYWHERE

Take a good, hard, analytical look at your business in light of the following questions: "How many opportunities are presented each day to connect with people? How about each month? Each year?" We're talking about every meeting, every phone call, every note, and every letter. We're not just talking about you but those who work for and with you as well. Every correspondence with every client or potential client is a connection opportunity and must be seen as such for you to optimize your production and effectiveness.

As Gary began to look at his company's opportunities for making connections he was blown away by the sheer magnitude of opportunities available. He found that his company, Van Kampen Investments, had over 750,000 phone calls to business partners or prospective business partners each year, and 500,000 such meetings face-to-face for a total 1.2 million connection opportunities each year. When you begin to look at each client contact as a connection opportunity, you become painfully aware of the need to train people in the art and science of making dynamic connections. This insight led Gary's company to begin to focus on developing the communication skill level of their sales force. From this came two programs, one that deals with consultative selling and a second that provides training on public-speaking skills, called Speak Performance. These programs are now in wide demand in the industry and are used internally to train wholesalers and representatives.

Chances are that you don't have 1.2 million human connection opportunities per year, but your business can no doubt grow, first by getting a handle on how many opportunities you do have, and secondly by optimizing each opportunity. When clients call with a question, do you ask questions to open up a new arena of conversation? When you call clients, do you ask about any new changes or challenges in their family or business? Do you exchange creative ideas for building business? When you stand up in front of a group of any size to talk, do you dump information or create opportunities for yourself? Do you query longtime clients about new ways of being of service to them, their family members, or others within their circle of influence? When you see your career as that of a financial specialist persuading people to do what is in their own best interest to do, you will refuse to allow any conversational opportunity to slip away.

You might surprise yourself with the number of connection opportunities available to you on a daily basis. Fill in the chart in Figure 1.1 and calculate the connection potential for your business. Have your associates and support staff calculate their client contacts and add to your business total.

This diagnostic activity has helped many people come to a greater awareness of the opportunities that are sitting right in front of their nose. Many brokers are alerted to the fact that they are missing opportunities each day by not being conscious of the potential of these conversations. Many others have found that they were not optimizing referral possibilities by just focusing on the problem at hand and not looking to expand the problem-solving call into a connection opportunity. As one financial professional put it:

FIGURE 1.1 | Calculating the Connection Potential of Your Business

Average number of calls outgoing each day _____

Average number of calls incoming each day _____

Face-to-face meetings each day _____

Average number of outgoing letters each day _____

Speeches or public presentations given each year _____

Approximate number in audiences _____

Subtotal _____ x 220 days per year = total _____

Totals from associates and support staff _____

Grand total _____

"It's helped me to change my attitude toward clients calling with problems. If the first step in creating change is to be disturbed with where you are at, then we have already crossed that hurdle when they call with a problem. Now I have the opportunity to play the problem solver. I have begun to see the upside in that instead of lamenting or trying to avoid the 'problem' call."

This attitude can help us all succeed. Start viewing every conversation, whether it is negative, neutral, or positive, as a test of your ability to connect. And, remember, you don't have to be talking. You simply have to be *focused*—focused on bringing about a positive response or reaction to the situation at hand—and focused on helping your clients to expand their horizons and overcome their tendency to procrastinate. Arouse your own competitive nature by viewing each and every conversation, even in conflict, as an opportunity to refine your connecting skills.

AN ADMIRABLE SKILL

What aspect of success in your career does not depend on your ability to connect? We must connect our clients so they will act in their best interests and to hold fast when the waters get choppy. We must connect with our boss(es) to convince them that the directions and paths we are taking will pay dividends for the company.

Beyond being essential to our careers, the ability to connect is also one of the most admired skills. Which of us does not admire those individuals who can stand up in front of a group, mesmerize their attention, get them in the palm of their hand, and lead them to act in their own best interests. We have all seen a preacher, a motivational speaker, a politician, or some other leader who possessed just such a skill and thought to ourselves, "If only I could do that!" With any degree of personality and likability at all, you can. Making dynamic connections is a skill that can be learned. We know, because we are constantly in the business of teaching this skill. We have seen people make remarkable progress when they applied themselves to excelling in the art and science of making dynamic human connections.

Ask individuals in the financial services business to identify one skill they wished they could possess, and the majority would most likely mention the ability to speak in public, to master the art of public persuasion. We have seen countless individuals build tremendous businesses by developing and utilizing this skill. Manifold doors of opportunity open to the articulate and persuasive presenter that would not otherwise open. If people are teachable, they can learn to be not just good, but great presenters.

But you have to be willing and able to go through the sometimes humbling process of examining your presentations and your presentation style.

Over the years, we have seen weak presenters (stumbling, disjointed, monotone, no eye contact) become good and confident speakers. We have seen naturally good presenters become powerful behind the podium and in front of their clients with some crafting and refining. Our goal for each person reading this book is the same as for each of the participants who go through the Speak Performance course—that they will emerge with a clearer idea of what constitutes a dynamic presentation, and that they will be able to stand and deliver with a persuasive sense of confidence and speaking ability. This we are sure of: everyone can improve upon their client presentation and public-speaking skills. Every inch of that progress will be rewarded with more clients, increased trust, greater admiration, and increased income. We are in the business of convincing people to act. People will act when we connect with who they are and what they really want.

In the next three sections, we will examine the dynamics of how to connect with both *who* people are and *what* it is they really want out of this relationship. In the final two sections, we will deal with *how well* your presentations connect with clients in both personal and public forums. Remember, no matter how good your intentions, those intentions will never come to fruition until you master the art of making the client connection. It's time to get serious about this business of making human connections.

CHAPTER 2

How to Meet, Greet, and Treat Your Clients

Understanding the Dynamics of Charisma

Ask yourself what it is that makes people most able to connect with others. In a word, it is likability. Those people practice relational skills that make people feel better about themselves and, consequently, about the person doing the connecting. This last part will focus on the relational skills necessary to raise your likability with clients.

Mitch was once asked by an insurance company to find out why certain, highly desirable clients never came over to their company, though it had pursued them for years. The company asking the question was a top-shelf firm with a strong history and a great business record.

Mitch sat down with the owners of the business in question and, instead of asking why they didn't do business with the company doing the inquiry, he began asking who they did business with and why. You can probably guess the answers he heard—they didn't talk about businesses they did business with, they talked about people. "I deal with Joe because we like Joe, he's always done right by us." "We're with Mary because she's easy to deal with, and if we have a problem, she's right there to take care of it." In fact, 95 percent of the time they talked about the relationship and the relatability of the agent. Mitch went back to the company with the following conclusion: spend as much time trying to recruit likability as you do ability. In the long run, people prefer to do business with people they like.

Yes, exceptions to this rule exist. But they are exceptions. We do business with some people who we can't stand or who drive us crazy, but we continue with them because they are highly competent or have the best deal in the marketplace. If an equal option ever appears, however, we will flee.

Some people are competent but not very likable. Some people are likable but not very competent. We all want to do business with people who are both competent *and* likable. People by nature would prefer to do business with people they like; yet, not enough people work as hard on their likability as they work on their ability. Consider the following vignettes gathered from clients.

Larry, Curly, and Moe

"I'm sitting in this advisor's office, and at least four times he either picks up a phone call or walks out of the room to go take care of something. The ironic thing about the two phone calls was that he immediately told them he was with a client and didn't have time to talk—so he was ticking us both off at the same time."

—Henry, client

"This advisor spent 45 minutes with me—30 of which were spent showing all the bells and whistles on his computer of some high-end portfolio management system he had. He was so proud of this thing, like it was the answer to all my problems. I'm sitting here thinking, 'Don't you want to know anything about me?' Are people really this stupid?"

—Susan, business owner

"Our friends told us to visit this financial planner and so we went. I don't know if this guy was having a bad day or what, but he was so uptight. He could hardly muster a smile. He seemed obsessed with business details and had this look on his face of feigned interest when we talked about something outside of where he was trying to steer the discussion. My wife and I just looked at each and knew we were thinking the same thing, 'This guy may be good, but if this is the way the conversations are going to go—no thanks!'"

—Curt and Rena, clients

Duh!

We should smile. We should listen and focus on the client. We should show enthusiasm about what we do. We should treat everyone with ultimate respect (as our kids are fond of saying, "Duh!"). But we often unwittingly abandon the basic rules of human contact and relational development when we are distracted, harried, overwhelmed, upset, or just having a particularly bad day. Do you think the client cares that you are distracted or harried or having a particularly bad day? Do you care that the server who just assaulted you while taking your breakfast order is having a particularly bad day or is overstressed? We doubt it.

When we talk to clients about who their money is with, we look for two things in their response. One, do they mention the name of the person or the name of the firm? Do they know the name of the financial professional? If they mention the name of the firm, we know the financial professional has done a good job of building the relationship. Two, how much enthusiasm do they display when talking about the financial professional? We're not as interested in how they talk about the financial professional's competence or skill as we are in how they discuss the individual's personality. We have noted that when clients speak enthusiastically about their financial professional, the individual almost always excels in his or her ability to relate to people in a genuine and enthusiastic way. They are "people people." They are likable.

IMPRESSIONS

We have often heard that you never get a second chance at a first impression. Well, you never get a second chance at a second impression either—or a second chance at a third impression. Every impression matters. Some financial professionals make a great first impression but don't follow through on successive impressions and, consequently, the client leaves. As we have stated earlier, every time you meet with a client you are confronting the longest yard—the critical three feet between you and your client. That three feet is a dynamic distance that is either shrinking or expanding every time you meet, greet, or treat your client with communication or action. Be vigilant of this fact: every contact and impression is as important as the first.

People come to financial professionals to fix problems, but they leave because of poor dynamics in the relationship. Which meeting or contact started that negative dynamic? Which word or look or bit of inaction opened the door in your client's mind that eventually led that client to walk out your door? Because determining which interaction sowed the seed of discontent is not always possible, we must become masters of every moment. We must excel at meeting, greeting, and treating our clients.

Pat Croce's Top Ten

Pat Croce is the charismatic former owner of the Philadelphia 76ers basketball team in the NBA. Unlike many of his peers, Croce does not restrict himself to his owner's box and press conferences. He mixes it up with everyone he can to make favorable impressions: fans, players, community, and the press. Croce believes that success with people boils down to simple but often ignored basics. Following are ten of those basics from Pat Croce's Top Ten Business Rules ("Top Ten Business Rules," *American Way* magazine, 1 Nov. 2000, p. 162):

1. *Hello—and good-bye.* Croce says that hello is a reflex, but good-bye has to become a habit. When you say good-bye properly, people come back for another hello.
2. *First name basis.* We live in an impersonal world. Anytime you oppose that attitude by using a first name, you make the world a better place.
3. *Listen, listen, listen.* I can't sell you anything until I listen to what you want.
4. *Communicate clearly.* Croce's philosophy in communication is to keep closing windows until what you want is crystal clear. Don't ever assume that people will understand what you mean or want.
5. *Be neat, clean, and fit.* Croce says that these characteristics help to communicate that you know what you're talking about.
6. *Be prompt and professional.* If you're late, you're rude.
7. *Be positive.* Being positive takes hard work. But it makes a difference.
8. *Give compliments.* Croce states that even in his business, the most highly rated, highly paid people in the world need to be complimented. If they do, how much more does it help the average Joe.
9. *Have fun.* Life is too short. You gotta have fun. Fun and a smile are contagious.
10. *Do it now.* Ideas are stolen. Promises are broken. Deals die. You have to move on.

People's attitudes toward you are inevitably linked to their interactions with you. You could possess all the persuasive power in the world but lack personal charisma—and fall like a rock in the one-on-one encounter; e.g., the public speaker we've observed who gets up and gives a dynamic presentation and then is heard afterward ordering his people around like dogs and talking to his audience members in a curt and condescending manner. No matter how persuasive that person may be in public, privately he will always be thought of as a jerk.

Some basic dynamics of personal charisma and likability will not only expand your circle of influence but will expand your circle of friendship as well. We would like to discuss five of those dynamics here:

1. Get real.
2. Treat everyone like a "10."

3. Live passionately and youthfully.
4. Exude positive energy.
5. Help people look forward.

GET REAL

Admit mistakes when you make them. Don't be afraid to discuss clients' emotions regarding money and life. Money is deeply tied to an abundance of life issues. People want to talk to a professional who is a real person. Don't hide behind credentials, awards, and professional jargon. The only people you'll impress are those using them.

Don't be afraid to talk about the lessons you've learned—and how you learned them. If you've never made any mistakes, I'm not sure I want you for my financial professional, because the odds are that I'll be your first.

Display pictures of your family, and ask about your client's family. Talk about your own journeys and dreams with your family. This conversation tells them you're living the same sort of grounded existence that they are—and you can relate.

Laugh easily. Laughter communicates many things—perspective, resilience, the joy of being, and the fact that you are real enough to be easily tickled. Laughter makes you likable and reachable at the same time.

People enjoy being with transparent people because of their desire to be transparent themselves. Finding people who are not hiding cards up their sleeve and playing the rest close to their vest is hard. When you meet someone who puts the cards up on the table and says, "Let's talk," it is refreshing. You get no pretense of greatness or arrogance, no illusion of knowing things we don't, no hubris of thinking that we're somehow above the troubles of the world. We're just regular people trying to navigate our way through uncertain times and sometimes troubled waters. Being real makes you worth trusting. Clients want to know they are not dealing with a mirage or PR invention. They want to know they're dealing with someone like themselves who knows more than they do in the important area of wealth building.

TREAT EVERYONE LIKE A "10"

We can't all be heroes. Somebody has to sit on the curb and clap as
    they go by.

—Will Rogers

Early in his career, Mitch had an older gentleman explain to him that every person he met was wearing an invisible sign around his or her neck but that most people didn't know how to read it. Every person, rich or poor, wears the same sign. He told Mitch that if he would learn to read the sign, he would succeed with people. The sign simply says, "Help me feel important."

Treat everyone like a "10." Remember the Bo Derek film *10*? The movie gave people a universal rating system for beauty. We would look at someone and say, "He or she is an '8.'" Our culture always seems to cater more to beauty than it does to brains, genuineness, or even ability. Watch the way the average businessperson fawns over a physically attractive individual versus the unattractive person. No wonder people become hypersensitive over a slight or by being dissed in a social setting.

People have an antenna up for the level of respect we are paying them when other, "more important" individuals enter the conversation or circle. Does our conversation suddenly wane when a more attractive, more powerful, wealthier individual enters the conversation? You've never thought about it? Better start watching your own programmed social reactions to beauty, wealth, status, age, and class distinctions. Trust us—your clients are watching for it.

We find that the elderly get less regard in society. We are talking about those who possess the most experience, wisdom, stories, and, oh by the way, the most wealth in our nation. Yet many of the retired are treated as has-beens or peripheral parties by society at large. Treat retirees like royalty in your office. Give them the deference, respect, and time that their age has earned them—they have earned the "10" rating.

LIVE PASSIONATELY AND YOUTHFULLY

Don't be afraid to display your nonprofessional side to your clients. Do you have pictures and artifacts in your office of the hobbies you enjoy and the places you've been? Do you have issues and causes in your community that you feel passionately about and are lending your life energy to? Or is all your energy consumed in acquiring money?

People today want to work with not only a competent professional but also one who understands balanced living. They want someone who can help them gain perspective as well as income. Are you able to demonstrate this to your clients? If so, how? We met a professional who called a brokerage office and told the receptionist, "My wife and I are into hiking, outdoor life, and helping others through our church. Do you have anybody like that in your office we could talk to?" Fortunately, that firm did have someone who met those "qualifications"—which was the beginning of a warm professional relationship. The financial professional talked enthusiastically with the couple about their mutual interests before they ever got to the topic of money. They wanted to entrust their wealth-building process to someone who shared the spirit of what they were saving for. This is human contact. Make human contact with your clients by exhibiting the things you are passionate about. Some will connect with your passions and others will simply admire your energy for life.

Whatever you do, don't start acting old. Don't complain about this and that. Don't moan and groan. It's a turnoff. Let people see youthfulness in you and your excitement about life and the possibilities in it. People want to be around a charismatic force. Your attitude is contagious—make sure it is something worth catching.

EXUDE POSITIVE ENERGY

You will not be a positive force in other people's lives by accident. Attitude is not a feeling you get—it is a direction you choose. People who have a consistently positive impact on others are deliberate and rehearsed in the practice of transferring positive energy. Each day, we are confronted with opportunities to speak critically of others— some people do and some don't. Positive people refrain for purposes both internal and external. Externally, positive people are aware that their listeners are wondering how they will speak of them when they're not present. Internally, they want to keep a fresh and vibrant view of life and people in spite of what life and people do to counter that view.

Any fool can complain, condemn, and criticize . . . and most fools do.

—Abraham Lincoln

It is almost as if positive people are living a "willful innocence." They know people can be stupid, cruel, selfish, and ridiculous, but they would rather look at their redeeming qualities. They choose humor and grace over criticism, and they choose romantic fascination with life over cynicism. These positive individuals are not blind to the things that are wrong and could be wrong, but they have found a better place to live. Beauty is in the eye of the beholder.

You can communicate contagious positive energy for life first in your eyes. When you meet a client, what are your eyes communicating? The client is looking and asking this question. Make sure that your eyes "smile" and communicate respect. If you are given to multitasking and extreme intensity in your work, you'll need to exercise an extra degree of caution here. If your eyes can smile, your teeth won't be far behind.

Almost worse than not seeing a smile when someone greets us is seeing a phony smile, which tells the person being greeted that the mind and the teeth are in disagreement. Check your thoughts about your client before you check your smile. A false smile can be the worst insult of all. Get the proper thought about getting to know this client fixed in your mind, let that thought travel to your eyes, and then to your facial expression. Then and only then can you communicate the warmth and respect that people desire and expect.

HELP PEOPLE LOOK FORWARD

Financial professionals Scott and Bethany Palmer describe their practice this way: "We are, above all, brokers in hope. People need to walk out of our office believing that the life they desire is within reach. If they don't, then we have failed to deliver."

How do you become a broker of hope? It starts with finding out where people are at and where they really want to be. A high percentage of Americans are stressed out in the effort to find balance between their working and personal lives. At the core of this problem, you will find unsure career choices, lopsided time allocations, and misguided finances.

Because of the ties between finance, freedom, and personal fulfillment, we believe that the financial professional has a great opportunity to partner with today's client in a meaningful and lasting manner. The majority of people are discontented with their working situation. Many hate their job, or parts of it, while many like their job but hate the hours. Although you may not be in a position to counsel their career choices, you are in a position to help pave the road financially for a transition to a more fulfilling work/life scenario. We have met many financial professionals who are now having conversations with their clients regarding the work/retirement dilemma and are setting up plans that work toward emancipating their clients into the kind of work or the kind of time allocation they can be happy with.

Money is a great servant but a poor god.

—Anonymous

You can give your clients hope when you help them to see that money is a utility to help furnish them the kind of life they desire. Life is not about making as much money as they can—money is about making the life they want. Financial professionals who can help introduce this perspective and then facilitate the process of purchasing this desired lifestyle have immensely raised their value in the eyes of their clients. Financial professionals who cannot do this will one day find that they have become obsolete as both their products and services have become ubiquitously commoditized.

Help your clients find a hopeful vision of life, with their money as the means instead of the goal, and you will be a certified broker of hope. They know they will need more money to bring this hope into their life and maintain it. Life is too short to waste it doing something eight to ten hours a day that does nothing but sour their outlook. People today, more than anything else, want their money to facilitate the process of meaningful existence. You can easily become their lifelong partner in this process simply by changing your focus and thus altering your job description.

Meet people at their level. Greet them with enthusiasm. Treat them with respect. Great financial professionals never stray from these fundamentals for winning this game of making human connections. Everybody matters—but not everybody treats them like they do matter. You can be the rare person who does, because you know how to read the sign hanging around their neck.

CHAPTER 3

The Emotionally Intelligent Financial Professional

Principles on Emotional Intelligence for making valuable human connections:

- Emotional Intelligence (EQ) will have more bearing on your success than will IQ.
- Emotional Intelligence begins with an awareness of our own emotional state and our impact on others.
- People make poor decisions when the logical part of their brain is hijacked by the emotional part of their brain.
- Financial professionals who lack resilience will choose the wrong motivations and give up easily.
- Emotional radar (empathy) is the skill that will help you to build rapport and trust with clients.

When an archer misses the mark, he turns and looks for the fault within himself. Failure to hit the bull's-eye is never the fault of the target. To improve your aim, improve yourself.

—Gilbert Arland

Current research shows that IQ influences at best 25 percent of people's success in their career. A careful analysis suggests a more accurate figure may be no higher than 10 percent and perhaps as low as 4 percent (*Successful Intelligence,* R. Sternberg, 1997). Recent studies in Emotional Intelligence, as reported in Daniel Goleman's landmark book entitled *Emotional Intelligence* (1995), demonstrate that EQ is a far greater predictor of success (80 to 85 percent) in the workplace and in life in general.

In 1960, psychologist Walter Mishel conducted a psychological test using marshmallows with four-year-olds. The children, at a Stanford preschool, were given a marshmallow and told that the teacher had to run an errand. If they waited until the teacher got back, they could have two marshmallows. If they couldn't wait, they would only receive one marshmallow. Some of the four-year-olds were able to wait what must have seemed an endless 15 to 20 minutes for the teacher to return. Those who waited used various techniques to survive the waiting period. They covered their eyes so they wouldn't have to view the temptation, rested their head in their arms, sang songs, talked to themselves, counted their toes and fingers, and even tried to go to sleep. This they did while the others swallowed the marshmallow as soon as the teacher left the room. Some even taunted those who restrained.

As a part of this study, all these four-year-olds were subsequently tracked down as adolescents and as they graduated from high school. The emotional and social differences between the eat-it-now crowd and the gratification delayers were quite dramatic. Those who had resisted the temptation at four years of age were, as adolescents, more socially competent, personally effective, self-assertive, self-reliant, composed under stress and frustration, likely to embrace challenges, confident, trustworthy, dependable, and self-initiating—and they were still able to delay gratification in pursuit of their goals. Even the SAT test scores of the waiters surpassed the grabbers by over 20 percent.

Systems based on IQ (Intelligence Quotient) have many positives; however, they cannot predict unerringly who will succeed in life. This fact is one of psychology's long-held secrets and industry's frustrations. A high-achieving student is not necessarily going to become the most productive in business. Put another way, can you think of someone who is really smart but really *stupid?* We often ask this question of our audiences, and of course, everyone knows someone who fits this description. When we inquire further into what they mean by "really smart, but really stupid" we hear answers like, "They lack common sense," or "They don't see the big picture," or "They're lacking people smarts," or "They just don't get it." Although their answers may seem a bit vague, when you distill them to their most basic level, you are left with a picture of someone who is intellectually astute and emotionally backward, awkward, or even dangerous.

People who fit this description seem to alienate others and have trouble controlling their emotional impulses. As a result, they cause offense to others because of their lack of resilience and social skills. A training program developed by Mitch's company to teach emotional competencies to financial professionals is called the ARROW Program™. This program expands and applies the five basic tenets of emotional intelligence. The five competencies are:

1. *Awareness.* Awareness of natural strengths and weaknesses and impact of our personality on others
2. *Recognition and Restraint.* The ability to identify negative emotions and restrain those emotions from affecting our behavior
3. *Resiliency.* The ability to rebound and grow from failure, setbacks, disappointments, and injustice
4. *Others (empathy).* The ability to discern feelings and motives; developing emotional radar
5. *Working with others (social skills).* The ability to communicate, resolve conflicts, and relate to and lead others

The ARROW Program places a fundamental emphasis on understanding core personality as a path toward developing three of the five emotional competencies: awareness, empathy, and working with others. Students of emotional competence need to understand the inherent strengths and weaknesses of their personality to develop personal awareness. Understanding others' personalities also plays a significant role in the development of empathy and social skills, which include listening, observation, interpretation, communication, and conflict resolution. Chapters 4 to 10 will deal with such issues as understanding the admirable and annoying aspects of your own personality, learning to read the body and tonal language signals of your clients, making the necessary adjustments in a selling or decision-making situation, and learning how to disentangle yourself from personality conflicts.

Figures 3.1 and 3.2 include the ARROW profile that participants use to assess their competency level in awareness, restraint, resilience, and social adeptness. Take a moment to fill out this profile and rate yourself in these five competencies critical to success.

Notes for processing: Draw an arrowhead at the far right of your line on the grid and an arrow tail at the far left of the line. This picture of an arrow serves as a metaphor for helping you define the specific areas necessary for raising your EQ.

Understand that every self-assessment has a built-in margin of error because of subjectivity and lack of awareness. For example, while an arrogant view of oneself would lead to an unrealistically high rating, a low opinion would lead to an unrealistically low rating. The 180 degrees column at the far right of the profile is designed for those who wish to have a significant other rate their competencies for them. Somewhere between your rating of yourself and a significant other's rating of you would be a fairly realistic assessment of EQ.

Emotional competencies are a product of both nature and nurture. For example, on the nature side, a personality that is very high on the empathy line is quite often below

FIGURE 3.1 | ARROW Self-Assessment

Directions: *Next to each question, place a number between 1 and 5, as per the scale below.*

1	2	3	4	5
Never		Some of the time		All of the time

SELF				180°
	A TOTAL	1. I am aware of why certain people like me. 2. I am aware of the things I do that offend or annoy others. 3. I am comfortable with who I am. 4. When in an uncomfortable situation, I can identify the emotion I am feeling. 5. I am aware of which emotions cause me the most trouble. 6. I am aware of why certain people are uncomfortable around me. 7. I am aware of the areas I need to work on. 8. I am aware of the effects my moods have on others.	**A TOTAL**	
	R TOTAL	1. I can find a solution when I am upset. 2. I am able to wait for something that I really want. 3. I can quickly pull myself out of negative moods. 4. I am able to express my anger to others in a proper manner. 5. I can talk honestly about issues that hurt or frustrate me. 6. I avoid taking out my stress on others. 7. I can remain calm when provoked. 8. I am able to persevere with unpleasant tasks.	**R TOTAL**	
	R TOTAL	1. I am able to refocus when others let me down. 2. I am able to accept events I cannot control. 3. I believe that mistakes are an opportunity to learn. 4. I examine myself rather than blaming others. 5. I am able to laugh at my mistakes. 6. I am able to put my failures behind me. 7. I maintain a positive and optimistic attitude. 8. I am able to persevere when treated unfairly.	**R TOTAL**	
	O TOTAL	1. I can easily sense what others are feeling. 2. I respond sensitively to the feelings of others. 3. I can sense what others are motivated by. 4. I am interested in other people's perceptions and opinions. 5. I look past my feelings to other people's feelings. 6. I can easily tell when people's words and body language do not agree. 7. I like spending time getting to know people. 8. I make an effort to listen when people are expressing their problems.	**O TOTAL**	
	W TOTAL	1. People feel at ease around me. 2. I am good at communicating with people. 3. I am good at resolving conflicts with others. 4. I am able to get people to work well together. 5. I am good at articulating thoughts and feelings. 6. I try to encourage and inspire other people. 7. I can remain friendly, even when in disagreement. 8. I am able to work well with people of differing opinions and values.	**W TOTAL**	

FIGURE 3.2 | ARROW Emotional Intelligence Profile

Take your score from the previous page and plot them on the corresponding lines/numbers connecting all dots. Then draw the feathers of an arrow on the left of your line, and the head of an arrow on the right of your line.

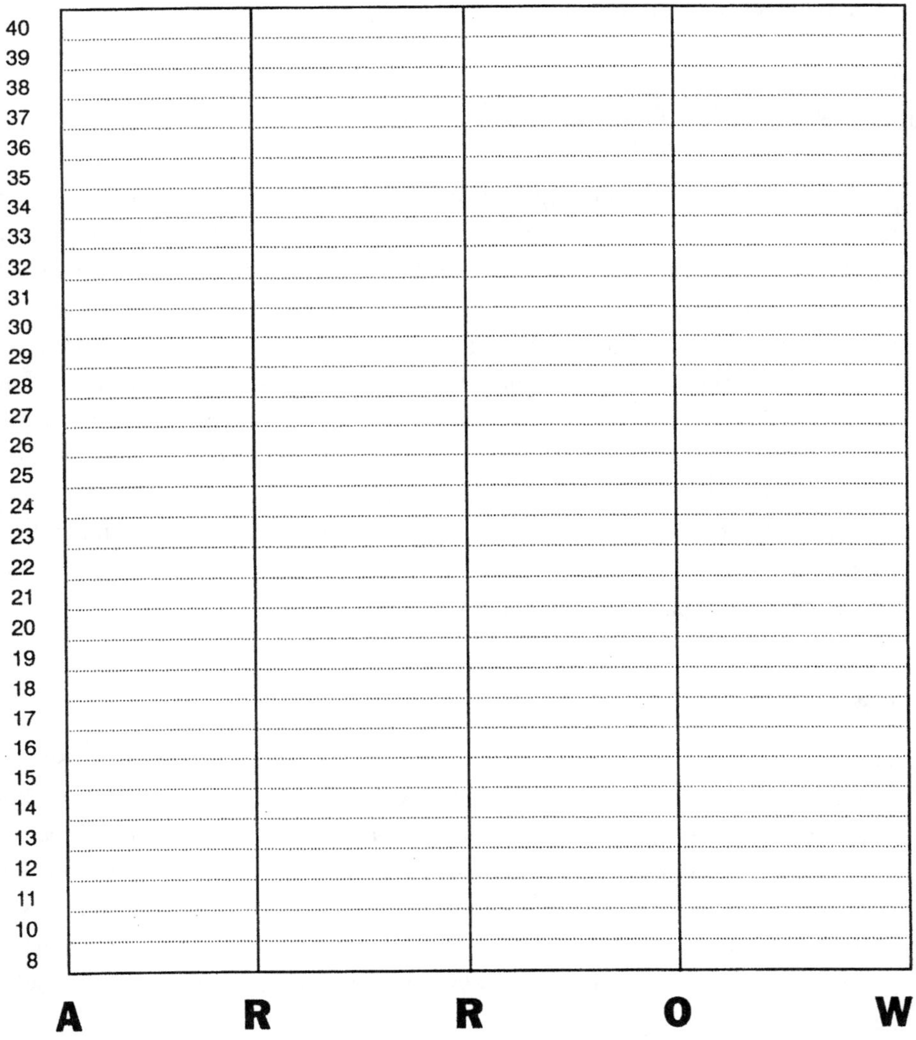
40
39
38
37
36
35
34
33
32
31
30
29
28
27
26
25
24
23
22
21
20
19
18
17
16
15
14
13
12
11
10
8
A
R
R
O
W

How far and how straight will your arrow fly?

The Arrow Program © 1999 PAGE 5 Peer Power

average on the resilience line and vice versa. For example, a person who is good at bouncing back from setbacks may not necessarily be the best listener by nature. On the other hand, a person who is sensitive and empathetic by nature may have difficulty dealing with disappointment. The good news about EQ, as opposed to IQ, is that, once recognized, emotional competencies can be addressed and raised. If you rate low on restraint, resiliency, or empathy, skills and processes can be learned to raise your level of competence in each specific area.

HOW EQ WILL HELP YOU SUCCEED

In today's marketplace, a premium has been placed on a financial professional's ability to relate to people—success in this business hinges more on relational skills than technical skills. Much of the modern financial professional's past value was based on technical and tactical skills that have been supplanted by emerging technologies. The positioning of the modern financial professional is that of facilitator of hopes and dreams and a source for financial insight and relational skills. In today's marketplace, the financial professional who hangs his hat on technical and tactical competence will be replaced quickly by one who is skilled at building relationships around clients' hopes and dreams.

These emotional competencies, when developed and practiced, ensure your superior ranking in the people skills necessary to win people over and maintain their allegiance in difficult economic periods. Following are short descriptions of the five competencies that can help you reach your career target.

Awareness

This skill involves understanding yourself and the kind of emotional response you evoke in others. For this sort of awareness to take place, you must confront both the strengths and weaknesses built into your personality. Each personality has built-in annoyances toward polar-opposite personalities. As a result, those who bother us the most—and are bothered by us the most—are usually our personality opposites. In Chapters 4, 5, 8, and 9, we deal extensively with this topic, and offer agendas for improving relations with all personality types as well as an agenda for improving any negative emotional impact that your personality type may cause.

This sort of awareness is critical when you consider the fact that a study showed over 87 percent of clients who left their financial professional did so because of "the relationship." (Prince and Associates) Ironically, out of this 87 percent of clients who left their financial professional, over 90 percent said they were satisfied with their financial professional's financial performance. Obviously, many of these financial professionals suffering the exodus of key clients were lacking an awareness of how their personality and style were repelling clients. We try not only to make financial professionals aware of the pitfalls of each personality style but also to offer an agenda for minimizing negative emotional impact with clients.

Recognition and Restraint

Most powerful is he who has himself in his own power.

—Seneca

Restraint is a sense of self-mastery—of being able to withstand the emotional storms without being swept away. Individuals with restraint are those who can control their negative emotions and not act or react inappropriately in situations. According to Daniel Goleman, "Keeping our distressing emotions in check is the key to emotional well-being" (*Emotional Intelligence*, 1995, p. 36). Daniel Goleman describes the loss of emotional control as the *amygdala hijack*. The amygdala is the anger center of the brain. When anger builds, it momentarily hijacks our rational function. The things we say and do in this hijacking period are the words and actions that cause us the most trouble—and regret.

The person who has a highly developed sense of recognition and restraint understands:

- The importance of being aware of the specific types of circumstances, personalities, and events that make them vulnerable to a loss of control
- The impact of unchecked emotion on their behavior and, ultimately, on their relationships with others

Individuals lacking in this particular competency are more prone to defending the words and actions that spill out in an amygdala overload. Their self-justification prevents them from addressing the core issues of recognition and restraint, which are the impacts these actions have on those around them as well as their own sense of personal confidence. They are either not fully aware of the circumstances or events that consistently trigger negative emotional reactions in them, or if they are aware, they have no game plan for avoiding these circumstances. The person with a highly developed sense of recognition and restraint can:

- Identify the specific moods, conditions, and stressful situations that commonly trigger negative reactions.

- Rehearse and prepare in their mind for predictable stressful events.
- Diffuse the brain circuitry overload with patience and redirection of energy.

The financial professional who has a firm grasp of the emotional competency of restraint is better qualified to help those clients who struggle with restraint issues—which ultimately affect their personal wealth-building process. Clients continually sabotage their financial success by acting on negative emotional impulses rather than calm and informed logic. The financial professional with a highly trained sense of recognition and restraint can help clients navigate the visceral labyrinth that stands between their present circumstances and true prosperity.

Resilience

Every problem introduces you to yourself. It shows you how you think
    and what you're made of.

—George Matthew Adams

Life is not about what happens; it is about what you make happen with what happens. Our level of resilience eventually defines success in any pursuit. To get an indication of your current level of resilience, rate yourself on the Resilience Rubric in Figure 3.3. Read each statement and circle the number that best describes you.

Martin Seligman in his book, *Learned Optimism,* demonstrates that optimism and pessimism are learned behaviors. By viewing the responses our role models demonstrated when faced with adversity, we begin to form a response pattern that is either self-defeating or self-improving. We all face three potential experiential sources of discouragement to varying degrees in life:

1. *Failure.* Where I am responsible for my situation
2. *Disappointment.* Where others have caused adverse circumstances
3. *Adversity.* Where circumstances have conspired to form an obstacle

When you deal with what people might term failure, do you beat yourself up and give up easily, or do you try to derive a lesson from the situation and move on? When others disappoint you, do you harbor bitterness and fantasize about revenge, or do you empathize with human weakness and forgive? When faced with adversity, do you tell yourself that something always goes wrong and you are just cursed with bad luck, or do you have a sense of gratitude for the things that remain and look for growth opportunities these adverse circumstances might provide?

FIGURE 3.3 | Resilience Rubric

Directions: *Read each statement and circle the number that best describes you.*

Approach to life/people...

1	2	3	4	5
Cynicism				Curiosity and wonder

When I am rejected, I...

1	2	3	4	5
Retreat				Move on

When things go wrong in my life, I...

1	2	3	4	5
Fix blame				Fix the problem

When I fail, I...

1	2	3	4	5
Internalize; give up				Change my approach

When I continue to fail, I...

1	2	3	4	5
Resist help/counsel				Seek help/counsel

When I get a good idea, I...

1	2	3	4	5
Talk myself out of it				Forge ahead with conviction

When I don't meet my goals, I...

1	2	3	4	5
Search for excuses/rationalize				Take personal inventory

When presented with challenging goals, I...

1	2	3	4	5
Complain & make excuses				Create plan for achievement

When circumstances conspire against me, I...

1	2	3	4	5
Feel unlucky/cursed				Salvage from the experience

My attitude toward each day...

1	2	3	4	5
Allow others to affect me				Set emotional compass

When I do something stupid or embarrassing, I...

1	2	3	4	5
Beat myself up				Laugh it off

When confronted with a mistake, I...

1	2	3	4	5
Rationalize my actions				Quickly admit my "error"

Total

[   ]

Ultimately, success is not about learning from life, but about learning the *right* lessons from life. If challenging circumstances teach us to withdraw, avoid risk, and insulate ourselves from vulnerability, then we are surely lacking resilience and are learning the wrong lessons from our experiences. In studying resilient financial professionals, these features are evident.

- *Resilient financial professionals choose curiosity over cynicism.* Cynicism is surrendering to the idea that no person deserves your trust.
- *Resilient financial professionals are curious about people.* Self-centered and self-serving individuals demonstrate lower resilience levels than those individuals who display a genuine curiosity and interest in others. This curiosity translates into sincerity and trustworthiness in the eyes of the client. These individuals also end up with more solid relational networking, which further strengthens their resilience potential.
- *Resilient financial professionals have learned to move past no.* They check the approach that led to the no. They study how they and others have gotten to yes, and they set realistic expectations to avoid zapping their initiative. Gary Mohammed, Director of Training at Lehman Brothers, has a creative approach to teaching his new recruits the advisory business. He reads Dr. Seuss's *Green Eggs and Ham* to them, and asks them to count the different ways Sam tries to close the deal. Gary understands that a lack of resilience in this area is often the result of a lack of creativity.
- *Resilient financial professionals recognize the transitory nature of extrinsic motivation.* They understand that material gain is a good motivator, but not when it leads to replacing values with valuables. They recognize that proving something to somebody is an extrinsic motivator that can lead to an obsession with being recognized—which can never be filled. They realize that controlling others is an extrinsic motivator that only adds stress and frustration as people and events elude our efforts at control.
- *Resilient financial professionals recognize the need for intrinsic motivation in their professional pursuits.* They understand that the most powerful motivators are a desire for excellence, the need to challenge ourselves, gratitude for every good opportunity, genuine curiosity about others and their lives, the thrill of overcoming adversity, and the joy of working with a higher sense of purpose.
- *Resilient financial professionals learn to view every negative situation as a test.* When assessing a negative situation, their competitive nature kicks in and they ask themselves, "What attributes of my character are being tested here?" and "How will I pass this test?"

- *Resilient financial professionals are coachable.* Many gifted individuals fail to succeed because they refuse to listen, learn, and change. They become victims of their own arrogance. Professionals demonstrating the highest levels of resilience display a teachable spirit, a desire to grow, and a flexible attitude toward change.
- *Resilient financial professionals have a ready wit.* They are not afraid to laugh at themselves, leading to quicker correction and better resiliency. Laughter is a sign of mental flexibility and is also a tonic for depressed moods. Laughter acts as a pressure valve for adversity and annoyances. It strengthens the immune system and relaxes the nervous system. In a study at Stanford, members of one group were given a lecture on positive attitudes, and the second group were taught to relax. Both groups then took an achievement test. The relaxed group scored 25 percent higher than the motivated group. Laughter is unbeatable in terms of relaxing our nervous system.

Empathy

You are in the minority if you have developed the ability to see past
the mirrors of narcissism. Those who can move past self-
absorption become skilled observers of those around them.

—T. M. Anthony

A critical emotional competence for building rapport, be it with one person or one thousand, is that of empathy. We like to describe empathy as "emotional radar." Emotional radar is the skill of reading and interpreting the motives and feelings of others. How important is having a finely tuned sense of emotional radar for today's financial professional? In our opinion, it is of paramount importance. The first step necessary in building lasting client relationships is empathy—the process of identifying emotionally with others. Empathy is also foundational in resolving conflicts. As demonstrated in Chapter 15, emotional motivators drive people's decisions. Empathy is the skill necessary to detect what those motivators are. Empathy is the ability to interpret the whys of what people do. It is the ability to read between the lines of conversation and ascertain what is really meant.

Empathy could also be described as political smarts or the ability to interpret the needs, motivations, and wiles of individuals in a corporate setting. The skill of empathy is articulated by our ability to tune in to and interpret nonverbal communication. In Chapter 6 we will discuss the body and tonal language signals that are instructive regarding how to approach a client.

One problem inherent in any sales-related industry is that sellers feel compelled to do a lot of talking. They believe that selling is in the telling. This approach is dangerous because while people are talking, they are doing very little observing. Observational skill, which is empathy at work, is a telling characteristic of a wise and seasoned financial professional. We don't know who we're selling to and what needs must be met until the questions are asked and the listening is done. Skills necessary for empathy development are:

- *Inquiry skills.* Asking questions that reveal feeling as well as fact (see Chapter 11)
- *Listening and appropriate response skills*
- *Recognition of body and vocal language skills* (see Chapter 6)
- *Interpreting and responding to body language signals* (see Chapter 7)
- *Understanding the role of perspective* (see Chapters 4 and 9)

Once you master observational skills, your emotional radar will be programmed to pick up the telling signals of what a client wants, how they want to be approached, and where their comfort zones begin and end. Rarely will a client depart the services of a financial professional who is tuned to their needs, wants, and hopes.

Working with Others

I have yet to find the man, however exalted his station, who did not do
    better under a spirit of approval than under a spirit of criticism.

—Charles Schwab

Recently, Mitch talked to a rancher who had sold his extensive land holdings and was looking for a financial professional to manage his wealth. When Mitch asked him how he came to choose the financial professional out of the many he interviewed, the rancher answered, "Well, we finally met one with a personality and decided he was a likable enough fellow to work with." This anecdote reveals that although people want competence, they also desire someone with social skills—someone who won't be a chore to converse with. The financial professional who is skilled at connecting with his clients understands that developing social skills is as important as developing professional competence.

We can't ignore these basic social skills critical to building and maintaining client relationships:

- How to meet, greet, and treat others
- How to disagree agreeably
- How to confront conflict with tact and diplomacy
- How to negotiate win-win compromises
- How to adjust your selling techniques to various patterns of personality
- How to create momentum by leading instead of pushing
- How to avoid land mines and tap into gold mines in personal relationships

Much of the relational separation and conflict we encounter with clients and coworkers could be avoided simply by being aware of the motivators and demotivators of each personality. Interpersonal stress and conflict arise when we consistently communicate or behave toward others in a manner that goes against their natural comfort zones. The emotionally competent financial professional knows how to identify the factors that motivate each person as well as those factors that cause discomfort and stress. This social skill is indispensable for building a client base that will endure. These skills are taught in Chapter 8.

Another key skill advisors need to develop is the diplomatic art of negotiating through conflict. We need to know how to move past blaming and attempts at manipulation to negotiating compromises that meet at the halfway point of personality DNA. If we do not learn to work with a client's personality, we will be met with frustration, resistance, and even hostility. The effective financial professional understands both how to confront these situations in the most positive manner possible and how to resolve them in diplomatic fashion. These skills are taught in Chapters 9 and 10.

Finally, in Chapter 7, we demonstrate the communication skills necessary for helping every client feel comfortable with the product you are selling. Our research with clients has shown that each personality style has a specific lexicon of language that they are comfortable with in a selling situation. Learning to adjust your presentation intuitively to the communicative comfort zone of your clients is a social skill that can and will pay rich dividends.

WORKING SMARTER

The good news about emotional intelligence is that it does not necessarily remain static. If we are willing to increase our personal awareness and address our areas of emotional weakness, we can become smarter in terms of EQ. A higher EQ translates into better relationships and a greater sense of self-confidence. As participants in the ARROW

Program have discovered, once you become more comfortable with who you are, your clients will start feeling more comfortable around you. Today's clients want to relate to a financial professional who can talk beyond the numbers and relate to them as human beings. The emotional competencies of awareness, restraint, resilience, empathy, and social skills all have a major bearing on your success or failure as a financial professional. In the realm of making successful client connections, the most effective financial professionals are those who are at ease with themselves and who have a knack for helping others feel at ease around them.

CHAPTER 4

Moving from Me to We

Understanding the inherent strengths and challenges in our own personality and making necessary adjustments are giant leaps toward developing connective power. We must gain a clear understanding of how our personality impacts others and is perceived by others. We must also learn to recognize the type of personality with which we are attempting to communicate so that we are not unwittingly arousing negative emotional reactions and shutting down the communication process. It is a matter of knowing yourself, knowing those around you, and knowing the adjustments you need to make. This is the process that allows us to move from me to we.

What we are talking about here is how to make the critical connection with our audience. Many times we find ourselves in situations similar to fitting a three-prong plug into a two-prong outlet—no matter how hard you try, you won't get a connection and certainly no electrical flow. The same holds true in developing critical connections with clients to create an emotional flow that leads to trust and loyalty with your clients. The only way this happens is when we begin to truly understand the important role of personality.

The intention of this chapter is to enable you to understand how you impact others at the level of core personality. Many financial professionals simply communicate at the superficial level of product features and benefits with a one-size-fits-all mentality. This approach is shallow and creates a weak psychological footing upon which to build client trust. As thefollowing illustrations show, your communication can go from superficial to profound by addressing clients' motives for investing and then ultimately addressing their core personality—the foundation from which all their decisions and reactions are based.

Awareness of our own personality's impact and greater concern for the comfort level of our clients are the basis for success in communication. When realized, these two objectives will minimize miscommunication, misunderstanding, and negative interaction with clients and serve as a basis for strengthened trust and improved relationships. This course, for many, has become a foundational communication skill for managing client expectations, reactions, and behaviors. Moving from me to we means we put our clients first by first understanding each client and ourselves.

The NYSE Rule 405 (know your customer) states that members must attempt to learn essential facts about every customer and account. This includes a financial profile, life profile, risk tolerance, investment experience, investment objectives, tax situation, and other considerations. A crucial component to the life profile, which is typically left out in our industry, is the personality profile of the client. If we cannot connect with the core personality of our clients, we will have a difficult time knowing our customers.

HOW TO TAKE THE PROFILE (SAMPLE)

By filling out the profile in Figure 4.1 you will discover your personality style. Remember that there is no right or wrong style—the profile simply reflects your personality makeup.

For each set, choose the word or phrase that *best* describes you. For best results, do not spend a lot of time on each answer—go with your first instinct. You may feel a sense of tension when you are forced to choose between two sets of words or phrases that describe you. This sense of tension is an integral part of the exercise.

THE PERSONALITY AXIS

While each personality style has many features—both positive and challenging—each personality has a simple and understandable axis around which it revolves. Understanding this personality axis or "spinal column" is a good first step toward understanding your own and others' personalities. The axis points for the four personalities are:

The Togetherness Axis—Feelings

First and foremost in the mind of the Togetherness personality are the issues revolving around sensitivity. How will others feel? How will this affect them? Did you show me respect and kindness? The higher your number on the T line, the more prominent this feature will be in your personality.

FIGURE 4.1 | T.E.A.M. Dynamics Personal Profile

Directions: Place the appropriate number next to each descriptive phrase.

MOST =	4	3	2	1	LEAST

A _____ True to friends   A _____ Understanding
B _____ Innovator   B _____ Takes charge
C _____ Thinks things through   C _____ Accurate
D _____ Energetic   D _____ Achiever

A _____ Thoughtful of others   A _____ Giving
B _____ Daring   B _____ Does own thing
C _____ Wants all information   C _____ Cautious
D _____ Laughs easily / Witty   D _____ Articulate

A _____ Will do as instructed   A _____ Humble
B _____ Risk taker   B _____ Refuses to give up
C _____ Wants things exact   C _____ Likes routines
D _____ Persuasive   D _____ Leads the pack

A _____ Listens and remains calm   A _____ Flows with the crowd
B _____ Wants to win   B _____ Strong personality
C _____ Deliberate   C _____ Dependable
D _____ Enthusiastic   D _____ Interesting

A _____ Hides feelings   A _____ Does not rock the boat
B _____ Courageous   B _____ Speaks openly and boldly
C _____ Has high standards   C _____ Plays by the rules
D _____ Likes to talk   D _____ Gets others involved

A _____ Friendly to others   A _____ Wants others involved
B _____ Decisive   B _____ Results driven
C _____ Wants order   C _____ Difficult time deciding
D _____ Outgoing   D _____ Optimistic

TOTALS: **A =** _____   **B =** _____   **C =** _____   **D =** _____

The Enterpriser Axis—Results

Enterprisers are most happy when they are accomplishing something and achieving results. They want to control their own destiny and are frustrated and unhappy when not in control. Individualistic in nature, Enterprisers live by the creed, "If you want to get something done, do it yourself."

The Analyzer Axis—Accuracy

Analyzers desire precision and accuracy in all they do. They want a linear and predictable process and want to see compliance with process. Their desire for accuracy leads to an intense desire to do things right.

The Motivator Axis—Energy

Motivators gravitate to where the fun and joy of life exists. They take a more random, less predictable approach to life and have great amounts of energy to burn. They love to be on the go, enjoy action, and like to be around people who exude positive energy.

DEFINITION OF ROLES

There is a proper and improper way to interpret your own or another's personality profile. The improper way to interpret a profile is to look at the highest letter (in Figure 4.2, T)

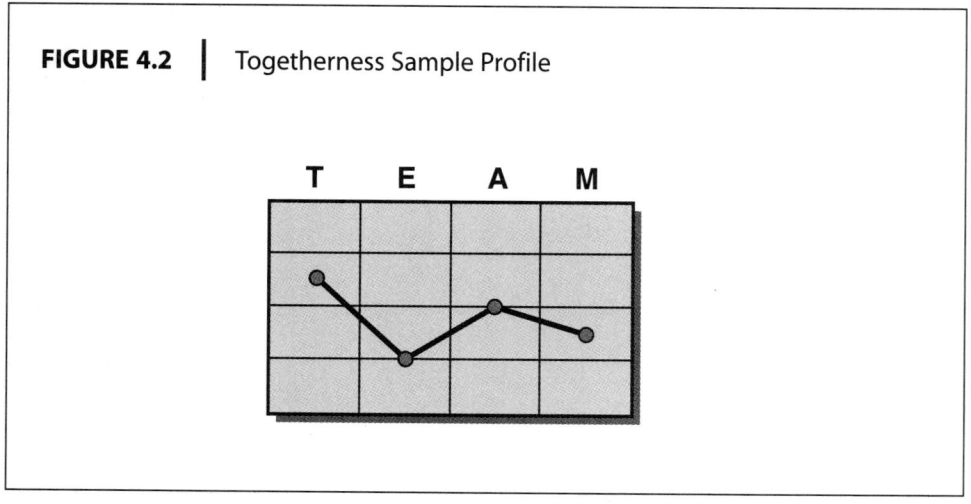

FIGURE 4.2 | Togetherness Sample Profile

and assume that the Togetherness profile comprehensively defines the individual in question. This sort of interpretation, while indicative of a personality tendency, oversimplifies the individual's personality.

The proper approach to interpretation is to look closely at the top letter (leading role), the second letter (supporting role), and the bottom letter (the villain role).

While some people will have just one definitive role, most people will have two roles that stand apart (see Figure 4.3). The most common combinations for leading and supporting roles are A-T, E-M, T-M, and E-A.

The more uncommon combinations for leading and supporting roles are E-T and M-A, the rarest combination. More information on the dynamics of these combinations is covered in our section on sample patterns. Following are definitions of the leading, supporting, and villain roles that will help you to understand your own personality pattern and the patterns of your clients, employees, and coworkers.

Leading Role

Your leading role is the most reliable predictor of how you will act and react on a daily basis. Your leading role can also be described as the comfort zone for your personality.

If you are performing work or fulfilling roles that are congruent with your leading role, minimal stress is involved. The opposite is also true, however. If your work requires tasks and roles that are not congruent with your leading role, you will feel higher levels of work-related stress.

An example would be the person with a leading role of Analyzer being in a position that required snap decisions. Another example would be someone with a leading role of Enterpriser who has to deal with detailed paperwork or slow and bureaucratic processes.

Supporting Role

Your supporting role is the complement to your leading role and plays a major part in your responses to stress and pressure.

For example, if your supporting role is T (Togetherness), you will tend to seek cooperation, sympathy, and help when under pressure. If your supporting role is E (Enterpriser), however, you will tend to become the rugged individualist under pressure.

The supporting role, A (Analyzer), will grow cautious and methodical, while the supporting role of M (Motivator) will raise their energy level and attempt to coach and persuade others.

FIGURE 4.3 | Sample Patterns

Common Personality Patterns

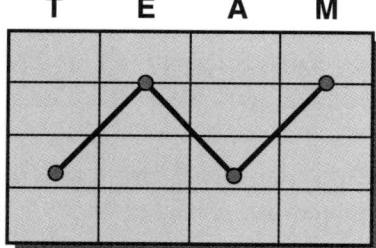

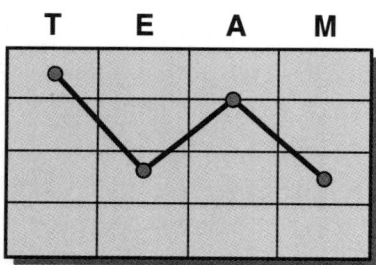

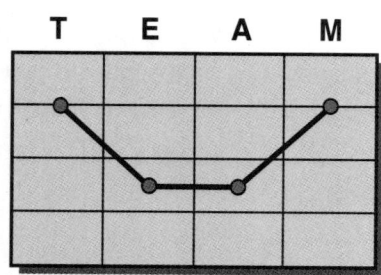

Uncommon Personality Patterns

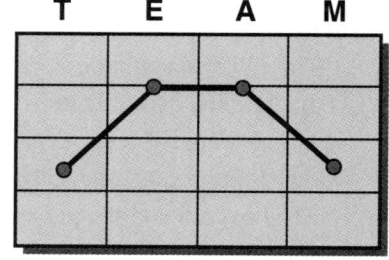

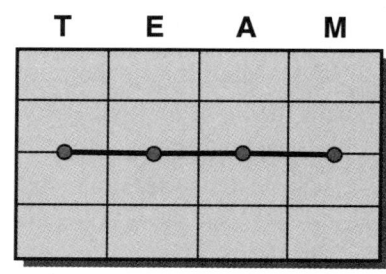

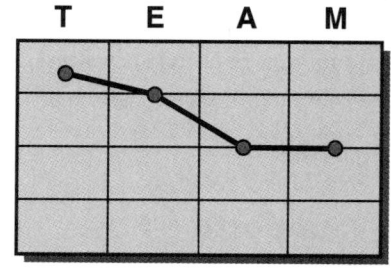

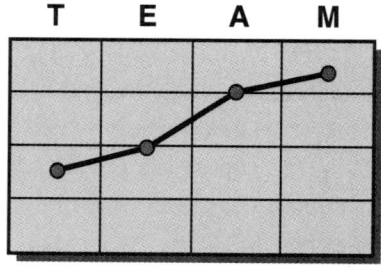

Villain Role

This is the personality style that causes the most stress and tension in your life. Because the level of this role is so low in your personality makeup, communicating with and working with a person of your villain role is an unnatural process for you.

Similarly, just as the individual you are working with fulfills your villain role, you may also be their villain role. Communication and understanding can be such strained processes for two people with opposing villain roles.

For example, if your villain role is T (Togetherness), you will become easily agitated with people who procrastinate, defend the status quo, and respond with oversensitivity. If, on the other hand, your villain role is E (Enterpriser), you will struggle with people who take charge and speak bluntly.

If your villain role is A (Analyzer), you will be easily annoyed by people who are very cautious, slow down processes, and overthink every matter that comes their way. Finally, if your villain role is M (Motivator), you will grow tense around people who are talkative, effervescent, and impulsive.

PREDICTABILITY—SIGNIFICANCE OF YOUR NUMBERS

The predictability of your personality or another individual's personality hinges on the level of the numbers on the T.E.A.M. Dynamics grid. In our sample (Figure 4.4), although both participants mapped out as high Es, the predictability of their behavior would show significant disparities.

In this case, John (E-35) and Judy (E-44) could claim that their leading role is E (Enterpriser), but their work style and behavior will show profound differences because of the level of their E.

John's style would be to take charge only when he felt that is what the other person or the group wanted. His leadership would be cooperative and empathic in nature.

Judy, however, would most likely take charge regardless of what others thought about it. In Judy, the E is a highly pronounced and definitive feature of her personality.

A 30 on any letter is the middle of the road or equator for that particular role. Once you get to around eight points higher or lower (38 or more, 22 or less) on any letter, you will fall into predictable behavior and response patterns.

Although there are four basic personality styles, each person is a unique recipe of those four basic ingredients. Each of us has within us all four personality roles to some degree—whether it be high or low—and is capable of responding in each role when necessary.

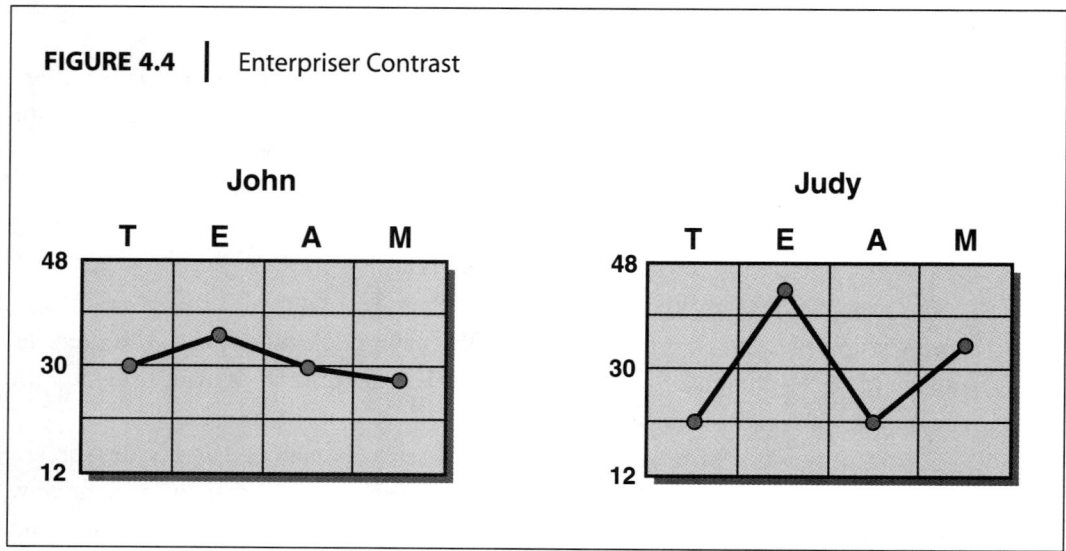

FIGURE 4.4 | Enterpriser Contrast

For example, a person with a 16 on the Analyzer line will dislike detail and usually avoid it, but is capable of becoming quite analytical if necessary. When sensitivity is called for, we can shift into the T side of our personality no matter how low it may be. When results and action are needed, we can shift into our E mode. When caution and careful planning are called for, we can shift into our A mode. Finally, when energy and optimism are called for, we can shift into our M mode.

When a person is high in one or two personality areas, these are good indicators of what their communication style and response to stress or pressure will be. One caveat: personality patterns are *not* a predictor of a person's values, beliefs, or temperament.

THE RECIPE FOR MAKING YOUR PERSONALITY

A helpful way to comprehend the balance of your personality is to look at the four personality styles as ingredients and the sum of these ingredients as the unique recipe that makes up your personality. Four basic personalities create an exponential number of possible combinations.

We should use this test as a means of understanding ourselves and others—not to stereotype them. No matter how low we are in one particular personality style, we still have some degree of that style. We can call upon that particular side of our personality in situations that demand such a response. For example, a person who is extremely low in the Analyzer personality could become quite analytical if flashing red lights came up behind him on the highway or if the IRS came calling.

A method for viewing your blended personality is to find the percentage of each of the personality ingredients. Divide the number of each personality style by 120. An example is shown in Figure 4.5.

Relational/Results Profile (Sample and Blank)

Of the four personalities, two are relationally oriented (T, M) and two are results oriented (E, A).

To get a snapshot of your personal relational/results orientation, add your T number to your M number and chart the total to the relational line on the grid shown in Figure 4.6. Next, add your E number to your A number and chart the total on the results line on the grid.

Interpreting the Relational/Results Grid

A majority of people will have totals within eight points of one another on the relational/results grid (see sample in Figure 4.7).

On the chart, we can see that this individual has an equal weighting of relational/results orientation regarding work and achievement.

A minority of individuals will have a grid that is heavily weighted toward relationships or results, as shown in Figures 4.8 and 4.9.

Extreme relational-oriented individuals will often maximize the time they spend conversing with and getting to know others and minimize their time in results-oriented tasks that are accomplished alone. We often call this type of individual a "people person."

FIGURE 4.5 | Calculating Your Personality Blend

Personality Style	Score	Division by 120 (Sum of TEAM)	Percentage
T—Togetherness	22	22 ÷ 120	18%
E—Enterpriser	44	44 ÷ 120	37%
A—Analyzer	16	16 ÷ 120	13%
M—Motivator	38	38 ÷ 120	32%

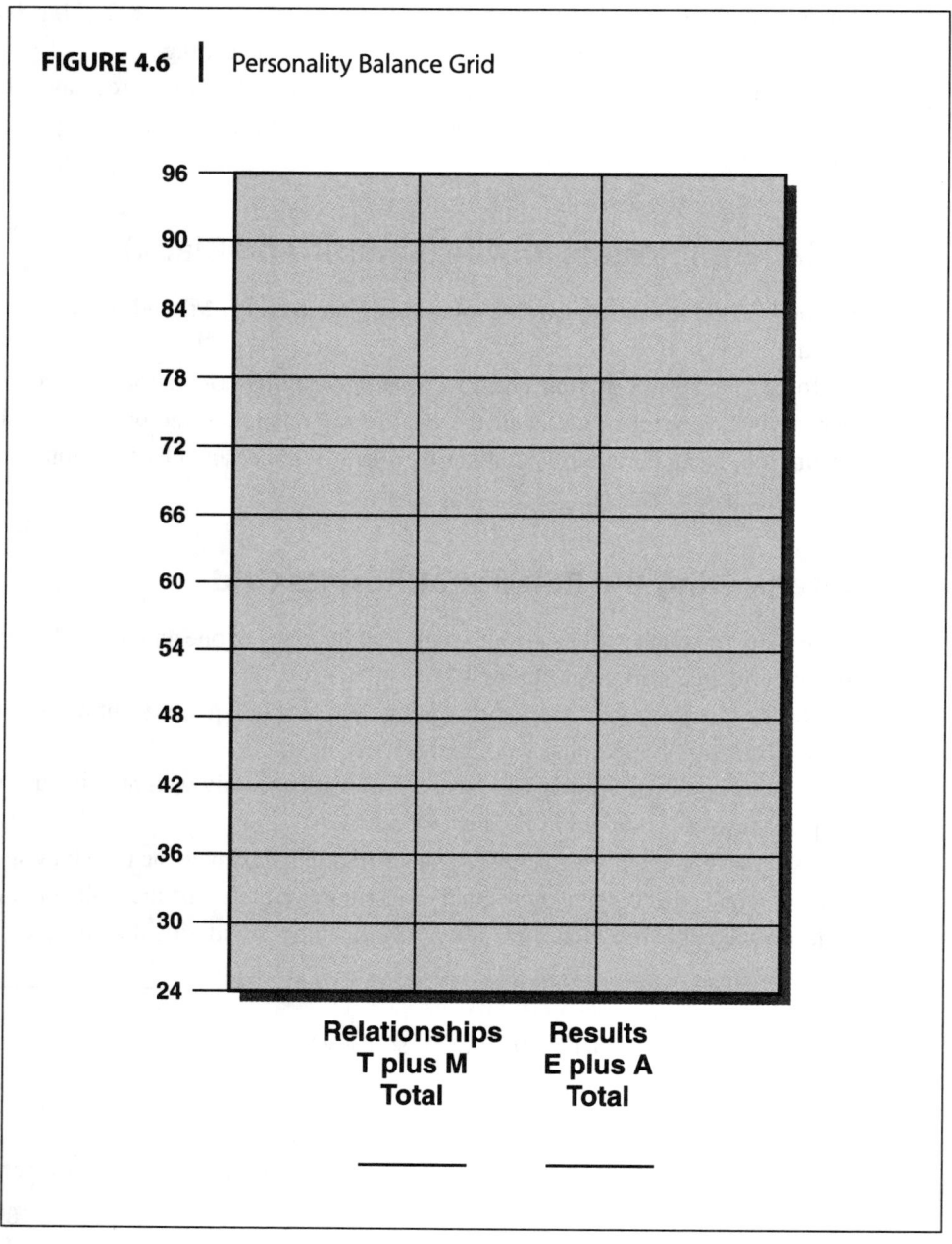

FIGURE 4.6 | Personality Balance Grid

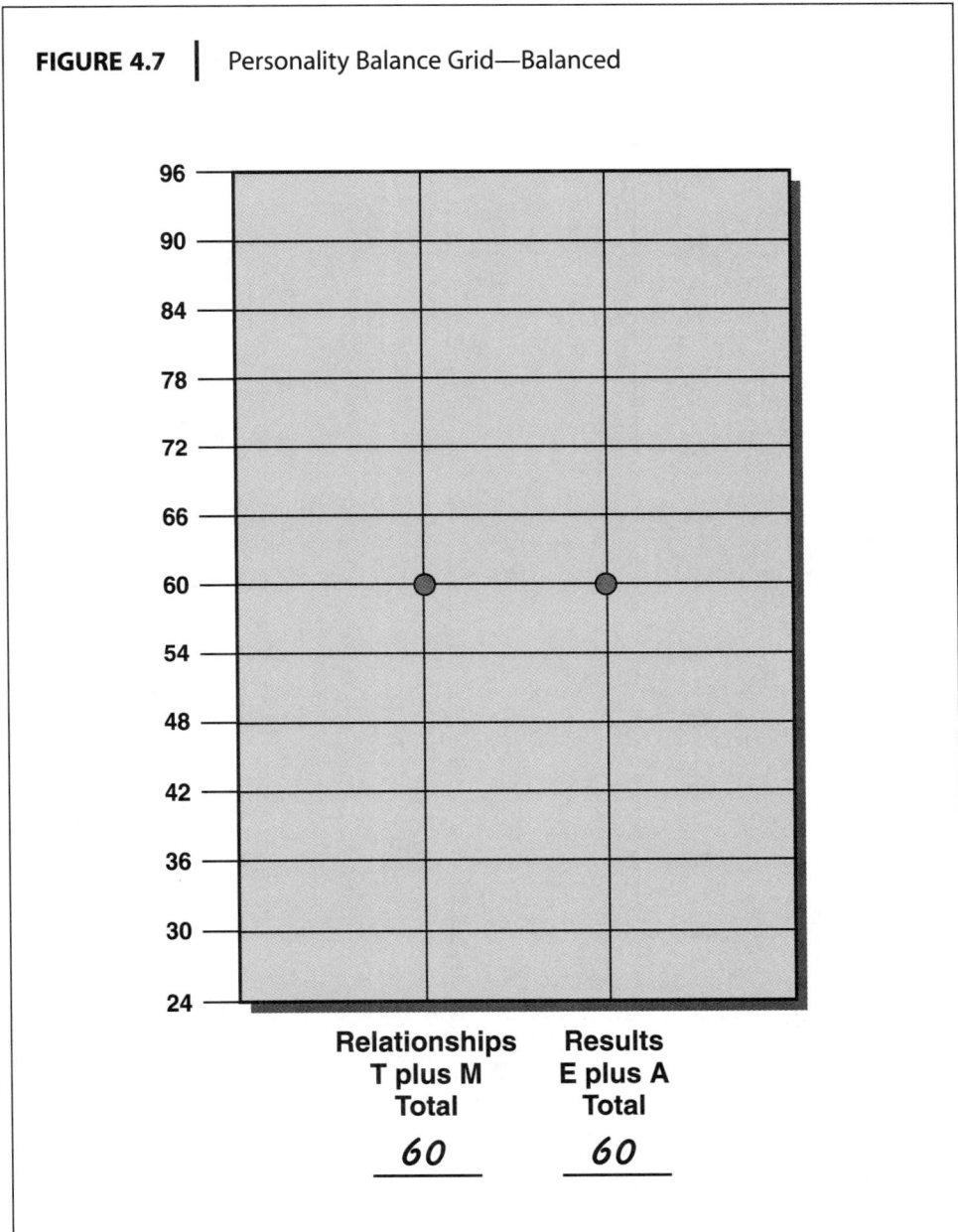

FIGURE 4.7 | Personality Balance Grid—Balanced

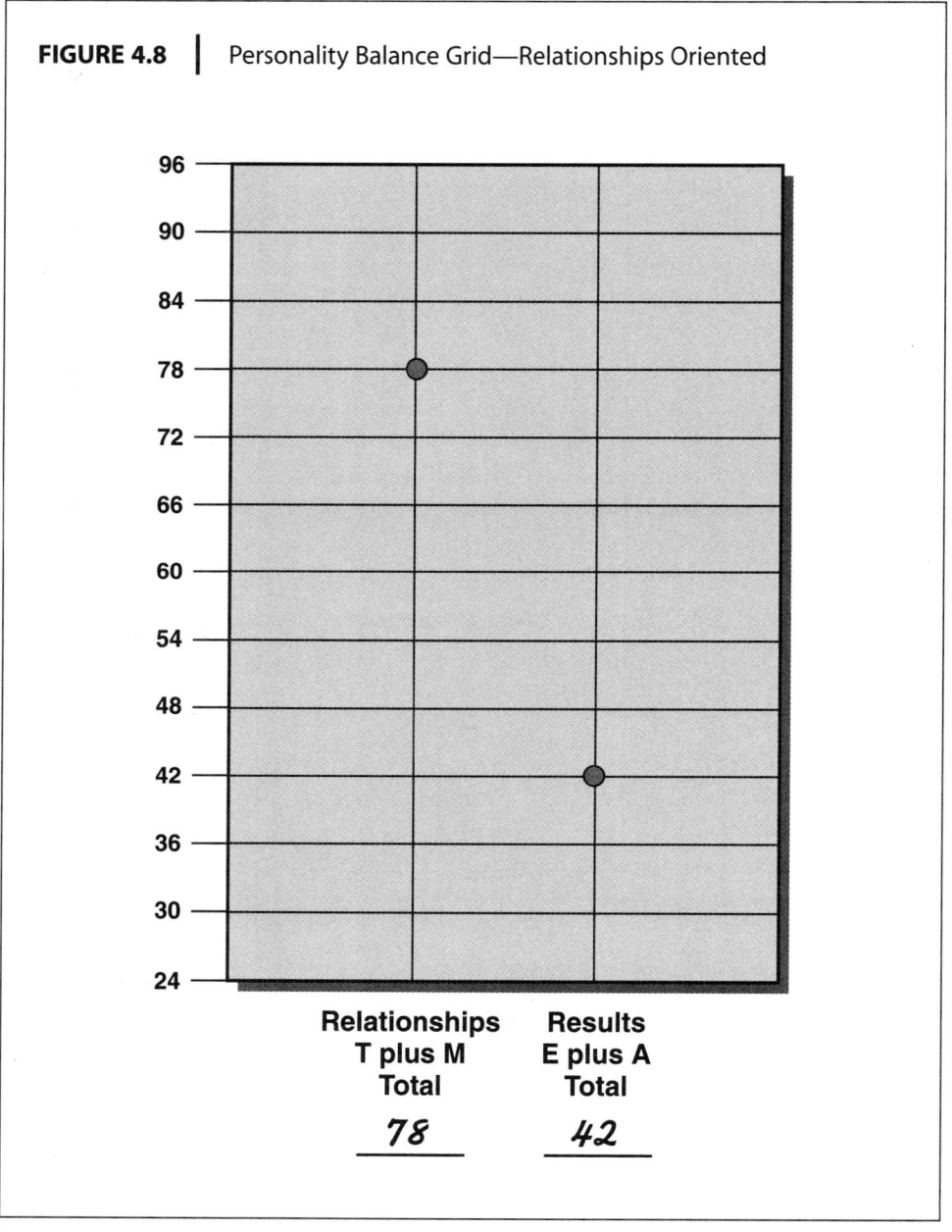

FIGURE 4.8 | Personality Balance Grid—Relationships Oriented

FIGURE 4.9 | Personality Balance Grid—Results Oriented

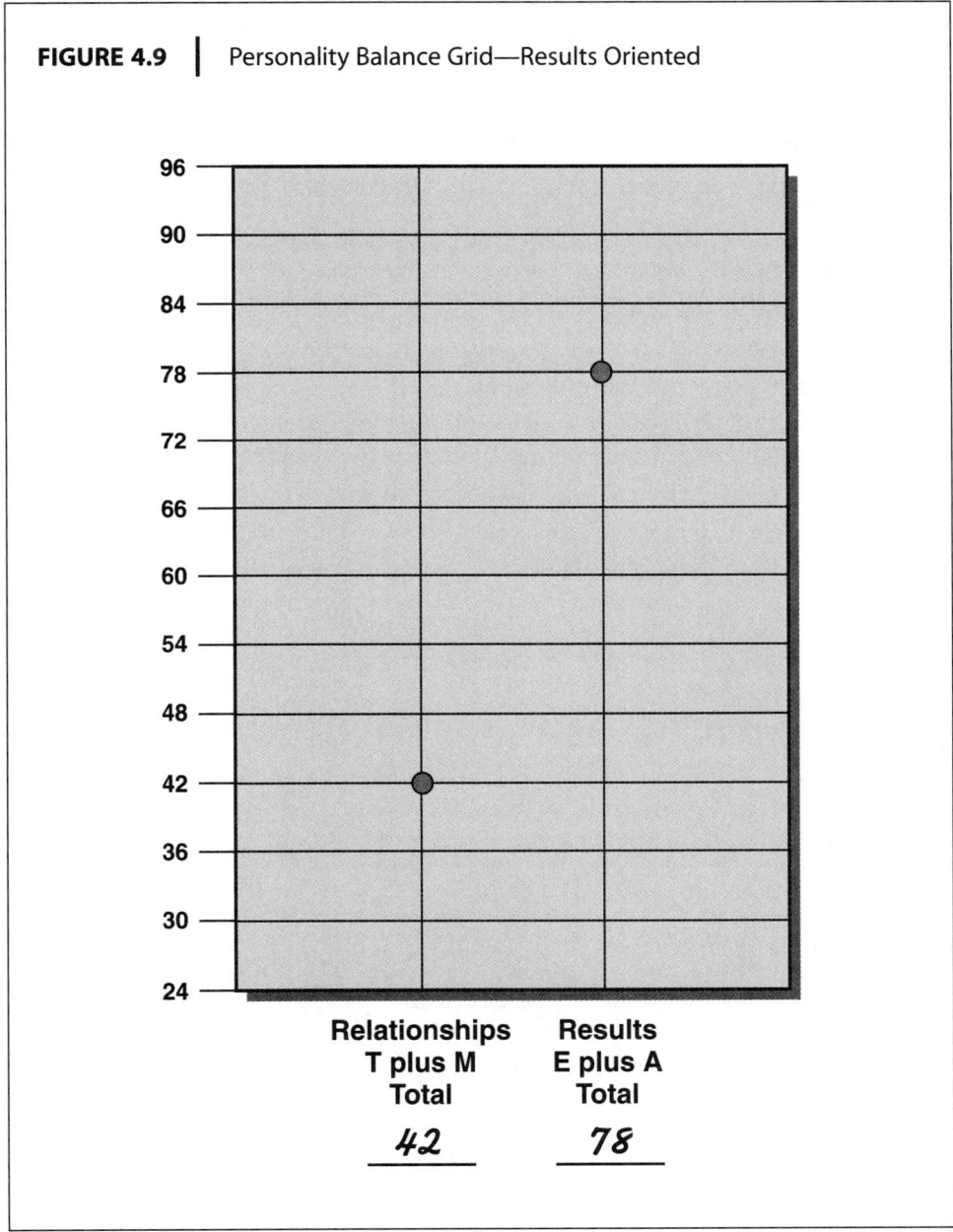

Extreme results-oriented individuals will be just the opposite. They will often minimize their time communicating and fellowshipping, and prefer to lose themselves in individual tasks and projects. Many engineers fit this profile.

POLAR OPPOSITES/ORIGINS OF CONFLICT

Much of the conflict we face is personality based. Our personality style in large part defines how we view people and events and how we respond to them. Two people of varying personality styles can view a single set of events and come away with completely opposite stories of what happened.

Many of the conflicts we face are simply rooted in personality differences. I am not wrong and you are not wrong—we simply perceive matters differently and, consequently, have different sets of priorities on how to resolve conflicts.

Figure 4.10 illustrates the natural opposite polarities of the four personalities. Ironically, up to 75 percent of married couples have been estimated to be personality oppo-

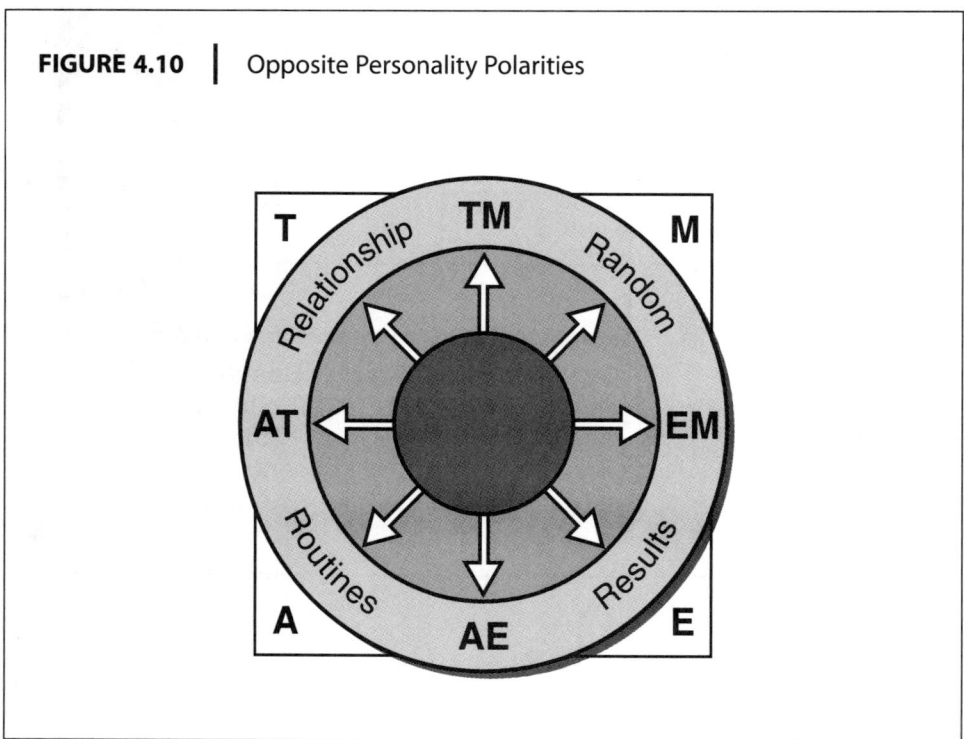

FIGURE 4.10 | Opposite Personality Polarities

sites. Why do we tend to marry our polar opposites? Maybe at the time, we were bored with our own personality and wanted to experience a different style. Then one day we wake up, look at our polar-opposite mate, and say, "So, you're going to be like this everyday!?"

A monumental leap in our ability to resolve conflict lies in understanding that much of it is rooted in personality. People are simply following the blueprint of their own personalities—just as we are.

Much of our disconnection with clients, lack of cooperation, and inability to persuade boils down to developing the ability to see matters from the other person's perspective. In the next chapter, "Understanding Personality DNA," we will explain the strengths, challenges, and areas of improvement for each of the four personalities. Once you understand these factors, your connection skills will improve as you begin viewing situations through the eyes of the client.

CHAPTER 5

Understanding Personality DNA

Personality is a person among persons. There is no personality of one
man on a desert island.

—Kilpatrick

You and I have no more control over the way our personality reacts to people and processes than we do over the color of our eyes or the shape of our noses. The same fact holds true for our clients. Every action, communication, and response is driven by our personality DNA—a psychological blueprint that we are born with. This personality DNA plays a leading role in determining the types of people and processes we are uncomfortable with. Once we come to an awareness of our own personality DNA, we suddenly realize why we click with some personalities and clash with others. We begin to realize why some processes drive us crazy, while others seem to revel in those processes.

The fact that our personality is blueprinted does not imply that we cannot adjust our behavior, communication, and responses. In fact, becoming aware of our personality DNA lets us recognize more readily where we need to adjust. We need to throttle back aspects of our personality when we are around certain types of clients, because those features will rub them the wrong way. With clients who match our own personality style, however, we need to let those particular features of our personality shine.

Awareness is the key we need to become great people connectors. Awareness is needed in three specific areas:

1. Who you are
2. Who those are around you and how they see you
3. What adjustments to my communication you need to make to build better connections or get plugged in

We need awareness of our strengths and challenges and areas we can improve. There is no good or bad personality pattern. We are what we are. Success comes when we are aware enough to recognize how our personality plays out to others and know how to temper features of our personality in given situations.

The truly mature financial professional is highly cognizant of her personality challenges and the inherent relational liabilities. In relationship building, this personal awareness is 80 percent of the battle. Many people keep making the same relational errors over and over and just don't seem to get it. On the other hand, being aware of your personality DNA will pay rich dividends because awareness will help you play to your strengths, avoid your liabilities, and focus on areas you can improve. Following is such an agenda for each personality.

THE TOGETHERNESS PERSONALITY

 Strengths:

- Strives for cooperation and consensus
- Keeps everyone involved
- Peacemaker
- Kind and caring
- Supportive and encouraging
- Amiable/tactful

Challenges:

- Wants to please everyone
- Has difficulty making decisions
- Has trouble standing up for feelings
- Easily offended
- Can be overly passive

Self-improvements:

- Make feelings clear
- Ask for clear directions
- Stop apologizing for opinions/ideas
- Take events in stride
- Focus on handling criticism with more emotional detachment

Strengths

The Togetherness personality has a feeling-oriented mode of relating. These people are always striving for consensus, harmony, and teamwork. They are easily rattled by conflict and are likely to play the peacemaker's role by saying, "Let's please try to get along."

The Togetherness style is led by a sense of caring and constantly tries to play the affirmer and encourager. Such people take a warm, personable approach and strive to avoid offending others. They are by nature understanding and responsive listeners.

Togetherness people try always to show respect to others and expect the same in return. They have their radar up for genuineness, sincerity, and amiability and tend to shy away from those who do not display these characteristics.

Challenges

The Achilles' heel of the Togetherness personality is a need to please everyone. By Achilles' heel, we mean an inherent characteristic of personality that causes 90 percent of our personal stress and relational frustration. We know of an Enterpriser whose idea of a good practical joke is to call Togetherness friends at 9 PM and tell them that somebody is mad at them. The Togetherness personality, because of their people-pleasing tendencies, won't be able to sleep all night. Enterprisers, on the other hand, would sleep like a baby knowing someone was upset with them.

Because of their tendency to want to please everyone, this personality often has a difficult time making decisions. They don't want anyone to be upset with the decisions they make. They also have trouble standing up for their own feelings. Mitch likes to say that you can never quite trust the smile of the Togetherness personality. They can smile benignly at you and simultaneously plan your assassination. They are unlikely to tell you how they really feel and are most likely to tell you what you want to hear.

Here are the common relational liabilities for the Togetherness personality:

- Procrastination
- Aversion to candor and straightforwardness
- Oversensitivity
- Lack of assertiveness
- Overseriousness
- Propensity for following the crowd
- Fear of rocking the boat
- Need for constant affirmation
- People-pleasing tendencies

Areas for Improvements

One of the first areas Togetherness people need to work on is dealing with issues in a more objective manner. They can bog down processes by overplaying the consensus card or by letting themselves be too easily offended. They must learn to not take every disagreement personally and try to handle criticism with a higher degree of emotional detachment. A person's comment may be simply about improving the process—not necessarily an attack on you as a person. The Togetherness person needs to work on stronger assertiveness skills. They often punctuate their ideas with physical and tonal question marks, as if to say, "I'm sorry . . . is it OK to say that?" They should practice speaking with conviction and resolve.

THE ENTERPRISER PERSONALITY

 Strengths:

- Results oriented
- Competitive
- Time conscious
- Candid
- Risk taking
- Thriving on pressure

Challenges:

- Impatient with people and processes
- May compromise quality for speed
- Overly individualistic
- Can be abrasive/tactless
- Autocratic tendencies

Self-improvements:

- Show more patience with people/processes
- Articulate more encouragement and support
- Make sure others see ideas before moving forward
- Listen
- Get help for detail work
- Get others involved
- Treat people with respect

Strengths

The Enterpriser personality is results oriented—and their list of strengths reflect that dynamic. Enterprisers are competitive by nature and they like to win. They are time-conscious and like to get as much done as they can in as little time as possible. Consequently, they are quite good at juggling projects and at multitasking. Their multitasking, by the way, often offends the Togetherness personality, who would prefer a more personal focus.

The Enterpriser is a risk taker and an agent for change. Their motto is, "If it isn't broken, *break it*. We've had it long enough." Enterprisers tend to be innovative thinkers. Another unique feature of Enterprisers is their ability to thrive under pressure. Enterprisers excel in pressure-packed situations, whereas such circumstances bring out tension and chaos in the other personalities. We often tell audiences that if they are ever in a burning building, they should follow the Enterprisers out, because they will find the most expeditious route out of the building. You don't want to follow the Togetherness individuals because they'll be apologizing to everyone that they aren't leaving with. You don't want to follow the Analyzers because they'll be trying to explain the fire marshal's code to the letter, as well as lining everybody up in alphabetical order.

You definitely don't want to follow the Motivators because they'll be cooking hotdogs and marshmallows, and making signs that say, "Burn, baby, burn!"

Enterprisers also tend to be practical, resourceful, and industrious. They simply want to get results.

Challenges

The Achilles' heel of the Enterpriser personality is impatience with people and processes. Things just never seem to move at the speed Enterprisers desire. Consequently, Enterprisers begin to get frustrated and begin pushing harder. They tend toward abrasiveness, harshness, and tactlessness in the name of, "Hey, you wanted the truth, didn't you?"

Often, because of their impatience, they will approach tasks in an individualistic manner, not wanting to be slowed down by the indecisive and status quo protectors. Enterprisers also tend to be autocratic because they are happiest when they are in charge. We asked a group of Enterprisers why they felt the compulsion to take over every situation, and one member of the group answered in a quintessential Enterpriser fashion, "Look," he said, "I'll make this real simple. People are sheep. Get it?"

Common Enterpriser relational liabilities include:

- Bluntness/insensitivity
- Impatience
- Autocratic manner/condescending
- Lack of affirmative input
- Propensity for giving ultimatums
- Confrontational style
- Misguided competitiveness
- Poor listening skills
- Compulsion for quick completion
- Frustrated with risk-averse personalities
- Sarcasm

Areas of Improvement

The Enterpriser needs to reach out and get others involved. As one Enterpriser put it, "Being a rugged individualist can lead to a lonely existence." Enterprisers would be wise to remember that although others may slow the process, they may enrich it as well.

Enterprisers need to be careful to display more respect, tact, and diplomacy. Some things may be true but are just not worth saying. They need to soften the harsh and blunt nature of their communication. Enterprisers need to help others see the vision before they move forward—offering them the needed encouragement along the way (without sarcasm).

Finally, Enterprisers need to get help with the detail work, the small stuff that makes big things happen. Enterprisers are most comfortable dealing with the big picture and will become frustrated or negligent if they do not get help with the small stuff.

THE ANALYZER PERSONALITY

 Strengths:

- Accurate
- Seeks proof and validation
- Plans projects in a step-by-step manner
- Focuses on facts
- Quality conscious
- Sets high standards for self/others

Challenges:

- Tends toward pessimism
- Can be critical/judgmental
- Has difficulty with spontaneity
- Rigid
- Paralysis by analysis
- Can be impersonal

Self-improvements:

- Open up to new ideas and ways of doing things
- Accept people for who they are
- Display more warmth and affection
- Restrain judgment
- Work on stress management
- Streamline communications

Strengths

The Analyzer is accuracy-oriented—they want to get things right. Consequently, they will be sticklers for proof, data, and evaluation. They are inclined to focus on facts about things and about people. They are quality-conscious and have very high standards, first for themselves and secondly for others they work with. They have a hard time understanding people who don't do their best to do things right.

It would be safe to say that everything as we know it in this world would self-destruct if not for the influence of the Analyzer personality. They are the architects and engineers who design, the specialized builders, the editors and specialists who make sure things are done and made right. Without the Analyzers, we would lose quality control.

Analyzers ask good questions, plan things out carefully, and are conscientious about following procedures. They are generally industrious and tenacious and try to stay logical in their approach.

Challenges

The Achilles' heel of the Analyzer is their propensity toward skepticism. Their skepticism serves them well in process development, but not in the people department. They are often guilty of snatching defeat out of the jaws of victory, telling people how and why they will fail and who will be responsible.

Analyzers also tend to be critical and judgmental. They see the world in black-and-white and have little patience with those who meddle in gray areas.

Two words you never want to say to an Analyzer are, "Hurry up." Nor do you want to imply haste. They will immediately begin to suffer a condition known as *paralysis by analysis.* Stress hormones freeze out their cognitive abilities when their time frames get shrunk. They don't believe you can do something well and do it speedily.

Analyzers also tend to be rigid in their approach. For them to change their way of thinking is difficult. Therefore, they will work vigorously to defend their present point of view. Analyzers can also be so consumed with facts, details, and processes that they neglect being personable and, as a result, relationships begin to suffer.

Here are the common relational liabilities of the Analyzer:

- Impersonal approach/appearance
- Values processes over people
- Resistance to change
- Pessimistic views
- Slow to change view

- Defensive
- Self-justifying
- Intellectual arrogance
- Propensity for criticizing and judging
- Tension and loss of composure under pressure

Areas of Improvement

The greatest need for Analyzers is to increase their flexibility, both with processes and with people. Opening up to new ideas and new ways of doing things is important. It's important to not panic when people or processes go off the linear track. Many Analyzers need to work on their stress management skills because they tend to become tense and frustrated when matters exit the realm of predictability.

Analyzers often need to improve their people skills as well. It's OK to smile, to laugh, and to show some enthusiasm. They should work at restraining their judgment, accepting people as they are, and displaying more warmth and affection.

THE MOTIVATOR PERSONALITY

 Strengths:

- Enthusiastic/high energy
- Likes variety
- Tries to create an amicable atmosphere
- Persuasive/articulate
- Spontaneous
- Laughs easily/fun loving
- Flexible
- Optimistic

Challenges:

- Impulsive
- Lacks discipline and follow-through
- Gets bored easily
- Can have several projects going at once, but few are complete
- Overlooks analysis

- Whimsical; may easily forget earlier commitments
- Overuses enthusiasm
- Has an aversion to small type

Self-improvements:

- Plan and see projects to the end
- Be careful in making commitments
- Get organizational support
- Listen and restrain commentary
- Don't take credit where it is not due

Strengths

The Motivator is energy-oriented. Because Motivators are social creatures by nature, they like to deal with people who are fun loving, flexible, and friendly. They like to take a playful and random approach to life and projects.

Motivators enjoy conversing, mixing with people, persuading others, and inspiring others toward their goals. They are naturally gifted at building excitement and enthusiasm. Motivators have a spontaneous nature and have an easy time making changes in midstream. Motivators also like a lot of variety and are easily bored with monotonous tasks.

Motivators are optimistic by nature and tend to see the possibilities more than the obstacles in every situation. Because Motivators tend to have their radar up for positive energy in others, they are quickly repelled by criticism, skepticism, and cynicism. Motivators like to keep energy levels up. They are naturally charismatic, articulate, and charming in their approach.

Challenges

The Achilles' heel of the Motivator is impulsivity. They are often guilty of leaping before they look. Many Motivators live by the motto, "Ready, fire, aim!" They often pull the trigger prematurely. Contrarily, the Togetherness personality's approach would be "Ready, aim, fire, because that's the way you're supposed to do it." The Analyzer would say, "Ready, aim . . . aim . . . aim . . . have we run this past compliance yet?" The Enterpriser would skip the "Ready" and just say, "Fire!"

Motivators often have trouble with freedom of thought (foot-in-mouth disease) and will blurt out words they later wish they hadn't. Motivators also tend to oversell when under pressure, dominate conversation, and have trouble focusing when someone else is talking.

Many Motivators struggle with organizational and detail issues, having an aversion to paperwork and fulfillment issues. They like to start better than they like to finish.

Motivators can also be quite whimsical, which leads to making promises and commitments they easily forget. This can and does lead to many relational conflicts. Once those conflicts arise, Motivators will then avoid confronting them.

Following is a list of the Motivator's relational liabilities:

- Easily bored
- Impulsive
- Lack of follow-through
- Empty promises and shallow commitments
- Disorganization
- Uses flattery to persuade
- Aversion to confronting conflict
- Inappropriate speech/obnoxious behavior
- Dominating conversations
- Overzealous appetite for attention and recognition
- Persuasive manipulation to achieve objectives
- Lack of discipline and self-restraint
- Taking credit for the work of others

Areas of Improvement

Motivators need to exercise discipline in fulfilling promises, sticking with projects and tasks, and following through on communication. For many Motivators, employing assistance with organization and detail work would be wise.

Motivators need to think through their ideas before promoting them. They need to be careful not to garner credit that should go to another person. Motivators also need to concentrate on getting past image and projecting more sincerity with people.

In our next chapter, we will show you how to read visual and verbal signals to know exactly which personality you are dealing with. Before you can adjust your communication to connect with a client's personality DNA, you must first learn the signals that tip off what that personality is.

PART II

Making the Personality Connection

You Have to Read Them before You Can Lead Them

Understanding Personality Signals

A research team once studied 1,000 sales interviews by putting a clock on the amount of time the financial professional was talking and the amount of time the client was talking. We know who did most of the talking; the financial professional talked 49 out of every 60 seconds.

One of the problems in a typical selling organization is that those doing the selling are usually passionate people. That passion is what makes them good at what they do, but it also leads many to believe that selling is in the telling. The truth is, however, we can really only sell after we've done the listening. When we're telling before listening, we haven't dug up the ground to sow the seed, and we might be throwing our seed on ground that isn't quite fertile. We can get so excited about whatever we're talking about, that we start telling before we've dug up the ground to find out who it is it we're talking to.

In Chapter 11, we will introduce the MVP Approach—a strategy for helping you to make lasting connections with your clients. Here is a brief introduction.

On the outer circle of influencing people are methodologies we have been taught in communicating and selling to others. These are the basic techniques that we learn regarding relationship building with clients.

A layer below that is values. The best way to learn about each person's values is to hear their experiences. Some of the best questions that you can ask clients are where they've been, where they've lived, and who they've worked for. By asking those questions, we begin to discover the experiences that are unique to each individual. You will find out what they want out of life and the kind of people they want to do business with. Keeping your antenna up for those kinds of values is important.

At the core is personality—or what we refer to as Personality DNA. No matter how people may try, they cannot get away from being the personality that they are. We once read a simple but brilliant gem of human wisdom on building relationships. It said, "Treat everybody like a "10."" It's the old Bo Derek reference. Very few people, however, upon meeting someone automatically think of that individual as a "10." We all have our biases about people. We rank one as more important than another. We have biases about the way people look, the way they look at us, the way they talk, where they've been, and where they've lived. We will provide you with the tools to get around those biases so that you can get closer to treating everybody like a "10." How do you accomplish that? By connecting with their core personality. That's where the next two chapters are headed.

Let's review the core of each personality style. We like to use the analogy of radar. Every personality has an antenna. Ask yourself what the antenna is looking for when you walk in the room. When Togetherness people walk in the room, their antenna is up for feelings. Their main concern is sensitivity—how something is going to play out to other people. An Enterpriser's antenna is up for results—"Are you going to help me get results?" If you are working with Analyzers, their antenna is up for accuracy. "Is this going to be right?" Experience shows that two words will make you a winner with Analyzers: *right* and *caution*. Use the phrases, "We want to make sure this is right" and "Let's exercise caution." The Motivator's antenna is up for energy. "How much energy can you bring to the table" and "How positive a person are you?"

BECOME A BETTER OBSERVER

Our objective is to help you learn to improve your observational skills. A major factor in preventing many of us from succeeding with people and building strong relationships is an inability to observe people. Remember the study about the average financial professional talking 49 seconds out of 60? If they are doing most of the talking, they have difficulty observing the other individual. We rarely learn anything while our mouths are moving. Those who win are the people who observe. The reason many do not observe is that they don't know what to look for. We now know what we're looking for—our client's motives, values, and personality. In this chapter, we are going to focus on personality.

To improve your observational skills, you must learn how to recognize the personality style of your clients and prospective clients quickly. This skill is really quite simple. Although it may sound complicated, after you identify the signals and begin observing those around you, you're going to be shaking your head at how obvious people really are. The natural follow-up is learning how to apply these skills in a selling situation, which is what Chapter 7 is all about—customizing your sales presentation for each personality type.

Recognition Tools

Ultimately, our goal is for you to make these observations intuitively. Our goal is for you to be able to walk up to any individuals, enter into a conversation, observe the way they talk, observe the way they look, make mental notes, and start adjusting your communication to their core personality. But in the meantime, we're providing you with a tool called the Client Conversation Profile (see Figures 6.1 and 6.2). You can use this profile in situations where you are dealing with prospective clients and you want to learn how to gauge their personality. After a conversation with a client, fill out the profile based on that conversation, and you'll have a strong indication of that individual's personality profile.

Take a moment right now and think of a client with whom you're trying to build a relationship. Think about the last conversation you had with this individual, and then go ahead and fill out the Client Conversation Profile. When you're finished, tally up the letters the same way you would on a T.E.A.M. Dynamics personality quiz. Tally up the number of Ts, Es, As, and Ms. The totals will indicate their lead and villain roles.

Do the results ring true for you about the person you just assessed? The Client Conversation Profile is a quick way for you to start figuring out what drives the clients you're dealing with. The reason this assessment works is because personality is automatic. What we mean by this is that personality inclinations are blueprinted in the DNA of our psyche. Our personality style is animated by our eyes, our demeanor, our faces, conversation, the style of questions we ask, and in our vocal patterns and pace. Our core personality simply sends automatic signals through our mannerisms.

We sat down and interviewed scores of clients from each personality group on camera. After watching the tape, we were almost inclined to believe that the people were scripted, because the individuals from each personality group gave the same types of answers in the same types of tones. However, the individuals were not scripted—the answers they gave were simply natural responses to questions that we asked them. We asked questions such as what qualities they were looking for in a financial professional, and as they answered those questions, we clearly saw their personality styles. We have developed a training on this skill set where we show this tape to financial professionals and they can see firsthand how obvious the personality signals are.

Start observing right away. As soon as you set this book down, turn on your observational skills. Start looking for these signals: demeanor, eyes, face, physical style, conversational flow, style of questioning, and vocal patterns. Start making mental notes. Don't just meander through conversations—observe!

FIGURE 6.1 | Client Conversation Profile

NAME OF CLIENT: _____

Directions: In the following groups, underline **one** phrase that is **most true** about your client. In the next column of the same group, underline **one** phrase that is **least true** about your client.

BODY LANGUAGE AND TONAL PROFILE					
1. Voice pitch:	**Most**	**Least**	**6. Style of questioning:**	**Most**	**Least**
• limited range	T	T	• asks "how" questions	T	T
• punches certain words	E	E	• drives to the "bottom line"	E	E
• monotone	A	A	• gathers information	A	A
• full range	M	M	• focuses on people issues	M	M
2. Tone of voice:	**Most**	**Least**	**7. Listening style:**	**Most**	**Least**
• agreeable	T	T	• receptive	T	T
• blunt	E	E	• fidgety, abrupt	E	E
• controlled, precise	A	A	• pays close attention	A	A
• friendly, upbeat	M	M	• moving/holds back energy	M	M
3. Pace of speech:	**Most**	**Least**	**8. Response to presentation:**	**Most**	**Least**
• slow, steady	T	T	• nods, cooperates	T	T
• fast, punctuated	E	E	• interrupts/draws quick conclusions	E	E
• slow, deliberate	A	A	• skeptical, hesitant, cautious	A	A
• loud, fast	M	M	• expresses feelings, wants openness	M	M
4. Conversational style:	**Most**	**Least**	**9. Eye and facial language:**	**Most**	**Least**
• amiable, plodding	T	T	• caring eyes, blushes easily	T	T'
• confident, driving, candid	E	E	• piercing eyes, confident defiance	E	E
• meticulous, reserved	A	A	• scrutinizing, poker face	A	A
• free-flowing, random	M	M	• happy eyes, big smile	M	M
5. During conversation, client . . .	**Most**	**Least**	**10. Physical style:**	**Most**	**Least**
• is calm and passive.	T	T	• polite, accommodating	T	T
• pushes toward the bottom line.	E	E	• restless, intense	E	E
• is uncomfortable with diversions.	A	A	• nervous, intense	A	A
• attempts to dominate.	M	M	• excitable, gesturing	M	M

FIGURE 6.2 | Client Conversation Profile—Scoring Grid

Directions: Add letters from the "MOST" column and record them next to the corresponding letter. (Take lead and support role from this column.) Add letters from the "LEAST" column and record next to the corresponding letter. Finally, determine the Lead Role (top score), Support Role (second highest number), and Villain Role (Lowest number), and record. (See sample scoring on previous page.)

SCORING GRID	
MOST:	T = E = A = M =
LEAST:	T = E = A = M =
LEAD ROLE: Highest score under MOST column	_____
SUPPORT ROLE: 2nd highest score under MOST column	_____
VILLAIN ROLE: Highest score under LEAST column	_____

THE TOGETHERNESS PERSONALITY

Let's begin with the visual clues that the individuals of the Togetherness personality style will give you:

- Their demeanor is friendly but not effervescent.
- They are calm and passive.
- Their eyes are soft, caring, and approachable.
- Their physical style is nonthreatening, and they typically will allow others to take the lead.
- They tend to mirror other people's mannerisms.

One of the clues to look for in identifying a Togetherness personality is the nod. An unconscious nod is always coming from the Togetherness personality.

During our camera interviews with scores of clients from each personality group, we observed how often the individuals of the Togetherness personality, after answering a question, would look at the interviewer with a questioning look as if to say, "Was my answer OK?" Instead of punctuating with an exclamation, they punctuated with a question mark. They are often looking for approval, which is a part of the Togetherness nature that they can't easily hold back.

What do you hear? The conversational flow of the Togetherness personality is responsive, respectful, and cooperative. Observe the types of questions they ask. You will hear role-oriented questions such as, "What is expected of me?" "What will you need from me?" "How will you support me?" We call these hand-holding questions.

It is also important to listen for the voice patterns of your clients. If you segregated people by personality, audiotaped their conversations, and then watched an audiometer, you would be able to see patterns that corresponded with each of the personality styles. The Togetherness pattern (see Figure 6.3) is slow and steady, like gently rolling waves—never too high or low.

FIGURE 6.3 | Conversational Clues: The Togetherness Personality

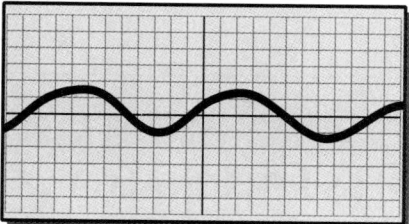

Voice Pitch: **Gently rolling waves**

THE ENTERPRISER PERSONALITY

With the Enterpriser personality, their confidence level comes through loud and clear. In the business world, Enterprisers are the ones doing a great deal of controlling. A great rule to remember for winning over Enterprisers is found in Mark Twain's writings—you have to walk the fine line between flattering and abusing them. Enterprisers have no respect for people who come along and just tell them what they want to hear. On the other hand, they need some flattery, because Enterprisers tend to believe they are God's gift to the world—there just aren't enough people talking about it. Yet Enterprisers only respect those who have the power to abuse them. But remember not to make the mistake of abusing Enterprisers too early in the process.

The visual clues Enterprisers will give you are as follows:

- They are candid and competent.
- Their eyes are laser direct and busy.
- They will often smirk and hold their head high.
- They carry their chin uplifted.

To help you identify the Enterpriser personality, think of the look you see at a poker table when somebody has really good cards. Enterprisers like to give that smirking impression that they have cards they're not playing yet. Even when they don't have the cards, they like to give you the impression that they do.

Enterprisers are restless and poised for action. Think of a viper ready to strike at any minute. In conversations, you'll hear them pushing for the bottom line. Enterprisers are notorious for constantly interrupting—to move the conversation along at a faster pace. Enterprisers are confrontational. For them, it's not about tact and diplomacy; it's about getting to the point of resolution quickly. They're abrupt in their speech and often ask questions about time and results, such as, "What's the bottom line?" or "How long will it take?"

Sometimes, differentiating between the body language of Enterprisers and Analyzers can be confusing, because both personality styles are good at the poker face. However, we know our approach with Enterprisers and Analyzers differs hugely. The difference between the two personality styles is their preference between quick and right. Enterprisers will push toward speedy results, while Analyzers will push toward accurate results. Their differing pace sets them apart.

Another way to differentiate between Enterprisers and Analyzers is their voice patterns. The voice pattern of the Analyzer personality style is very controlled. The voice pattern of Enterprisers is also controlled, but just when you think they've settled into an even pattern, they'll punch a word for effect (see Figure 6.4).

FIGURE 6.4 | Conversational Clues: The Enterpriser Personality

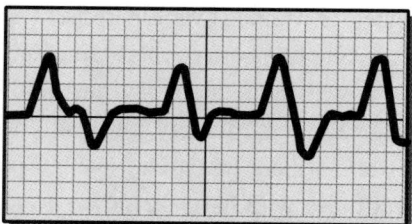

Voice Pitch: Punches certain words

THE ANALYZER PERSONALITY

What are some clues that will help you identify your Analyzer clients? First of all, look at their eyes. Their eyes are serious and intense, almost as if you can see question marks in them. Their eyes seem to ask, "What are you talking about here?" Their eyes seem to beg for clarity. They have the look that says, "Explain that one more time." The visual clues Analyzers will give you are as follows:

- Their demeanor is reserved, meticulous, and nervous.
- Their eyes are scrutinizing, scanning, and squinting.
- Their face is controlled and nonemotional—a poker face.
- Their posture is rigid.

The conversational flow of the Analyzer is very deliberate and intensely focused. Notice the hesitation in their speech and choice of words. While Enterprisers want to finish sentences for others, Analyzers meticulously look for the perfect word to express what they're thinking. Analyzers ask more questions than any other personality style. They like to ask detailed questions and begin them with who, what, when, where, and why. But remember, all their questions are really about the one big question, "Is this the right thing to do?" Using the words *right* and *caution* with Analyzers is very powerful.

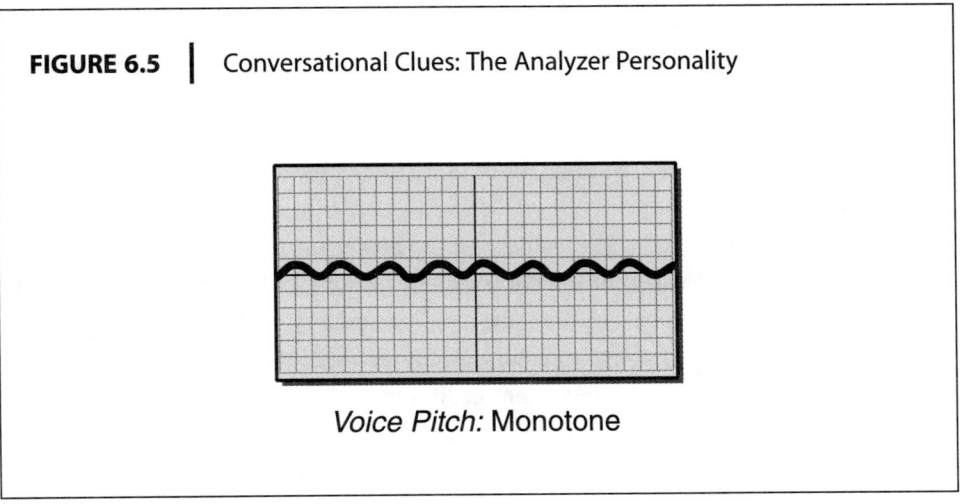

FIGURE 6.5 | Conversational Clues: The Analyzer Personality

Voice Pitch: Monotone

You can see from Figure 6.5 that the voice pattern of Analyzers is precise, sometimes monotone, slow, and deliberate—and always controlled. Remember, that's what it's all about for the Analyzer; they like to be in control of their own emotions.

THE MOTIVATOR PERSONALITY

With the Motivator personality style, life is all about having fun. You'll observe a great deal of motion in their body language. A conversation with Motivators is like dancing—a lot of lingual moves are going on. From many Motivators' point of view, work is just something that gets in the way of having fun. For the Motivator personality, getting a result, signing a contract, or making a deal is almost just an aside. "Why were we here again?" they might ask, then remember and say, "Oh yeah, let's do it." Some of the visual clues Motivators will give you are as follows:

- Their demeanor is free flowing, playful, and animated.
- Their eyes are happy, dancing, and wide open.
- Their face and physical style is warm and energetic.

The Motivator's conversational flow is flexible and random. It is hilarious to watch Analyzers and Motivators in a meeting—that is, if you're not involved. Analyzers have to deal with everything in a linear fashion: A, B, C, and D. Motivators, on the other hand, do not even know how to spell linear. For Motivators, conversation jumps all over the map. A good talk to Motivators is like a pinball game. During this random conversation, their greatest pride is remembering where they were, "Oh yeah, that's what we're here to talk about." Motivators can also be fidgety. Because they have so much energy under the hood, a lot more horsepower is there that they're not showing to you.

Keep in mind that Motivators use the power of personality to get things done. Because of that, Analyzers and Motivators can literally hate each other. To better understand the difference between the two personality styles, remember that they have different routes to achieve results. Analyzers achieve results through processes; they define a clear process to get the result and stick to it. Motivators, on the other hand, do not believe in processes as much as they believe in the power of personality to get things done. Motivators know that if they are engaging and charismatic, they will win people over. So, who's right here? They both are—they've just got to learn to deal with each other.

Motivators also like to network and ask questions like, "Who are you working with? Who do you know? How big is this thing going to be?" Because Motivators look great when they're telling a good story, you can win them over by giving them a story they can tell to others.

As you can see from Figure 6.6, the Motivator's vocal pattern is all over the map, a wide range with lots of ups and downs.

FIGURE 6.6 | Conversational Clues: The Motivator Personality

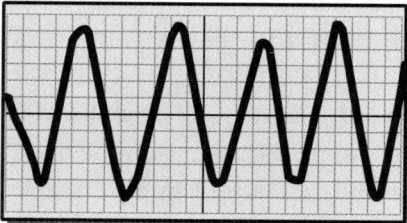

Voice Pitch: Has a full range

In reading others, start with the eyes, which are truly the gateway to the soul. Core personality shines through the eyes. An individual's core personality also manifests itself in posture, facial expression, and tone and pace of speech. Becoming a keen observer of these mannerisms is intriguing. You will be both informed and entertained by the predictable signals your eyes have been opened up to. Once you know who your clients' personalities are, you're better prepared to deliver a laser-specific presentation. The next chapter will show you how.

For information on obtaining T.E.A.M. Dynamics profiles for personal awareness, hiring, managing, and sales adjustments, contact Mitch Anthony at http://www.mitchanthony.com.

CHAPTER 7

Keys to Connecting with Personalities

In this chapter, we will address emotionally intelligent methods of communicating with each personality to optimize each connection opportunity and to minimize confusion, conflict, and misunderstanding. These goals are accomplished by learning to view scenarios through the clients' perspective and to communicate in such a way that strengthens trust and cooperation. Too often, brokers and financial professionals are perceived to have placed their own interests above their clients. Through the T.E.A.M. Dynamics approach, clients are assured that their core needs and comfort levels are understood. This approach ensures the improvement of existing relationships and a sound footing for developing relationships.

The wise financial professional understands that at the very center of a client's actions and reactions is the core personality that drives behavior and communication. Once you have discovered the personality orientation of your client you can choose a communication path that leads to clarity, understanding, and teamwork between financial professional and client.

The classic mistake that many professionals make is to assume that every client will automatically plug in to their style of communication. They won't. This leads to communication breakdown and the disintegration of trust, which is at the heart of the financial professional/client relationship.

This chapter will take you through the subtle adjustments that are necessary with each personality style to improve the quality of your communication with your clients.

Communication Challenges and Obstacles

In the following segments, we will highlight the nature and orientation of each personality style, the adjustments necessary by the sales professional, and the words or phrases that affect the emotional comfort zone of the client.

Each personality style will be profiled regarding the communication approach they are most comfortable with, including the type of presentation they prefer. Also profiled will be the likes, dislikes, risk tolerance, and challenges of communicating with each personality.

We have surveyed hundreds of members of each personality group and asked the question, "When in a sales situation, how do you like to be approached?" The following pages give their answers in insightful detail. Their varied answers reveal the diversity of the needs necessary to connect with each personality style. A strong correlation exists between a client's personality style and the appropriate categories of investment to suggest. For example, two of the personalities are risk-averse by nature, Togetherness and Analyzer, and two are comfortable with risk, Enterpriser and Motivator.

The changes you make in your communication approach, though simple in nature, will be profound in effect because they will help your clients to be comfortable with the information and ideas you are sharing. You may find, to some degree, that you already have been making these adjustments with people on an intuitive level and the following information affirms those communication strategies.

CRITICAL SELLING ADJUSTMENTS—
THE TOGETHERNESS PERSONALITY

Remember the following communication guidelines in dealing with the Togetherness personality:

- Demonstrate respect by paying close attention when they talk.
- Demonstrate sincerity. They want to like you before they work with you.
- Demonstrate a concern and caring for people.
- Go slowly; wait until they trust you.
- Ask about their feelings regarding your product or services and its applicability.
- Do not force them into a buying decision. Avoid pressure tactics.
- Tread lightly because offending the Togetherness personality is easy.
- Allow them time to think things through.
- Refer to your satisfied clients.

- Use statements of commitment and seek a commitment.
- Identify specific steps and time frames.

Many Togetherness financial professionals have approached us and told us how they were having trouble in their closings. What we do is sit them down and ask them to practice their close. Nine out of ten times they give the company's standard close, but their eyes seem to be backing up and apologizing the whole time—and their clients are seeing it.

What works much better for these financial professionals is a tailor-made close that fits their personality style—a close that lets the client know, "I'm going to be there for you. I'm going to pay attention to all the details that you're too busy to watch." Their eyes are now into the close. Unless they're saying something they can believe in, their eyes are apologizing while they're trying to close the business.

Let's take a look at some of the critical adjustments you want to make with the Togetherness style. Remember to go slowly and pay close attention when they talk. If you don't pay close attention when individuals of the Togetherness style are talking, you turn them off right away. If you're distracted while they are speaking, that's it. You may have jeopardized the whole deal. If you're a multitasker or have professional-level attention deficit disorder, you are going to offend this personality.

Demonstrate the concern you have for your other clients. The stories you tell should illustrate this concern. Remember to use statements of commitment. Remember to ask how they feel about your product.

Close with specific steps and time frames. Don't paint your close with a broad brush stroke—paint it with specifics. "So what we're going to do is this, one, two, and three, and then the time frame for number one will be this and the time frame for number two will be this. . . ."

Do not force a buying decision. One of the things members of the Togetherness personality have told us is that they'll let you know they're ready to be closed. They'll lean forward, start nodding, and say something to let you know that they are ready for you to hold their hand through the process. If you try to close them *before* all their emotional issues are dealt with, it's not going to work. Because one of the problems with the Togetherness style is the inability to say no, clients may say yes but not mean it. None of us wants to see that sort of buyer's regret.

Brent S., a financial professional who fits the Togetherness personality style, tells of going shopping for a mattress and how the salesperson pushed all the wrong buttons with his personality.

"We walked into a store and asked for a specific type of mattress and what their best price would be. The salesman gave us a price and assured us that this was the best they could do. I told him I could get the same mattress across town for $200 less. He said, 'Don't leave. Let me talk to my manager about this.' So, he came back and told us that he could now beat their competitor's price. I said, 'No thanks,' and walked out. I didn't feel like he was being sincere with me the first time and that he was going to take us for an extra $200 if he had the opportunity."

This story typifies the Togetherness approach. This personality style has its antenna up for honesty, integrity, sincerity, and respect. They are quickly scared off by those who fail to demonstrate those abilities.

Here is an overview of what the Togetherness personality wants in dealing with others:

I Want:	• A reliable, stable relationship
I Don't Want:	• To be coerced or pushed into a decision (I have trouble saying no)
	• People to be upset with me (I have trouble when others are not pleased or approving of me)
You Must Convince Me:	• How your product or service will bring simplicity and security into my life
	• That you will be there to support me when I have questions or problems

Remember that the Togetherness personality places the highest premium on the quality of your relational skills. Their antennae are up and alerted to insincerity, affected presentation, disrespect, impatience, pressure tactics, and opportunistic approaches. They are looking for supportive and secure business relationships where the financial professional will take the time necessary to explain the process and to answer questions that arise in a personable and caring manner.

Here are some words in the Togetherness personality comfort zone:

• We, Let's	• Commitment
• Concern	• Security
• Sensitivity	• Step-by-step
• Teamwork	• Long-term

The emotional comfort zone of the Togetherness personality is dealing with people who will take the time to establish a relationship and not be in a hurry doing it. They can be offended easily, so watch the type of humor you choose and avoid controversial topics.

Most important, however, is to demonstrate that you are a nice person. Work hard to demonstrate respect and sincerity. Members of the Togetherness personality style are bothered by people who are abrasive, overly individualistic, hurried, and seemingly unconcerned for the well-being of others.

Is word choice significant when working with the different personality types? Absolutely. In researching each profile, we asked them to tell which words made them feel comfortable or nervous. If our job is to make our clients feel good about who we are so that they'll do business with us, we certainly don't want a vernacular that's going to make them nervous during the conversation.

The preceding list reveals the words that appealed the most to the Togetherness group. If you're selling to a Togetherness person, make a note of a couple of these words that will help you, particularly as you open a discussion with them.

The word *we* is particularly significant to the Togetherness personality. When you use *I* with them, their response is typically to assume that you're ego driven. If you say *you* too much, they may feel like you're putting too much pressure on them. *We* is also very important to the Togetherness personality because it connotes partnership and collaboration. Remember, if you're an Enterpriser, the Togetherness personality style is most likely your villain role, so to start using these words will be even more important for you.

CRITICAL SELLING ADJUSTMENTS— THE ENTERPRISER PERSONALITY

Following are communication guidelines for presenting to the Enterpriser personality:

- Don't talk about your company before you ask what they want (concisely).
- Uncover their top concern/priority.
- Stress bottom-line benefits.
- Establish context up front. Start with the end result and work back.
- Don't waste time with small talk.
- Paint a broad brush stroke. Enterprisers will make decisions with a small amount of information.
- Ask for their opinion and affirm it without sounding like you are pandering.
- Do not try to connect with the high Enterprisers by long stories or with overly enthusiastic presentations. They see this as contrived and phony.

- Prepare for a quick decision based on facts.
- Allow them a way to win.
- Give options and possibilities and let them decide.
- Don't contradict unless you have information and the confidence to back it up.
- Appeal to the ego.
- Allow them to talk themselves out of a position rather than to be talked out of it.

Here are some of the adjustments that the Enterpriser is looking for. Establish your competence and philosophy quickly. These are the magic bullets when you're working with Enterprisers.

If you want to sell to an Enterpriser, walk in the room and, instead of making a presentation, say something like this, "First, I want to establish my philosophy." What this telegraphs to the Enterpriser is: "If we agree on investment philosophy, we might have something to talk about, and if we don't, let's not waste your time or my time." They will immediately say, "I agree with that," or they may add an addendum to it. But as soon as they buy into the philosophy, the rest is gravy. We've seen it work many times. Enterprisers want to get to your philosophy quickly, and they want to know that you're competent.

Another key to establishing your competence with Enterprisers is to look the part. If you think there's even a chance that you don't project a look of confidence when you walk into a room, then fake it. Get your chin up in the air, look directly into people's eyes, and put some force into your words. If you don't, the Enterpriser CEO chairing the 401(k) committee will look right past you. Enterprisers demand competence.

Inquire about their achievements—it's all about them. Put an Enterpriser behind the wheel. You should always give Enterprisers the feeling that they're controlling the whole deal, that they're the boss. Pick up the pace. Don't be a slave to your script, and paint with a broad brush stroke (remember to allow them a way to win). You also better be able to pinpoint when it's going to get done and then follow through quickly. Show them that you mean it.

Suzanne B., a financial professional who fits the Enterpriser personality style, tells the following story about a neighbor who tried to sell her on some nutritional supplements:

> "This neighbor of mine belongs to one of those multilevel marketing things that sells vitamins and such. So he comes to me and says he wants to tell me about this opportunity that he's sure I would be just great at. He's a nice guy and everything, but he gave the worst stumbling, bumbling presentation I have ever witnessed. He goes on and on, and can't string together a coherent thought process. The whole time I'm thinking, 'This guy is so weak, I wouldn't buy Girl Scout cookies from

him.' The funny part of it is his products were actually something I could probably use, but there was no way I was going to buy from this bozo."

Suzanne's comments reveal several key aspects of the Enterpriser personality. The Enterpriser looks for both competence and confidence in the people they work with and buy from. They smell weakness like a shark smells blood. Act the least bit unsure of yourself, and they'll be gone in a flash. As is quite apparent in Suzanne's story, Enterprisers want you to be able to make your pitch well and be able to get to the point fast.

Here is an overview of what the Enterpriser personality wants in dealing with others:

I Want:	• To be in control
	• Results
I Don't Want:	• To be taken advantage of
	• To be slowed down
You Must Convince Me:	• Of what your product will do for me
	• The results I will see

The Enterpriser personality places the highest premium on achieving results in a timely, efficient, and orderly fashion. Enterprisers are rarely willing to relinquish control. They can quickly perceive self-interest or a lack of results orientation on the part of the financial professional. Enterprisers typically are comfortable with risk but want to be informed in candid terms of what those risks are. Enterprisers will become more tolerant, patient, and relational once the advisor has demonstrated competence. They will quickly and often harshly confront any inconsistencies, perceived misrepresentations, or omissions on the part of the financial professional.

The Enterpriser wants the best choice in the least amount of time. They are often multitaskers who like to accomplish as much as possible each day. They do not like to be told what to do and often take a flexible approach with rules. They are most comfortable working with people who are risk takers, think for themselves, and don't indulge in meaningless talk and activities.

Projecting professionalism and confidence in your ability to get things done is important to the Enterpriser. The emotional comfort zone of the Enterpriser personality is to work with individuals who are competent and confident. This personality quickly sifts out those who do not know their stuff or who lack confidence in their company or themselves. Enterprisers are also bothered by slowed progress, too much bureaucracy, beating around the bush answers, and lack of follow-through.

Here are some words in the Enterpriser comfort zone:

- Results
- Customized solution
- Innovative
- Efficient
- Highly competitive
- Research
- Unique
- Expedite

The most important word to an Enterpriser is *you*. "You are the man." "I want to know what you think." "What has been your experience?" Even when high Es know that their egos are getting stroked, they still like to hear it. Enterprisers typically figure that at least you are smart enough to recognize how brilliant they are.

They want to hear the word *results*. They want to hear that you'll get it done. They like customization. Enterprisers don't want a boilerplate plan. Their point of view is, "I have my own specific situation, customize your plan for me." They like the words *innovative, efficient, highly competitive, unique, expedite,* and *quickly.* Those words are magic with Enterprisers. If you're a Togetherness person, your villain is most likely the Enterpriser, so commit these words to memory and use them in your presentations to Enterprisers.

CRITICAL SELLING ADJUSTMENTS— THE ANALYZER PERSONALITY

Following are communication guidelines for presenting to the Analyzer personality:

- Slow your pace—listen intently.
- Be accurate. Don't approximate or round off numbers.
- Do your homework. Be prepared to give every detail about your products or services.
- Set the stage for trust using data.
- Explore their interests (the latest technologies, etc.)
- Support each feature/benefit statement with logic and rationale.
- Never say or imply with body language, "Hurry up!"
- Summarize your presentation carefully.
- Detail how you'll follow through.
- Don't ever say, "I know you'll like this."
- Avoid hyperbole and animated presentations.
- Allow time for decisions.

It's all about facts with Analyzers. Analyzers are a tough group to sell to, so slow your pace and listen intently when working with an Analyzer. Never go into a meeting with an Analyzer without having a pad of paper and a pen. One of the things that really impresses Analyzers is that while they're talking, you're taking copious notes. We advise that you practice this. You could be drawing a picture of Mickey Mouse for all they know, but the fact is, taking notes is going to impress them.

Do your homework. It's not sufficient to tell an Analyzer, "The returns from this fund last year were in the midteens." That's not even close to being good enough for them. And, let's be honest here, how may deals have we not closed because we didn't have one or two critical facts about that client? We found out later what they really wanted to know. We make our final presentation, and we get a letter back saying, "Thanks, but no thanks, because . . ." That "because . . ." is often something that we could have found out if we had done our homework. Research that we don't do and questions that we don't ask prevent us from winning Analyzer accounts. One of the simplest yet most brilliant demonstrations of this principle that we've heard of is one financial professional who always asks the Analzyer CFO, "What are the important issues for you—the issues that you need to be sure are addressed?" He does that because he doesn't want to have to discover that information later on—in a rejection letter.

Avoid exaggeration, emotion, and overpromising. Analyzers just go crazy when people get really passionate about something. We have heard many Analyzers say, "I read enthusiasm as a lack of training." (Conversely with Motivators: if you don't have enthusiasm, they won't give you the time of day.) Don't be derailed when an Analyzer seems unenthusiastic, because they are famous for their poker face.

Summarize your presentation carefully. Use those notes that you took to summarize exactly what you heard during the meeting: the main concerns, the direction you discussed, and the time line. Summation telegraphs to Analyzers that you paid attention. Also remember to give them time—don't try to close the deal too soon.

Arnie Z., a financial professional who fits the Analyzer description, tells this story about dealing with a car salesman:

"I went into a car lot because I was pretty well set on buying a model they had on their showroom floor. A salesman comes over to me—he's all smiles and handshakes—and starts telling me how great this model is. I'm annoyed immediately because I already know this is a good model. Right away he says, 'Why don't you take it for a drive?' I decline and say, 'Well, I have a few questions first.' So I sit in the car, and he sits with me. I see a couple of buttons on the dashboard that I'm unfamiliar with and ask what they are for. He says he doesn't know and why don't I just look at the owner's manual after I take it for a drive. This guy is trying to sell me a $35,000 product and doesn't know a damn thing about it! No matter what I ask him, he doesn't have the answer. Finally, about the fourth time he suggests I take a test-drive, I gather my information pieces and leave."

Arnie's response is very characteristic of the Analyzer personality in a selling situation. Arnie wanted information, not emotion. He wanted his many questions answered before he got behind the wheel. He didn't like dealing with someone who was unprepared, uneducated, and who kept pushing to a close.

Here is an overview of what the Analyzer personality wants in dealing with others:

I Want: • Accuracy, assurances, and proof

I Don't Want: • To be criticized
• To be hurried

You Must Convince Me: • On the logic of investing in your product
• On your track record

Analyzers are very logical and linear in their relational style. Analyzers are not often interested in what other people do or what they prefer, because they assume others do not possess the same high standards that they possess. They will present logical questions and want factual answers. Analyzers will increase in skepticism when witnessing hyperbole, zealousness, and anecdotal evidence. They will be interested in your background credentials and performance record as well as the rationale behind your efforts. This relationship will quickly falter when the financial professional uses pressure, hastens decisions, or is critical of the Analyzer's judgment. The wise financial professionals will take a logical, organized, and linear approach and base their recommendations on accurate data. Understand that the Analyzer has a natural hesitancy, resistance to, and discomfort with changes.

The emotional comfort zone of the Analyzer personality revolves around accuracy and predictability. Establishing credibility and trust takes time, and the Analyzer is not willing to take a risk without thorough safeguards and preparation. The Analyzer tends to see things in black-and-white and harshly judge an action or statement that does not appear to comply with the guidelines or rules. Analyzers are bothered by tactics used by many in the sales realm: overcommitment, hyperbole, shifting attention away from the issue, and trying to charm people with personality.

Analyzers are most comfortable with factual, logical approaches delivered calmly and patiently. They are interested in seeing accuracy and follow-through with commitments.

Here are the magic words to soothe the Analyzer's highly charged nervous system:

- Caution
- Research
- Projections
- Proof

- Logical
- Analysis
- Thorough
- High standards

Particularly if you're a Motivator, and if Analyzers are your villain role, start using some of these words: *analysis, thorough,* and *high standards.* Remember that Analyzers have very high standards for themselves, and they have difficulty dealing with people who don't have high standards for themselves. Use the word *consistent.* Analyzers detest processes and people that are whimsical—here today and gone tomorrow. They want to hear about consistency.

The biggest concern that Analyzers have is doing the right thing. This is why they ask so many questions. Your job in persuasion is to help them find the right products and assure your Analyzer clients that they are right for them.

CRITICAL SELLING ADJUSTMENTS— THE MOTIVATOR PERSONALITY

Following are communication guidelines for presenting to the Motivator personality:

- Pick up your pace and energy.
- Talk about the potential of your product and services.
- Describe your benefits and program with passion.
- Use storyselling, illustrations, anecdotes, metaphors, and true-life experiences.
- Be prepared to respond to a quick decision.
- Ask lots of questions about your client—their histories, their victories.
- Provide an opportunity for your clients to vocalize their goals.
- Remember, they are sold more on your enthusiasm and convictions than they are on features and proof.
- Use an informal and sociable approach.
- Avoid small print and thick presentation.
- Focus on payoffs for them, e.g., recognition, excitement, or income.

Start off with a smile. They need to see you smile. Try to be a little informal, a little playful about what you're doing, even if it's not easy for you. Lightening up signals to them that you'll be enjoyable to work with.

Ask about their histories, their victories, and their goals. Motivators love to tell their stories. Lead with passion, and follow with features and proof. Isn't it amazing what a completely different mode you have to be in if you're presenting to an Analyzer instead of a Motivator? The things Analyzers hate, Motivators love—and vice versa.

Use stories, anecdotes, and metaphors. Motivators love a good metaphor, illustration, anecdote, or an analogy. Those things really resonate with the Motivator style, because they bring dry facts to life.

Avoid small print and thick presentations. We're not joking here. When you put small print in front of Motivators, what happens? They back up, and they feel tense. Their nervous system gets rattled when they have to look at small print or a thick presentation. They're thinking, "Oh no, we're not going to do all that." This sort of presentation does not play well to their short attention spans. Never write a detailed letter to a Motivator. In written correspondence, use bullet points for the Enterpriser and Motivator personality styles, and use details for the Togetherness and Analyzer personality styles. Also, remember to end with a playful note or a joke in communications with Motivators.

Emphasize the payoff for the Motivator. The Motivator's antenna is up for, "What's my payoff here?" and "How is this going to be good for me or make me look good?"

Remember, negativity is a deal killer. Don't walk into a Motivator's office complaining. Don't exercise your cynical wit in front of Motivators. They want to know you're a positive person. They want to deal with optimistic people who are going to get the job done—not with people who are always whining and complaining.

Jacqueline T. is a financial professional who fits the Motivator personality style. She told us the story of how a peer tried to sell her on working for his firm.

> "I was at a point in my career where I felt I needed a change, so I accepted an invitation for an interview with another firm. What a total turnoff that was! The guy who interviewed me never smiled or laughed—he took himself so seriously. He just talked about expectations, guidelines, and the competitive advantage he felt his firm had. I remember thinking to myself, 'I wonder if everyone in this place is as boring as you.' I couldn't imagine working for or with someone who took himself so

seriously. I mean, the money would have been better, but I think I would have hated every minute."

Jacqueline, like other Motivator personalities, has her radar up for friendly, flexible, fun-loving, and optimistic people. Motivators are more concerned about people than they are about processes. They want to know that they will enjoy and look forward to working with you. Motivators seem to be looking for positive energy in others that they can connect with. They want to squeeze all the enjoyment out of life that they possibly can.

Here is an overview of what the Motivator personality wants in dealing with others:

I Want:	• To be noticed
	• To persuade and influence others
I Don't Want:	• To be rejected or ignored
	• To get boxed in with detail
You Must Convince Me:	• Who is using your product
	• How I can promote it to others

The Motivator personality is the most intuitive in its relational style. Motivators try to get a feel for the type of individual they are dealing with. They're quite vigilant about finding positive energy, which is expressed in optimism, enthusiasm, and a congenial manner. While Motivators expect financial professionals to understand and be in control of details, they do not want to be bothered with any of the details. They want them to paint broad brush strokes, use illustrations, and provide real-life testimonials of the services they provide. Motivators feel a need to articulate their ideas, experiences, and opinions regarding the presentation they are hearing. The wise financial professional needs to accommodate this need to articulate and not get flustered when the presentation or meeting goes offtrack.

The emotional comfort zone of the Motivator personality is working with people who are friendly and flexible in their approach. They are frustrated by people who are married to routines, engage in great detail, and are overserious in the approach. Motivators enjoy the art of conversation, learning about you, and talking about themselves. The social aspect of doing business is important because they feel it reveals who you really are and your level of flexibility. Motivators do not like being forced or confronted. They are very conflict-averse and will avoid confronting negative issues. They want to work with people who are easy to work with and who have a sense of humor. Motivators are also turned on by competition and possibilities.

Here are some words in the Motivator comfort zone:

- Quick
- Easy
- Innovative
- Fun
- Big, exponential
- Cutting edge
- Competitive
- Possibilities
- Fluid, flexible
- Opportunity

One magic word for Motivators is actually quite humorous. Listen for the word *great.* Walk into an office and listen, and wherever you hear *great,* that's where your Motivators are. "Oh, that's great!" you'll hear them say.

Easy is another magic word for Motivators. They also like the words *innovative, creative, big,* and *exponential.* Get a thesaurus and search for synonyms for big and exponential. Motivators like statements such as, "This is going to be huge!" Other magic words for Motivators are *cutting edge, competitive, possibilities, fluid,* and *flexible.* When presenting your ideas to Motivators, let them know that if they change their mind, there won't be any problems: "This whole idea is very fluid; it's very flexible. We can move this in and move that out." This approach makes Motivators feel very comfortable. Motivators don't want to get locked in.

Another magic word for Motivators is *opportunity.* Motivators by nature are optimistic people, and they want to believe that they can do something bigger and better. They love to hear motivational speeches about doing the impossible. They want to reach the goal that's never been reached, so talk in terms of opportunity and achievement.

AT THE CORE OF MAKING HUMAN CONNECTIONS

Remember that at the core of people is a personality blueprint or personality DNA that drives their perspectives, their communication, and their responses—including their responses to you. Masters at connecting learn to adjust their communication intuitively to a level that causes their clients to feel comfortable at the core of their being. Use these personality insights, and see the difference in how clients begin responding to you.

Pushing the Right Buttons

The next thing we need to understand in the process of communicating with different personalities is to find out what the specific land mines and gold mines are for each personality style. By land mines we mean those triggers that bring stress to an individual, and by gold mines, we mean those triggers that motivate an individual.

Developing an awareness for avoiding these personality stressors or land mines is important. We all have to face the reality that each day, we accidentally and unwittingly step on land mines with certain personalities. Although we may not mean to, we say certain words that trigger something in our client's brain that says, "Don't talk like that to me." Conversely, we trigger gold mines with other personalities, causing a magnetic chemistry. That's when people start nodding and smiling and think, "Yeah, you're right on the money there. I've had an experience just like that." Developing an awareness for each personality style's unique set of land mines and gold mines will keep you from offending existing and prospective clients and help attract people to you.

For years we have been surveying thousands of clients, managers, and financial professionals on their particular set of personality stressors and motivators. We have separated those people by personality group and asked them to answer these two questions:

1. What things bother you the most or stress you out in working with others?
2. What things motivate you to want to work with others?

The answers we hear are amazingly consistent for each personality pattern. The stressors are indeed land mines. If you push these buttons you will end up with shrapnel in your face and have difficulty building a relationship. The motivators are truly gold mines. You will help people feel comfortable in your presence and increase their desire to work with you.

Following is a list of the stressors and motivators for each personality style, as well as some tidbits of wisdom from those who have learned how to avoid relational land mines and tap into relational gold mines.

THE TOGETHERNESS–DOMINANT PERSONALITY

STRESSORS

- Dealing with change
- Having to be candid, aggressive, or assertive
- Being singled out publicly
- Having to lead
- Making autonomous decisions
- Completing complex tasks without feedback
- Not being appreciated
- Lack of time because they have trouble saying no

MOTIVATORS

- Providing support to others
- Working cooperatively with others
- Giving thorough explanations
- Receiving verbal or written recognition
- Dealing with likable and considerate individuals
- Low pressure, noncompetitive environment
- Being consulted in planning stages (team approach)
- Specific steps and clear time frames

Whenever you're talking to individuals of the Togetherness personality style, you need to be especially conscious to put all your energy and focus on them. Your focus signals that you appreciate and respect them. Enterprisers frequently push this stressor by multitasking, which unintentionally sends a signal of disrespect to the Togetherness personality. Motivators trigger the stressor by being easily distracted.

Individuals of the Togetherness personality get stressed when they don't receive appreciation and/or approval. They like to act as team players and require a degree of recognition to feel good about their involvement. Although both the Togetherness and Motivator personalities desire recognition, they are vastly different. For example, individuals of the Togetherness personality want you to put a little flashlight on them at the meeting and say something like, "I want to thank Sylvia for the fine job she's done." On the other hand, Motivators want the floodlight on them—to be on the Jay Leno show or in a ticker tape parade.

The Togetherness personality also becomes stressed when you interfere with their comfort zones. They become comfortable with a certain way of doing things and become extremely uncomfortable when somebody comes in and messes up their routines. The Togetherness personality needs time to adjust to change.

Another stressor for the Togetherness personality is being forced to be candid or to deliver bad news. They also are stressed by being singled out publicly and having to lead. The Togetherness personality wants someone else to be the pioneer trailblazer, and then they will join in completing tasks without feedback.

Individuals of the Togetherness personality have difficulty when no one is telling them whether or not they are doing the right thing. Enterprisers often let down the Togetherness people by not offering enough affirmation. Enterprisers need to practice telling the Togetherness individuals that they are doing a good job.

Individuals of the Togetherness personality resent not being consulted in the planning stages. Therefore, before deciding on a plan, consult with them instead of just handing them the finished project and telling them, "Here's the plan, now do it." The Togetherness personality also prefers a low-pressure, noncompetitive environment. Working cooperatively with others is a motivator for the Togetherness personality as is having a team situation to work with.

THE ENTERPRISER–DOMINANT PERSONALITY

STRESSORS

- Being in a predictable and monotonous circumstance
- Listening to detail
- Dealing with red tape
- Waiting for change, waiting on decisions
- Others withholding true thoughts or feelings
- Being dominated or controlled, appearing soft or weak
- Financial professionals beating around the bush, lack of candor
- Projects not being finished
- Working with overly cautious, procrastinating people

MOTIVATORS

- Having control over situations
- Atmosphere where candor is encouraged
- Working with creative individuals
- Working with pragmatists
- Deadlines and pressure situations
- Being autonomous—not having to depend on others
- Being in a leadership position
- Improbabilities, extreme odds, challenges to the ego

In one way or another, not being recognized is a stressor for all groups—but in different ways and for different reasons. Enterprisers are not attention freaks. They don't need people to pat them on the back; they just need others to tell them what a genius they really are.

Enterprisers are stressed by having to work with people who are not passionate about their work and who are not doers. A dangerous land mine for the Enterpriser personality style is dealing with red tape. Overly cautious and worried Analyzers make Enterprisers go crazy, suffering through all those details and having to wait. The Enterpriser personality is stressed by unfinished projects and by working with procrastinators. Another stressor to the Enterpriser is being in a predictable and unchallenging situation. This lack of challenge drives Enterprisers crazy.

Because Enterprisers are stressed by others withholding their true thoughts and feelings, they are motivated by an atmosphere where candor is encouraged. Enterprisers love being in situations where everybody tells the truth and tells them exactly where they're at, and they can just charge on ahead. Enterprisers love being in leadership positions. Deadlines and pressure situations motivate Enterprisers, as do improbabilities, extreme odds, and challenges. They love going on the mission that's never been done before. The Enterprisers will be the ones who say, "We can do that!"

THE ANALYZER–DOMINANT PERSONALITY

STRESSORS

- Oversimplification
- Being pulled off task
- Listening to multiple inputs
- Working with impulsiveness
- Having to persuade or sell others
- Having to stretch routines
- Having other people not follow through with tasks
- Being held responsible for others' work or mistakes
- Being questioned about quality of work or performance
- Having to make subjective, personal responses
- Dealing with time-related pressure
- Working with random, unfocused, and unpredictable personalities

MOTIVATORS

- Being right
- Approaching tasks logically and systematically
- Going at their own pace
- Being in control of their performance factors
- Being in thought-provoking conversations
- Working with those who stay on track
- Working with people whose standards are high (quality conscious)

A major stressor or land mine for the Analyzer personality is in dealing with other people's lack of attention to detail. They want follow-through and focus all the way to the end. While Enterprisers want to get it done for the sake of getting it done, Analyzers want to get it done *right*.

Another Analyzer land mine is oversimplification. Salespeople aggravate Analyzers by saying, "It's going to be easy, no problem, we can do that," without telling them how.

Analyzers dislike being pulled off task. Here's a group that suffers from tunnel vision. They can get so microfocused that everything around them can look like chaos because they're stuck in this tunnel mode.

Of all the personality styles, Analyzers struggle the most with having to sell to or persuade other people. They hate being questioned about quality and are stressed by having to listen to multiple input and deal with time-related pressure. Analyzers are stressed when they are given something to do and not given enough time to finish, although it often seems that no amount of time is enough.

Analyzers are motivated by thorough, thought-provoking conversations and by working with people with high standards. Being in control of performance standards motivates them. Analyzers want to write the rules, and they want to make the rules. This causes conflict with both Enterprisers and Motivators, who like to break the rules. Analyzers get along with Togetherness individuals because they are good at following rules. Analyzers are motivated by being able to go at their own pace.

THE MOTIVATOR–DOMINANT PERSONALITY

STRESSORS

- Dealing with detail
- Listening to slow, monotonous presentations
- Overserious approaches
- Negative and critical conversations
- Pessimistic people and surroundings
- Repetitive and inflexible surroundings
- Working alone
- Complexity
- Not being recognized
- Long, drawn-out processes
- Having to follow through to the end of a task

MOTIVATORS

- Opportunities to talk
- Having the spotlight
- Opportunities to convince and persuade
- Social environment
- Playful approach
- New challenges
- Incentives for achievement
- Competing with others/inspiring others
- Frequent change
- Optimism

The Motivator personality has quite a long list of stressors. For starters, they don't like abrupt people. Motivators don't like talking to nonlisteners, which is ironic, given their typically short attention span. In their mind, the conversation belongs to Motivators—so don't interfere! They are born articulate and feel they should get more airtime. Have you ever gotten the feeling around Motivators that they're in love with the sound of their own voice?

The worst thing you can do with Motivators as soon as they throw out an idea is to start putting out negative and skeptical eye/body language. Motivators demand creative, not constipated conversations. They feel that all great ideas come from that creative conversation, and you just never know what you'll stumble into. We use the slogan *playing outside the box* for Motivators.

Another Motivator land mine is dealing with an overly serious approach. They avoid people who don't smile. When you're with Motivators, take it easy and act a little more playful in your pursuits. Motivators avoid negative environments and inflexible surroundings. They hate doing the same thing over and over. Monotony is a motivator killer for this personality style. They also hate long, drawn-out processes and having to finish projects. They are also stressed by not being recognized for how wonderful they are.

What are the gold mines with Motivators? First and most important, Motivators like a playful approach. They also like optimism, incentives, and little perks. They enjoy opportunities to talk and to inspire others. When others get into a difficult situation, the Motivator personality loves to be the inspirer, the motivator, the cheerleader, and the person to get everybody fired up about possibilities. Frequent change and new challenges energize them. They enjoy kick-starting new ideas, being in the spotlight, and having opportunities to lead.

Wouldn't it be great if your brain was programmed so well in the right hemisphere, as far as relating to people, that as soon as you walked into any situation—click, click, click—you would recognize each individual's personality DNA and never do anything to cause anyone stress. But the problem is, we all live predominately in a world of mirrors. By nature, we're all narcissistic to varying degrees. We're concerned first about ourselves and meeting our own needs. We don't want to stress ourselves out and we want to stay motivated. It's awkward at times for us to switch our approach and become the kind of individual who won't cause stress. But we have found the more we practice these adjustments, the less stress we will cause others, and others will become all the more motivated to work with us. However, inevitably, despite all precautions, we're going to be faced with confrontational situations. In the next two chapters, you will discover the secrets of those who have learned to handle conflict successfully.

CHAPTER 9

Turning Conflict into Opportunity

In this chapter on personality-based communication skills, you will learn the skills critical to positive relationship management, namely how to minimize conflict scenarios and diffuse existing personality-based conflicts.

Most of us would agree that much of the conflict we experience with clients, employees, and coworkers is personality based. In this chapter, we will teach effective approaches that factor in the predictable actions and reactions of the four core personalities. We will also highlight techniques of tempering one's own personality—based on biases that tend to surface in conflict scenarios. We will demonstrate simple steps toward compromise and consensus building as means for diffusing or preventing conflicts. We will also identify the predictable behaviors of each personality in conflict scenarios as well as effective communication methods for reversing a negative climate.

THE POWER OF EMPATHY

The first and most crucial emotional competence necessary for resolving conflict is empathy—the process of identifying emotionally with another person. In fact, empathy may be the cornerstone of all conflict management. Empathy is certainly a skill demonstrated by those who have mastered the art of keeping themselves disentangled from conflicts.

In Daniel Goleman's landmark research on the emotional intelligence found in highly successful individuals, five areas of emotional smarts were identified: awareness, restraint, resilience, empathy, and social skills.

Before we cover the social skill of personality-based conflict resolution, let's understand that empathy is a foundational need for resolving personality-based conflicts. Because of our core personality, forcing ourselves to feel events the same way another person does can be difficult. However, we can at the very least understand that others feel events differently than we do, and that they are neither right nor wrong. The good news is neither you nor the other party is wrong for seeing events as you do, as the perception and response are rooted in your core personality.

The reality is, if you want to resolve those conflicts, your first step is toward empathic identity and understanding of the other person's vantage point. By taking this first step, you bring down their defenses and they are more willing to meet you halfway.

The Lens of Personality

A good metaphor for developing understanding when dealing with opposing personalities is to realize that each personality sees the world through a unique lens (see Figure 9.1). The Togetherness personality sees the world through a wide-angle lens—always trying to capture that "Kodak moment"—and is always concerned about others in the process. The Enterpriser personality sees the world through a telescope and wants to keep moving toward a distant shore (his goal). The Analyzer personality sees the world through a microscope and is constantly trying to get a closer, more detailed

---

FIGURE 9.1 | The Lens of Personality

| Togetherness Personality | Enterpriser Personality | Analyzer Personality | Motivator Personality |

view. The Motivator personality sees the world through a kaleidoscope and captures the fun, spontaneity, and excitement of life.

Using these metaphorical lenses can help us to view a conflicted situation through the eyes of the other person, even if that person is our personality opposite. Understanding the perception of the other party is the great empathetic leap that makes most conflicts reasonable and many broken relationships reconcilable.

Johnny Falls Down: A Parable

The following parable illustrates the phenomena of personality-influenced perceptions and their role in conflict.

Johnny and his four friends were riding their bicycles when Johnny fell down. Here is how his four friends responded to the situation:

> **Togetherness Friend:** "Are you OK? Can I help you?"
>
> **Enterpriser Friend:** "Where did you learn to ride a bike? Hurry up, we're going to be late!"
>
> **Analyzer Friend:** "You'd better not move. You could have an internal injury. You know, you wouldn't have fallen off if your shoe had been tied."
>
> **Motivator Friend:** "That was cool! Did you see that flip? Unbelievable!"

The next day at school Johnny's four friends gave their idiosyncratic accounts of what had happened:

> **Togetherness Friend:** "I really wonder if these are people I want to be friends with. Johnny falls off his bike, and one person is yelling at him to get up, another is criticizing, and another is laughing at him. Those people have no sensitivity."
>
> **Enterpriser Friend:** "Johnny is such a klutz! Just because he can't ride a bike, we're late and end up with the worst seats. Next time he doesn't get invited."
>
> **Analyzer Friend:** "Johnny is so careless. I still think he should go see the doctor. Sometimes these internal traumas kick in late. I mean, I've heard of people dying."
>
> **Motivator Friend:** "It was hilarious! He goes flying, does a flip. I give him a "10"—Olympic quality. There was blood everywhere!"

Moral of the Story. We often think conflict arises because we can't agree on a solution. Johnny's story illustrates that, because of our core personalities, we have trouble just agreeing on what happened, even when we all witness the same event.

The Other Person's Perspective

Many of our conflicts are due simply to this phenomenon of personality-based interpretation and response. The first and most powerful step in conflict management is to allow yourself to see the event through the vantage point of the personality you are dealing with. The chief question we need to ask in conflict is not, "What do you think we should do?" but rather, "What did you see happen?" or "What is the problem from your vantage point?"

Too often, conflicts escalate as we argue over the proper response while we have not yet agreed on what happened (through one another's eyes) in the first place. As our parable illustrated, each personality witnesses a different set of events within one event as biased by their core personality. Until we understand the other person's interpretation of the event, our attempts at resolution can be futile.

A large percentage of our continuing conflicts are rooted in core-personality perceptions. Just how much is rooted in personality is debatable because of the subjectivity of conflict. We know that personality plays a substantial role in the amount of personality conflict we experience with coworkers, employers, and clients.

WHOSE FAULT IS IT? THE ROOTS OF STRESS IN THE WORKPLACE

Once each person's actions and reactions can be traced clearly to their core personality, our approach toward coworkers, employees, and clients can shift from blaming and attempts at manipulation to negotiating compromises—meeting at the halfway point of two personalities.

An individual's core personality is like the DNA that drives their behavior. Attempts at altering the DNA of an individual's core personality will be met with resistance, frustration, and even hostility. Certain modes of behavior are so far outside the comfort zone of their personality that they cannot enter those modes without becoming tense and stressed in the process. The financial professional or manager who constantly forces these modes on the employee who constantly resists these modes soon becomes the focal point for conflict.

Resolving core personality-based conflict plays a significant role in both production and management issues. Following are some examples of how core personality comes into play in our everyday affairs:

- *Scenario One.* The high E (Enterpriser) manager barks orders at a high T (Togetherness) financial professional, who is highly sensitive by nature of personality.
- *Scenario Two.* This same high E client frustrates a high A (Analyzer) financial professional by pushing for closure on a project but not providing necessary details.
- *Scenario Three.* Another example of a common workplace agitation is the high A manager who takes an impersonal approach, focusing only on process to the neglect of personal relationship, thus alienating both the relationally focused T and the M (Motivator) personalities. (The inverse of the above scenarios would also be true.)
- *Scenario Four.* A high T client is easily offended by the high E's candor, and that same Enterpriser is frustrated by the high T client's indecisiveness.
- *Scenario Five.* The high M financial professional feels that the high A client impedes progress with pessimism, need for detail, and constant second-guessing.

To diffuse conflict in all of these scenarios, each personality involved must meet the other halfway in establishing a comfortable mode of working and relating for both parties. For example, we have seen individuals in similar scenarios improve their workplace relations by:

1. Confronting personality-based tensions
2. Establishing halfway-point personality compromises

Negotiating Core-Personality Compromises

Scenario One: High E Manager and High T Financial Professional

ENTERPRISER COMPROMISES

- Find diplomatic ways to state case.
- Ask—don't order.
- Pause and inquire when you observe frustration.

TOGETHERNESS COMPROMISES

- Don't regard Enterpriser's candor or abrasion as a personal attack.
- Write directives down and reiterate.

Scenario Two: High E Client and High A Financial Professional

ENTERPRISER COMPROMISES

- Try to understand the Analyzer's need for thoroughness.
- Wait for the Analyzer's input before pushing to completion.
- State case in open-minded manner.
- Demonstrate patience with tone and body language.

ANALYZER COMPROMISES

- Find areas of agreement and restrain impulse to judge.
- Listen to and consider innovative input.
- Play devil's advocate without being negative or cynical.

Scenario Three: High A Manager and High M Employee

ANALYZER COMPROMISES

- Try to be more personal in approach.
- Understand that processes are most successful when people are enthused.
- Allow time for a little socializing.
- Ask for creative input.

MOTIVATOR COMPROMISES

- Get help to organize ideas before presenting.
- Prepare a plan for follow-through.
- Understand the Analyzer's need for detail to be comfortable.
- Stay focused (take notes) when the Analyzer is giving input.

Scenario Four: High T Client and High E Financial Professional

TOGETHERNESS COMPROMISES

- Understand Enterpriser's need for action and results.
- Keep a sense of humor regarding candor (Enterprisers can take some ribbing).
- Ask for Enterpriser's input and give a time frame for your decision.

ENTERPRISER COMPROMISES

- Be mindful of high T sensitivity before responding.
- Talk through both options and consequences with Togetherness personality.
- Temper opinionated tone.

Scenario Five: High M Financial Professional and High A Client

MOTIVATOR COMPROMISES

- Don't express ideas to the Analyzer that are not well thought out.
- Slow down presentation and make a short outline.
- Regard pessimism as helpful troubleshooting rather than shooting down.
- Ask the question, "What will we need to do to make this work?" (Take notes.)

ANALYZER COMPROMISES

- Ask the Motivator where you can get the details you desire. (Don't expect to get the details from the high M.)
- Be prepared to hear big-picture concepts.
- Be willing to play around with ideas.
- Make sure your expression is not communicating negativity or tension.

Unreasonable Expectations

It was said of Alexander the Great that the more he got to know people, the more he loved his dog. Expecting everyone in your workplace to adjust to all of the quirks and characteristics of your personality style is unreasonable. Those with a similar pattern as yours will be comfortable with your natural form of relating. With these people, few compromises are necessary, and you can just be yourself.

Diplomacy, restraint, and compromise enter in most often when we are dealing with those of opposite patterns. If we refuse to restrain and compromise our own personality habits when dealing with those of conflicting personality patterns, we will be met with the equally powerful forces of resistance and resentment.

If you are willing to temper your own personality impulses, you can reasonably expect that the other parties—sensing a step in their direction—will alter their response. A reasonable expectation is to negotiate compromise by first demonstrating compromise. As the above scenarios demonstrate, one party cannot negotiate compromise for both parties. True compromise involves both parties taking equal steps toward the halfway point of a working comfort zone.

PERSONALITY-BASED CONFLICT TENDENCIES

Because of the four different personality styles, we see radically different responses to conflict. A financial professional should understand these tendencies to incisively diffuse the existing tension. People often become angry with one another because of the way they react—not understanding that many such reactions are programmed into the DNA of the core personality.

Following are some of the common conflict responses of the four personalities.

Common Conflict Responses: The Togetherness Personality

In conflict situations, High Ts are likely to:

- Avoid interpersonal aggression.
- Become quiet.
- Tend to freeze up (may flush with frustration).
- Become emotional and/or defensive.
- Will express frustration and feelings to people other than the offending party.
- Give in or feign agreement to avoid losing approval.

The financial professional must recognize the signs of escalating conflict or frustration with the Togetherness personality. They are often subtle in their method of disagreement, and as a result, either they are overlooked or attempts are made to superficially placate them. Conflict is building when the high T personality begins to clam up, starts to flush, displays a lost or bewildered look in the eyes, or responds in a defensive manner.

In conflict scenarios with Ts, the wise financial professional will:

- Inquire about their thoughts and feelings in the situation.
- Demonstrate concern and respect with good listening skills.
- Outline the necessary steps in resolving the conflict.

Common Conflict Responses: The Enterpriser Personality

In conflict situations, Enterprisers are likely to:

- Take a direct, aggressive approach.
- Rapidly escalate the level of confrontation.
- Create win-lose outcomes if cooperation is lacking (competitive).
- Attempt to clear the air at one sitting.
- Solve problems with more regard for closure than feelings.
- Listen to creative input in order to solve problems.

Because of their propensity for candor, Enterprisers will wrestle conflict head-on. Some people appreciate their straightforwardness, while others find it offensive. Enterprisers often operate with a what-you-see-is-what-you-get mentality and abhor any pretense—especially in a conflict scenario. This personality style is not afraid of hurting people's feelings if they feel the resolution is right, and are often heard saying, "They'll get over it!" in regard to emotional responses. Because of their intense desire for closure, however, Enterprisers will listen to creative input that solves the issue and will quickly move to resolve issues rather than stew and harbor resentment.

In conflict scenarios with Enterprisers, the wise financial professional will:

- Avoid arguments, listening to complaints and ideas for resolution.
- Ask for the best ways to solve the conflict.
- Own up quickly to any mistakes made (without trying to make up excuses).
- Be ready to put the situation behind and move forward.

Common Conflict Responses: The Analyzer Personality

In conflict situations, Analyzers are likely to:

- Increase resistance and shift into passive/aggressive behavior.
- Overpower others with facts and logic.
- Become defensive.
- Withhold information.
- Respond with "What if?" questions and "Prove that!" statements.
- Judge their adversary and the situation in black-and-white (critical) terms.

Resolving a conflict with the Analyzers is going to be a different experience altogether than with the Enterprisers. Whereas the Enterpriser wants a quick resolution, the Analyzer wants a thorough resolution. Analyzers examine all the events that led to the conflict, then carefully lay out the groundwork to prevent this scenario from recurring. Analyzers will not readily change their views without overwhelming evidence. The Analyzer's first response in conflict will be defensiveness, and they will quickly attempt to prove that they are right. High As may withhold necessary input for solving the conflict or even refuse to participate at all in the resolution process.

In conflict scenarios with Analyzers, the wise financial professional will:

- Not force or push the resolution process (adopt a patient approach and move slowly and cautiously).
- Avoid debate and blaming.
- Take notes and ask for their critique of the problem and input in preventing future conflict.

Common Conflict Responses: The Motivator Personality

In conflict situations, Motivators are likely to:

- Avoid the scene when negativity is sensed.
- Try to dismiss or smooth over the situation (adapt a superficial fix).
- Become emotional and offended, taking criticism or conflicts personally.
- Seek control or revenge by persuading others to side with them.
- Openly joke about or trivialize the conflict (but be internally upset).
- Overwhelm their opponent with monologue.

The Motivator personality is quite uncomfortable in confronting conflicts, which goes against the grain of their take-life-in-stride nature. Motivators are good at rallying people to their cause and trying to win by virtue of a majority. They are also inclined to use superficial fixes by making light of the situation to restore an air of amicability quickly. Motivators avoid people whose tone communicates anger, frustration, and impatience. Criticism is often taken as a threat to their image, and they may respond by attacking the adversary or venting their frustrations. Motivators may also act as if the problem is solved when an undercurrent of conflict remains, in hopes that it will pass.

In conflict scenarios with the Motivator personality style, the wise financial professional will:

- Approach the client in a friendly and positive fashion.
- Use self-deprecating humor to ease the tension.
- Frame a *we* approach to the conflict instead of an *I* or *you* approach.
- Ask for their thoughts and ideas for resolution and listen without interruption.

As we have illustrated in this chapter, much of the tension and conflict we experience with others is a result of a naive and misdirected focus—we focus on what happened instead of why. When we look below the surface of people's actions and reactions, we see deep-seated personality patterns. We believe that learning to recognize these personality tendencies gives us a great deal of leverage in placating and resolving conflict situations.

The effective financial professional recognizes that each personality has an idiosyncratic comfort zone and that conflict will happen when we violate those zones of comfort. With such recognition comes opportunity. The opportunities are for us to demonstrate that we understand our clients' barriers for comfort and security as well as demonstrate our own willingness and flexibility to meet them at their point of comfort.

CHAPTER 10

Connecting
in Conflict

When most people think of the word *confrontation,* they immediately associate it with negative emotions and the escalation of conflict. Confrontation, when handled properly, can be a very positive emotional process that results in not only resolving the conflict but in preventing future conflicts as well. The crucial step is in the approach.

We recently heard a story about a business owner who had an irate contractor pacing in his reception area. He fit the stereotype for his trade—a stout, muscular man with a stern demeanor that advertised the brevity of his patience. He told the receptionist that the business owner owed him $30,000 and he wasn't leaving the building until he had a check in hand. His tone was harsh enough that the receptionist figured he meant to become a permanent fixture if not satisfied with payment. She called the business owner's office to apprise him of the situation. To her surprise and to the surprise of the contractor, he said, "Oh, send him right in."

Twenty minutes later, a stunned staff watched as the contractor exited the business owner's office a transformed man. He was wearing a jacket with the company's logo on it and holding a check for $3,000 in his hand—and couldn't say enough about what a great guy the business owner was. He shared with the receptionist how the business owner was all smiles and handshakes and so glad to see him—the opposite of what he had expected. The owner listened to the contractor's complaint and assured him of how important it was for him to maintain a good business relationship with him, especially as the business was growing. He told the contractor of the cash flow challenges they were experiencing with their growth and got him to agree to take $3,000 today and the balance in 60 days. He then fitted the contractor with a jacket and sent him on his merry way.

We have found that with a will to listen and some diplomatic charm, you can turn your worst adversary into your greatest advocate. We have studied personalities who seem to excel in the art of confronting difficult situations and have noted the patterns of diplomacy that they exercise. We will call these patterns Confrontational Rules of Thumb. Follow these rules in difficult, testy, and trying circumstances and experience the magic of capitalizing on conflicts rather than suffering from them. The wise financial professional recognizes the opportunities that await the captain who can successfully navigate through choppy seas. By following these simple but efficacious rules of confrontation, you will earn admiration, confidence, and trust.

CONFRONTATIONAL RULE OF THUMB #1: BE TRANSPARENT

One of the best ways to initiate motivation for the other party to work through a conflict is to start with a clear and honest agenda. People often fail to work with us or to work things out because they're suspicious of our motives. They're thinking to themselves, "Yeah, this is going to be good for you, but what about me?" To obviate such problems, clearly address why you're there by saying something like, "The reasons I want to work through this situation are . . ." When people are not honest in admitting their motives, the mind's suspicious radar will try to detect their real angle. As we are all aware, the common cry of "What's in it for me?" has become the law of the jungle—people rarely set out on a course of action without some hope of personal payoff.

Any attempts at confronting and resolving a conflict should commence with a transparent admission of why you're there and what your payoff is. The payoff you seek may be emotional in nature such as, "I wanted to talk today because I think I may have miscommunicated, and I don't want to have any tension or mistrust in our relationship. I was hoping we could talk through this matter and come to an understanding. I value you as a client and want this relationship to continue and grow."

The other party likely will retract their suspicious radar with this introduction because you have laid your cards on the table. You have demonstrated that you want to keep their business and remove any tension from the relationship. If you were to approach the same situation with, "I think we need to talk about such and such a situation. . . ," the client will begin to wonder, "Why do you want to talk about this?" Without transparency in confronting conflicts, suspicions begin to fester, and communication erodes into a defensive jousting match.

CONFRONTATIONAL RULE OF THUMB #2: GIVE THE CREDIT, TAKE THE BLAME

The common, narcissistic urge in most people is to gather glory when things go well and spread blame when things go wrong. People within corporations and organizations often build up years of resentment based on these behaviors. People have an innate need to be recognized for their contributions and to be approached diplomatically and gracefully when they make mistakes. Only the secure and confident financial professional can sincerely accept responsibility when communication fails and processes falter.

Emotionally intelligent financial professionals understand that their leadership styles in times of tension establish a pattern for the entire organization. The financial professional who accepts blame and distributes credit recognizes the crucial importance of a team dynamic in organizational success. Motivation is quickly diffused when people energetically contribute and receive little or no recognition or gratitude. This demotivating spiral is accelerated quickly when the financial professional harbors the credit for their efforts. Workplace history shows that such disingenuous and narcissistic behavior erodes relational trust and loyalty, leading to increased conflict and resistance to cooperation.

> "I have watched many advisors try to walk a tightrope with client confidence by pounding their chest and blowing their trumpet when the portfolio saw notable gains, and then blaming the markets when the portfolio experienced losses. My mentor, Morry, taught me just the opposite. When his clients had a great year he would tell them, 'The markets were kind to us this year,' and the client would walk away thinking, 'That Morry is sharp. I'm glad I know him.' When these same clients had a down year, Morry would say, 'I just wasn't on top of my game this year, but I think we can turn it around.' And the client would walk away thinking, 'It was a bad year in the markets. I would have done even worse somewhere else.' I never heard him brag about success, and I never heard him whine about failure, and people trusted him implicitly. I've followed the same approach."
>
> —Everett C., independent financial professional

When a person is always right, there has to be something wrong.

—Anonymous

The world is full of people who want to take credit for what others do right, and those same people want to blame somebody else for everything they do wrong—which is the root of many business conflicts. Take a look at those people with whom you work that you just want to run away from. This second rule defines what is wrong. Many people, because of insecurity, are living unconsciously by the rule, "Take the credit; give the blame." Sit back and observe the magic that happens when you start saying things like, "You know this situation fell apart, and I've got to look in the mirror first. I've got to ask myself where I screwed up. What did I neglect to look at? If I'm going to be in a leadership position, such as a financial professional, I've got to be ready, able, and willing to take the blame for what happens on my watch."

Alternatively, when things go right, start hearing these words come out of your mouth, "Yeah, I was involved, but if you didn't do what you're doing and my staff didn't do their part, this wouldn't have worked so well. This is a team game we're playing here." Behind every great story is a team of people making it happen. Start uttering these beneficent words and observe how magnetic a personality you become to other people. People want to be around secure individuals who are giving credit and taking blame.

Here's the magic of taking blame—it disarms your adversary. An old saying instructs, "When you know you're going to be accused, accuse yourself first." By accusing yourself, you remove the arsenal from your adversary. You go from a metaphorical whipping to a metaphorical self-flagellation by saying, "I really screwed up here. I'm sorry to say it's not the first time, and do you know how I screwed up? Let me tell you about the time. . . ." Now you're disarming your adversary—you're literally disrobing your mistake and they're beginning to feel like, "Yeah, I agree, but hey, that's enough!" We've also noticed the phenomenon of accusing yourself first. When you start saying, "Here's where I'm culpable," all of a sudden they start saying, "Well, yeah, but it wasn't just you . . . I mean I could have done . . ." Most fights are a ping-pong match of, "You did this" and "No, I didn't do that." Avoiding this frustration is simply a matter of taking the blame *before* it is offered.

CONFRONTATIONAL RULE OF THUMB #3: KNOW WHEN IT'S AN I OR A WE PROBLEM

In potential and actual conflict situations, paying close attention to the subtleties of our speech is important. If a problem is the result of our own making or negligence, and we say to a coworker or client, "We've got a problem," we are implying that the problem is equally of their making and that they share responsibility to fix it. This approach will meet either outward or veiled resistance.

On the other hand, if there are equal and proportional contributions of negligence, then stating, "We've got a problem" or "I've got a problem," is a smart approach for the manager, as it infers a team approach and a willingness to help.

If the cause of the problem is squarely on the shoulders of the other person, avoid saying, "*You've* got a problem," which isolates the individual in a negative spotlight. This approach is kind of like watching yourself do a belly flop in a slow-motion replay—a painful experience. The safest and best approach is to say, "*We* might have a problem here" or "*We've* got to figure out a solution." By using we, you are showing them they are not alone in this situation but rather on a team, and that you are there to help resolve the situation.

When you know you caused the problem, the scenario is not a we problem, it is an I problem. Since I caused a problem, it is my problem, not our problem. Then it is important to say something like, "I have a problem. I goofed up. Can I get some help from you?" or "Unfortunately, I caused this problem by myself, but I can't fix it by myself. Is there any way you can help me?" How do most people respond to an approach like that? If they've got half a heart, they'll help you. What do you do, however, if you are being blamed for a situation in which you've done nothing to cause the problem? As regrettable as it is to be blamed unfairly, you can win friends in both situations by:

1. Asking for help after admitting culpability when you caused the trouble
2. Sharing and shouldering the responsibility even when others caused the problem

CONFRONTATION RULE OF THUMB #4: USE SELF-DEPRECATING HUMOR

A physiological fact is that laughter and tension cannot occupy the same space at the same time. For example, if you lifted a 100-pound weight and someone told you a funny joke, you would drop the weight because laughter diffuses the tension that allows you to lift it. This illustration translates into a good metaphor for the baggage people carry in the workplace—which often translates into interpersonal conflict. Approaching these conflicts with a self-deprecating sense of humor can help to diffuse the tension that prolongs the conflict.

Blessed is the man who can laugh at himself; he'll never cease to be amused.

—Anonymous

If we had to pick out one rule in life for becoming a more likable person, we would keep this rule: Learn to laugh at yourself. People are attracted to those who don't take themselves so seriously that they can't have a laugh at their own expense. People who can make fun of themselves are easy to communicate with and easy to be around. People are attracted to laughter and smiles, and self-deprecation indicates a secure and self-confident individual. The fact that you can joke about your shortcomings and foibles tells people that underneath the surface, you're a fairly confident individual—without any pretenses.

A perfectionist is someone who takes great pains—and gives them to
   others.

—Anonymous

Why do so many people, especially those who take themselves too seriously, put up pretenses in conflict situations? Many people feel the need to keep up their image—they're afraid of exposure. In the study of psychology, this defense is called the imposter syndrome. Many people are afraid that others are going to find out what they really know or who they really are. If you're in a situation where the potential for conflict exists, and you say, "I guess I was kind of a dope yesterday," that sort of self-deprecating opening creates a pretty good starting point. You'll arouse fewer defensive instincts with this approach. If they respond by saying, "Yeah, you were a dope all right," instead of becoming defensive you say, "At least we have agreement on that." Now you're getting somewhere. Behind all this lightheartedness, a significant psychological shift is taking place. When you cease to take yourself so seriously, your adversary is inclined to do the same. Self-deprecation acts as a tension-releasing lever—once you pull that lever, the conversation can take a more edifying tone.

To summarize, the advantages of a humorous approach are as follows:

- People who can laugh at themselves are easier to communicate with in conflict situations.
- Laughter releases tension and acts as a stress valve.
- People are attracted to laughter and smiles.
- A self-deprecating sense of humor indicates a secure and confident individual.

CONFRONTATION RULE OF THUMB #5: USE A HUMBLE APPROACH

It's what you learn after you know it all that counts.

—John Wooden

These kinds of statements indicate a humility-based approach.

- "I may have messed up here."
- "I think I goofed."
- "Did I handle that properly?"
- "Do you think there's a better plan?"
- "I apologize."
- "I'll need some help for this to work."
- "Did I follow through on the way we'd talked on that project?"

People who are not accustomed to such an approach may struggle with such prefaces at first but will soon be convinced by the change in tone and response from the other party. In the T.E.A.M. Dynamics approach to conflict, each person recognizes both the natural strengths and flaws of each personality style. Once we realize that certain flaws or challenges are inherent in each style, we can more easily adapt a sense of humor and humble demeanor regarding those flaws.

Tension and conflict build when we take the opposite path of accusation and self-justification. This path only breeds resentment, even when we are in the right. Bjorn Borg's sporting maxim of "Win without bragging and lose without excuse" also serves well in the realm of managing conflicts.

If we could deliver a key idea to every sales professional in the world, it would be to remember the letters *HHH,* which stand for humor, humility, and hunger. Those three intangibles produce selling success. People want to know you're hungry, and they want to know you have a sense of humor. Humility will bring you more success with people than will stubborn pride. Humble people are grateful people. Humble people appreciate where they started and where they are today. A person who possesses humility doesn't need to make pretenses. Simply put, people connect with and trust those who possess humility. What's not to like about those individuals who are in touch with their own weaknesses as well as strengths? Their humility encourages a humble and responsible response on your part. Humility demonstrates that you value the relationship and that you have an open mind.

Humility is as scarce as an albino robin.

—A. W. Tozer

Some good words to practice are, "I'm sorry, I made a mistake," or "I could be wrong here," or "Please forgive me for what I said or did." Having the humility to say such words adds cohesiveness to your relationships. People are more at ease and want to deal with people who can articulate such modesty. Humility indicates a secure, confident, and realistic person—the kind of person everyone wants for a financial professional. Client trust and loyalty will flourish with such an approach.

The Humble Cognition

Emotionally intelligent managers possess an equal awareness of their personality's assets and liabilities. Each of the four personality styles (Togetherness, Enterpriser, Analyzer, and Motivator) have natural inclinations and features that spell strengths on one side and challenges on the other. Being cognitive of these personality liabilities makes each individual easier to work with and, consequently, more adept at resolving personality-based conflicts.

Following are the four personality styles with a description of their inherent liabilities that cause relational friction.

The Togetherness Personality

- Procrastination
- Aversion to candor and straightforwardness
- Oversensitivity
- Lack of assertiveness
- Overseriousness
- Propensity for following the crowd
- Fear of rocking the boat
- Need for constant affirmation
- People-pleasing tendencies

The Enterpriser Personality

- Bluntness/insensitivity
- Impatience
- Autocratic manner/condescending
- Lack of affirmative input
- Propensity for giving ultimatums
- Confrontational style
- Misguided competitiveness
- Poor listening skills
- Compulsion for quick completion

- Frustration with risk-averse personalities
- Sarcasm

The Analyzer Personality

- Impersonal approach/appearance
- Values processes over people
- Resistant to change
- Pessimistic views
- Slow to change view
- Defensive
- Self-justifying
- Intellectual arrogance
- Propensity for criticizing and judging
- Tension and loss of composure under pressure

The Motivator Personality

- Easily bored
- Impulsive
- Lack of follow-through
- Empty promises and shallow commitments
- Disorganized
- Uses flattery to persuade
- Aversion to confronting conflict
- Inappropriate speech/obnoxious behavior
- Domination of conversations
- Overzealous appetite for attention and recognition
- Persuasive manipulation to achieve objectives
- Lack of discipline and self-restraint
- Taking credit for the work of others

Here are a few of the many advantages of approaching conflicts with a humble demeanor:

- A humble approach is based on an open mind.
- A humble approach demonstrates an awareness of one's own weaknesses as well as strengths.
- A humble approach encourages a humble and responsible response.
- A humble approach demonstrates that you value the relationship at hand.

In any confrontation situation, if you practice these five rules of thumb, people are going to be more inclined to work with you and to find a way to work it out with you. These rules of thumb are emotionally intelligent methods for diffusing conflict situations. Too often, conflicts are intensified because of ill-advised approaches toward resolving the problem. A people-smart approach to confrontation is important. We have found that people are more inclined to help you when they find a reason to like you.

The story is told of a conflict that Ben Franklin was having with a member of the first Continental Congress. To move forward on an important idea, Franklin needed this individual's agreement; however, his foe would not budge even an inch. Franklin searched for a tactic to put himself in the good graces of this man. Franklin decided that this man needed to view Franklin in a different perspective for any change to take place. He tried to think of some favor he could do for this gentleman and then came upon the idea: "To win another person over, it is best to allow them to give you a gift or favor than for you to give them a gift or favor." If he did a favor for the man, that favor could easily be misconstrued as a briberous act, but if he asked this man to do him a favor, it would only be interpreted as an act of grace. Franklin learned that this man had in his possession a rare volume of a book that he desired to read, so he went to his adversary and implored him about the possibility of reading this rare book. The man was only too happy to extend this favor and to display a more congenial side of himself to Franklin. Once Franklin had read the book and they had discussed the author and contents, a more friendly dialogue had been established between them. This amicability led to a compromise that helped Franklin move his cause forward. Ben Franklin's example helps to affirm our chief principle regarding confrontation, namely that people are most inclined to help you when they find a reason to like you.

Confrontation skills come down to our ability to put relationships in their proper priority—above and beyond winning an argument or getting our way. What do we really gain by winning an argument when winning breaks down a relational connection that could have contributed to our future prosperity? In laying out the confrontational rules of thumb, we do not intend to imply that these approaches or responses will be easy. We are all human, given to whims and occasionally carried far from logic by our own self-justifying emotions. Consequently, we will be tempted to plead our case, even if by doing so we pave the path to greater conflict. By practicing the principles we have laid out, however, you will see the world of conflict through a different set of eyes. You will see that most people do not want arguments, disagreements, and the accompanying tension. You will see that people desire resolution and peace of mind. By following these principles, you can diffuse tension, bring clarity, and quickly move forward from negative situations.

These small, subtle steps in communication lead to great strides in creating a team dynamic within your organization. People feel assured that their mistakes will be repaired quickly because the focus is on fixing the problem, not placing the blame. Cooperation and teamwork flourish in such an environment, and the wise financial professional sets this *we* tone in the organization. Also, make sure that your tone and your body language communicate cooperation as well as your words. Insincerity with team-building phraseology is just as, or more, destructive than blaming and irresponsibility. Most conflicts find their roots in poor communication. The effective financial professional understands this and works toward communicating that he or she is going to be easy to work with.

FINAL NOTE

Great persuaders are not measured merely by their ability to stir large crowds, but by their ability to positively influence every person they meet. Their influence is felt one to one, on the teams they work with and the crowds they stand before. No matter what the situation or who the audience, our skill in connectivity is in communicating who we are, where we are headed, and how we can help at every available opportunity.

PART III

Connecting with the Individual

The Human Drama

Act I—Revealing the Characters and Dramas

Every man is, in certain respects, (a) . . . like all men, (b) . . . like some other men, (c) . . . like no other man.

—C. Cluckholm and H. Murray

The presentation process to an individual is in many ways like a three-act dramatic play. In the first act of a play, both the characters and the dramas between them are introduced. In the second act, the various dramas unfold and in the third act the conflicts are resolved. Sales professionals are familiar with a kindred process: the discovery phase (revealing the characters and the dramas), the presentation (addressing the dramas), and the advancing stage (closing), which resolves the conflicts.

Just as an audience judges a dramatic presentation on the quality of these dramatic essentials, so they will judge your performance by how well you present yourself in these stages of connectivity and presentation. When we watch a movie or a play and the characters are developed in a superficial way without revealing much of their character, we immediately lose interest in the story line. When the dramas unfold in a predictable, formulaic manner, we quickly get bored because it looks like a hundred other movies we've seen. We must somehow relate to the story for it to maintain our attention for 90 minutes. If the movie leaves conflicts hanging in the lurch at the end, we walk away dissatisfied. These emotions are very close to the emotions that play out in the typical financial professional-client dialogue. How do you measure up in the three acts of a client presentation?

Act I—Revealing the Characters and the Dramas

Do you take the time to get to know who your client really is, or do you just cover the fact-finding basics and try to push ahead to your product presentation? In your first act, if you hope to build a relationship that will last, you must dig to find out who your client really is and what it is your client really wants. How much of yourself do you reveal in your presentation? Do you present a presence that is both professional and personable? Do you have an ear tuned in for the money-related dramas that are playing out in your client's life? Are you making a correlation between what your client needs and what you have to offer?

Act II—The Dramas Unfold

Is your presentation formulaic and monotonous? Does it sound like the kind of pitch your clients could and would hear from a thousand other financial professionals? If so, they will quickly lose interest in your story line. Do you bring a passion and believability to your role as advisor? Are you and your material one? If you have absorbed your role, your presentation will be much more convincing than if you are reading from a company script. People are drawn to those advisors who bring a palpable passion and intensity to their work.

Act III—Resolving the Conflicts

Have you helped your audience to walk away feeling like they will live happily ever after? Do they leave your presentation with a greater sense of hope than when they arrived? This is why people come in the first place. They want a better, freer life. They want to solve big problems. This only happens when you uncover *and* resolve their conflicts. People may try to minimize or pretend they have no conflicts, but this denial is simply pretense. They would not keep an appointment and make the journey if they did not have money-related conflicts lurking just below the surface. For you to advance the sale, your products and services must resolve these conflicts. Your presentations will close properly when you learn to make the emotional connection between what you do and what they want and need.

WHO ARE THESE PEOPLE?

"I often tell my peers that they should imagine a scenario of a businessman walking down the street and being stopped by another businessman who bluntly asks him, "How much money do you have?" The first man responds, "That's none of your business. Why do you want to know?" The second man responds by telling him of all his financial credentials and years of experience in managing other people's money. He even mentions the names of some people that the first businessman is familiar with. He closes by telling the man that he can accomplish great things with his money. The first businessman tells him that his accomplishments may all be well and true but he hasn't accomplished much with him. I have witnessed some presentations in my industry, which seem just as obtrusive and offensive as this story. What I tell my cohorts—especially young advisors—is this, that every client wants to feel unique and valued. It's not about their money; it's about them."

—Simon J., financial professional

Before we delve into the discovery process, we first must establish what we are looking for. All financial professionals spend time digging out facts. These facts are about balances, income, goals, and expectations. But we have found that the most successful financial professionals go a layer or two below the factual surface and seek to discover more about their clients than just their possessions and plans. They have learned that building trust hinges on finding out who their client is—not just finding out what they have. These financial professionals are using what we like to call the MVP Approach to advising, as shown in Figure 11.1.

M—Methodology. Successful financial professionals have a tried-and-tested method for ascertaining the knowledge they need to make a presentation that scores a bull's-eye with the client. They use a sales process they are comfortable with—and that their clients are comfortable with as well. Although these financial professionals have a methodology for presenting their products and services, they also understand that this approach is surface oriented and cannot replace the other necessary elements of discovery.

V—Values. Successful financial professionals understand that the worth of their clients cannot be measured in strictly fiscal terms. Each client has a set of values and principles that defines their pursuit of success. The wise financial professional understands the necessity of asking questions to uncover these values.

P—Personality. At the core of everyone is what we call a personality DNA defining the type of people they are comfortable with, the types of risk they are willing to take, the kind of communication they prefer, and the sorts of processes that either stress or comfort them. We have found that this knowledge is absolutely essential to

FIGURE 11.1 | The MVP Approach

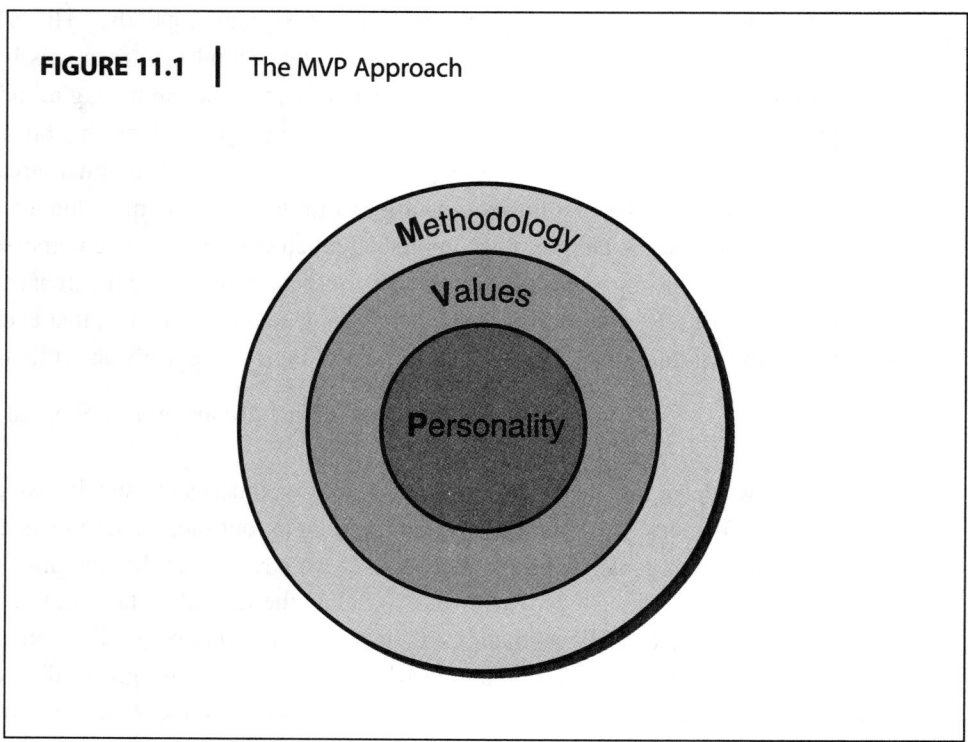

keeping clients happy. If you learn this particular people skill, you will be in the successful minority that has uncovered the key to successful communication with clients. We have dedicated an entire section of this book to the study of this indispensable client connection skill.

Discover Their World

I've never learned a thing while my mouth was moving.

—Anonymous

We met a financial professional who has been the number one producer in his firm (which employs hundreds of financial professionals) for almost ten years straight. At an awards dinner, we were told that not only was he perennially the top producer, but that a wide chasm always lay between him and the number two producer. We asked him to try to define in succinct terms what he thought the key to his success was. His answer was surprising but brilliant. He said the key for him was *curiosity*.

"I've always been extremely curious about people," he told us. "I want to know where they came from, where they are today, where their journey has taken them, where they would like to go in the future, what kinds of things stir their passion, and where their children have gone or are going. I just like to know as much as I can about everybody. It's not a put-on for me—it's just the way I'm made up. I think people see my sincere interest and curiosity and are drawn to it."

How much curiosity do you demonstrate toward your clients—and not just toward their assets, but toward the life that built those assets? Think of the most recent time you had a conversation with someone who wanted to find out everything they could about you—a person who seemed genuinely interested in you. If you can't remember such a conversation recently, you're not alone! This phenomenon is easy to explain—people are narcissistic by nature, and they would prefer to talk about themselves. The best definition of narcissism we know of is the fellow who said, "Enough of me talking about me, how about you talk about me now?"

Selfish: Devoid of consideration for the selfishness of others.

—Ambrose Bierce

We once heard a presentation by a consultant who studied the amount of time that sales professionals and clients talked out of every 60 seconds they spent together. Figure 11.2 shows the disappointing results of that study. Not only did the sales professionals use the majority of the airtime, they *dominated* it. How can we explain such a statistic? Would this statistic also be true in the financial services world? Is the average financial professional under the impression that she is more important than her clients? Are some financial professionals in love with the sound of their own voice, or are they simply practicing the only method they know—which is talk, talk, talk, and talk some more?

How do you feel when someone dominates 82 percent of the conversation? Angry? Frustrated? Bored? These emotions are prevalent, but they all lead to the core emotion, which is feeling unimportant. If we refine our discovery skills for no other reason, we should do it for this purpose—to help each client feel like our most important client.

Uncovering Values

In their book, *Storyselling for Financial Advisors,* Mitch and his coauthor, Scott West, set out to find the best questions that top financial professionals were asking their clients. They were looking for the type of questions that would help financial professionals uncover their clients' background, values, and the principles they held dear. One of

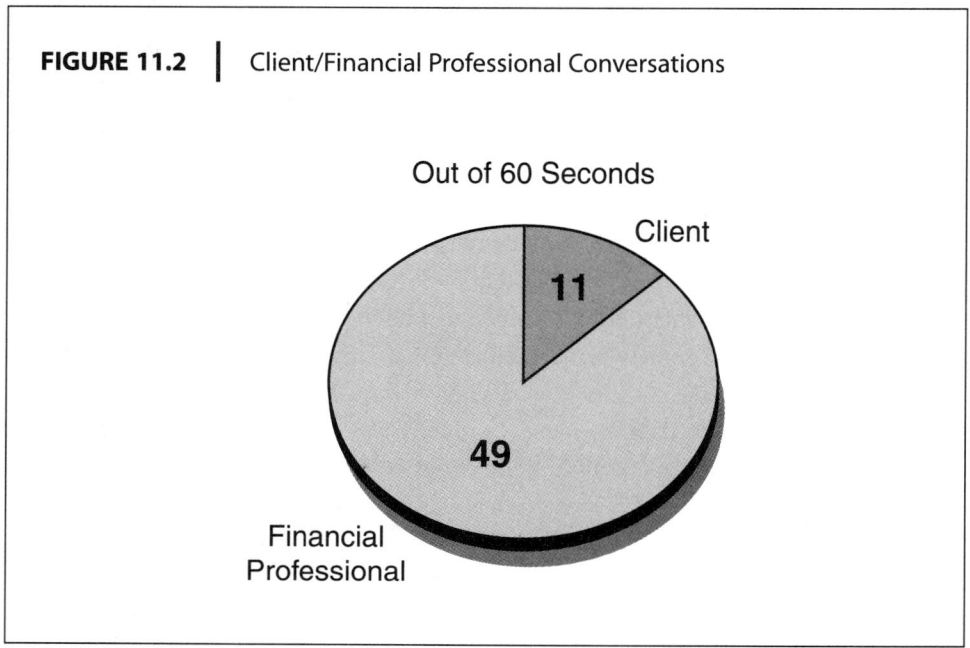

FIGURE 11.2 | Client/Financial Professional Conversations

Out of 60 Seconds

the facts of life every financial professional can relate to is the danger of not asking the right questions. For example, a financial professional can run into trouble when un-knowingly bringing up a stock, a company, or an idea that causes offense to the client. We call these trouble spots *land mines,* as they can cause a presentation to blow up in your face. When you begin asking the questions we are about to prescribe, you end up tapping into *gold mines,* areas of need that a client will reveal when we ask the right questions. The difference between the financial professional who walks into land mines and the one who walks into gold mines is found in the questions they ask. Following are ten of the best questions they found for generating gold-mine conversations.

Where are you from? This simple question will reveal much. First of all, people enjoy talking about their roots—especially the mature client. Second, a certain set of values is associated with growing up in specific areas. Growing up on a family farm is a far cry from living on 12 different military bases, as children of military personnel do. What you're really looking for are ways to connect with the client. Just a few degrees of separation put you apart from any other person in the world. One financial profes-sional told us how amazed he was to see how often his clients knew someone that he knew—that discovery resulted from asking this question. By talking about where they're from, clients reveal some of their values and often expose some common connection.

Tell me about your life's work. Here is where the client will reveal the path life has taken up until the present. Clients reveal their values and priorities as they tell you about the career opportunities they have embraced and rejected. Not only will their answers reveal values, but they will also give you a clearer picture of their personality, ambitions, and hopes. Many people derive a major portion of their identity from the work they do or did. By failing to query into their occupational history, you can miss an opportunity for a relational connection. Some may even have an ego need for others to respect or acknowledge their accomplishments. Many people have unusual career paths and interesting stories to tell. Wise is the financial professional who asks and listens.

Tell me about the best financial decision you have ever made. When you ask this question, you are giving your clients permission to gloat just a bit and possibly to confess the antithesis—the worst financial decision they have made. People like to talk about their personal victories. Some also like to get some financial baggage off of their chests. Their answers reveal the depth and breadth of the client's financial savvy and possibly some insight regarding the level of risk they are comfortable with.

What principles do you endeavor to follow with your money? We have found that this question helps to reveal clients' sources of learning, whether from parents, relatives, friends, financial letters or magazines, radio, television, or the Internet. You'll also get an indicator of their personal guidelines toward investing. Are they spenders or savers? Do they want to leave a vast inheritance to heirs or charity, or spend it all before they die? Some simply want to protect what they have, while others are willing to roll the dice. Some want to retire as soon as possible, while others plan on never fully retiring. You often will be able to ascertain where your clients stand on these issues through their answers to this question.

Do you avoid some investments as a matter of principle? This question is important for today's client. When we ask audiences of financial professionals how many of them think this is an important question, only about 10 to 20 percent agree. However, when we ask clients if they had strong aversions to certain investments because of personal scruples, 60 percent said that they did. Socially Responsible Investing (SRI) is an idea that is gaining popularity. SRI is an approach where investors only invest in companies that live up to determined environmental, ethical, or moral codes. *The Wall Street Journal* reported that the Domini Social Equity Fund was one of the 65 best funds with a three-year annualized return of 32.6 percent. People read this and begin to believe that following a set of values with your investments can be both morally and financially rewarding.

If you could teach one financial principle to your children/ grandchildren, what would that lesson be? The answer to this question reveals the essential guidepost in your client's financial life. Financial professionals who ask this question hear answers like, "Easy come, easy go—the harder you work to get it, the harder you work to keep it," "Use your money to enjoy your life, your best memories will not be about savings account balances," and "Make sure your money works as hard as you do." Two powerful things happen by asking this question. First, you are demonstrating that you value the lessons they have learned, and second, you are demonstrating a keen appreciation of wisdom regarding financial issues. Today's clients, especially prosperous mature clients, are looking for more than knowledge—they are looking for wisdom.

What do you want your money to do for you? Money is not an end—money is a means. We are not here to serve money—money is here to serve us. The question is *how* we want money to serve us. Money and wealth building are always tied to deeper emotional issues. Are we trying to purchase freedom, security, a legacy, or opportunities? By inquiring in this way, you can become a partner with your clients in building for the dreams that they have for their money, rather than simply being a mechanical facilitator in the process.

What other people have you assumed some financial responsibility for? This question is highly pertinent for the times in which we live, especially for the baby boomer who is facing a responsibility crunch. Because many boomers waited until later to have children and their parents are living longer, many are feeling the squeeze of financial pressure. Many clients in the boomer age group have assumed a sense of responsibility for parents who don't quite have enough to live the way they would like to in retirement. An additional $300 to $400 can make a substantial difference for many retired parents of baby boomers. Some are beginning to set up "parental pensions" and other such support mechanisms for aging parents. You can start to become a facilitator for these processes and for college savings programs simply by asking this question.

Have you ever thought about how much money is enough? For some, there will never be enough money; for others, who prefer to live a simple lifestyle, their current means are more than adequate. Many are interested in leaving some sort of legacy with their money. This may involve the development of trusts, endowments, etc. A generation of baby boomers is constantly striving to add new layers of meaning to their lives. Many will seek to use their money to find a sense of purpose through charitable involvement. Smart financial professionals have learned that by opening up this dialogue, they can make a profound connection as well as aid in this process.

What do you expect from a financial professional? John Sestina, a veteran financial professional and mentor to other financial professionals, asks all his clients a version of this question, "If we were to work together and it's now 12 months later, looking back a year, what did I do for you?" Sestina reports that no matter what expectations the client spoke about in the previous hour, his truthful expectations get elicited with that question. This is a great closing question, because it is comforting for both parties involved when at the close of a consultation, the financial professional has a clear idea of the client's expectations.

As mentioned earlier in this book, 87 percent of the people who left their financial professional did so because of the relationship. The best way to obviate problems with your clients is to ask them for their idea of a job description for you. If it isn't realistic, you can correct it then and there. At the very least you are now aware of what it will take to meet their relational expectations.

It's all about life. Gary likes to teach that the questions we ask act as a framework for the picture we will paint with our presentation. Great presentations can be a work of art requiring creativity and inspiration. But most of all, they require understanding the subject from all angles. On the other hand, building a frame is a constructive task— it is a process of precise query and workmanship. The questions we presented in this chapter are effective for building this framework. The four sides of the frame you want to build for every client are: understanding their life, their work, their values, and their expectations (see Figure 11.3). When you have built this framework through intelligent inquiry, you are ready to begin your presentation.

We call the preceding questions the LIFE Inventory (Life Inventory of Formulative Experiences) because discovery should be all about your client's life. Discerning a person's investable assets takes nothing more than a calculator. However, understanding how a person obtained those assets and where they want those assets to take them someday takes something more. It takes curiosity, intuition, intelligence, imagination, and sincere interest in your clients. Once your clients get the sense that you understand what their life is all about, trusting you with their financial management is a very short step.

If your discovery process goes well, it will have revealed the various dramas being played out in each of your client's lives. Now you're ready for Act II, where you begin to address these dramas with the products and services you have to offer.

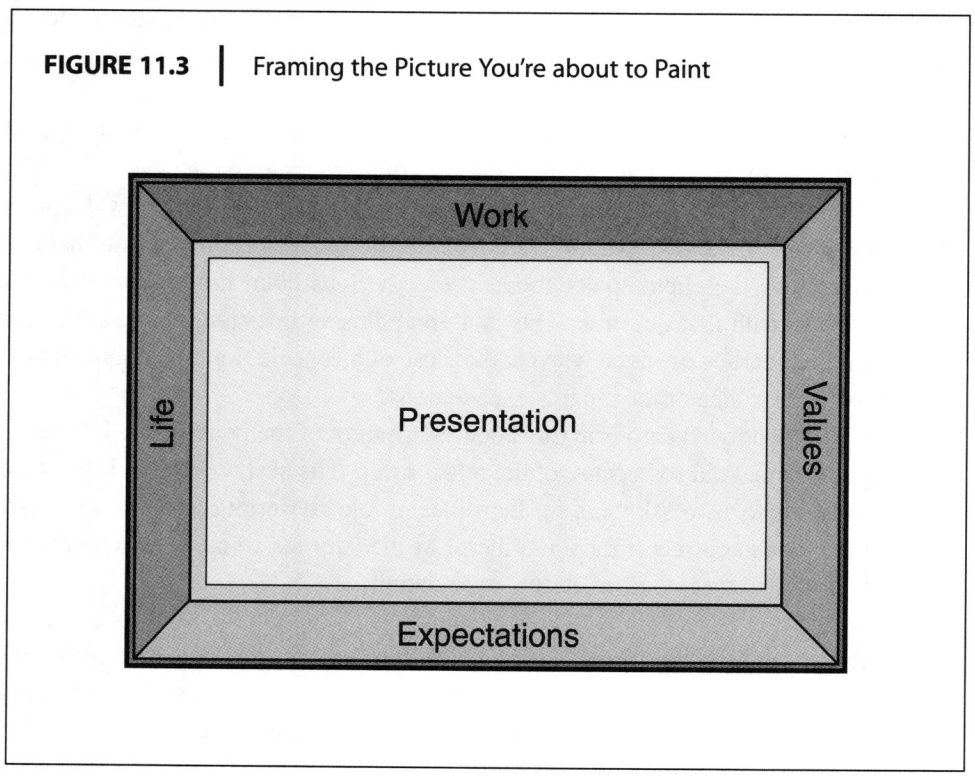

FIGURE 11.3 | Framing the Picture You're about to Paint

CHAPTER 12

The Human Drama

Act II—Addressing the Dramas

Anything you say in your product presentation that is not directly related to the personal needs of your client is a waste of time and breath. Even if your presentation materials are in four colors and laminated, without life relevance, they are a waste of ink and laminate. What really moves a client to take action is *relevance*. Every word that comes out of your mouth in your presentation of product and service must hit a bull's-eye in the mind and emotion of the client.

How well you meet the client's agenda will depend entirely on how well developed your skills of inquiry and observation are. If you follow the advice in the last chapter and ask questions which reveal who your client is as well as what your client has—and then listen very closely to the answers they give and how they give them—you will be well prepared to give your presentation. There will be little guesswork. You will know that every word you speak will find a willing and receptive audience, because your client has already revealed his needs. Your presentation must play to the dramas unfolding in the life of your client. In this chapter we will share principles to help you focus your presentation directly on the issues that the client is facing.

PRESENTATION PRINCIPLE #1: KNOW YOUR TARGET

Gary recently had an experience that illustrates how easily the opening comments of a presentation can miss the mark. This experience shows how, if your opening statement doesn't connect, you have just flipped off the relevancy switch in the client's brain. At a major boat show in Chicago, Gary and a friend were looking at a boat that caught Gary's eye. The salesperson walked over and made this opening comment, "If you have any technical questions on the specifics of this boat, I'll be over to answer those technical questions." Now that may be a good opener if your prospective client is an engineer or a 30-year navy veteran who wants to know all the specs of the motor, boat design, etc., but it is certainly not a good opener for a guy like Gary. Gary has a high-energy, highly motivated, fun-loving, and garrulous personality. The last thing he wants to talk about are the specs of the engine or any other details—he wants to talk about how he is going to use the boat.

Gary's friend, who is also a sales professional, was slack jawed at how badly the salesperson had missed his mark and turned off Gary in a nanosecond. This opener proved to be very costly for the sales professional. He failed to use the skills of discovery to find out *why* Gary would want to invest a considerable sum of money in a boat. He failed to use the skills of observation to get a feel for the type of personality Gary is. Consequently, Gary and his friend walked away—and the salesperson was clueless as to why. Any line of a presentation, including the opener, is a waste of breath if it is not immediately applicable to the life and personality of the client. Our first rule of thumb for a can't-miss presentation is this: Don't present a word until you know how your product or service will fit your client's life.

If you are not sure, then you should still be asking—not telling. In the above story, the sales professional could have started an engaging presentation with Gary by asking one simple question, "If you were to own this boat, how would you use it?" How people survive in a sales profession without being in touch with the law of the jungle—the What's in It for Me (WIIFM) principle—is beyond us. Yet thousands of vendors of products and services launch into presentations all the time thinking only about what's in it for them. What they fail to realize with this self-serving approach is that they have created a huge blind spot in their psyche, which prevents people from wanting to do business with them. People intuitively will choose to do business with those professionals who demonstrate that they are in touch with serving their clients' spoken and unspoken interests. If you are not sure of their needs, don't be tempted to begin presenting. Continue your discovery process until you are sure of what they need and why they need it. Great presentations are not about throwing darts in the dark—they are about launching laser-guided missiles.

PRESENTATION PRINCIPLE #2: ASSUME NOTHING

Give a presentation that results in a successful human connection based on knowing both what your client needs and knowing why they need it. Every person does not set up an investment plan for the same reason. They may all be looking at one means but have a multiplicity of ends. One person sets up an investment plan because he wants to quit working, while another sets up an investment plan so she will never have to quit doing the work she loves. One person invests so she can someday spend money on leisure and fun, and another invests because he has needy family members for which he feels responsible. One person invests because she is afraid of being old and broke, and another person saves because he loves packing money away and watching it grow. We point out these contrasts because knowing how your presentation will sail is much easier when you know which way the wind blows.

The following story illustrates the dangers of walking into a situation with a product and assuming you know why the client would want it.

An insurance agent sat down with my wife and me and began to tell us that a major motivator for purchasing a life insurance/investment policy should be to provide for your children's college education. We thought it was rather presumptuous of this fellow to tell us what our motivations should be rather than ask us how we felt about funding our children's education. Both my wife and I had worked our way through school with negligible aid from our parents. We had discussed this issue and felt the experience had helped to fortify our work ethic and mold our character, and we both had seen too many of our classmates on a free ride from their parents fritter and party away their opportunity to learn. We had decided that our children would (1) earn money toward college, (2) receive matching funds from us based on their earnings, and (3) take out a student loan for the shortfall. Had the insurance broker bothered to ask, we would have explained our philosophy.

He didn't get our business.

The next agent that visited us started by asking the story of our life. That was the best move he could have made. He discovered that my wife had lost her first husband to cancer after six months of marriage when she was just 21 years old. Before he died, he had forgotten to sign a document that would have reassigned the benefit on his life insurance policy from his parents to his wife. For some unimaginable reason, his parents kept the benefits after his death, leaving his widow both bereft and broke.

Consequently, my wife had a morbid fear of another complication in her support should I precede her in death. With the way she felt, no amount of life insurance was enough.

Because he bothered to ask, that agent got the sale.

—Mitch Anthony and Scott West, *Storyselling for Financial Advisors,* pp. 63–64

As the preceding story illustrates, when you assume you know what your clients want or why they want what they want, you are skating on thin ice—and it's just a matter of time before you fall in. The most successful presentations are those that already incorporate this sort of intelligence.

Questions before Answers

Most of us can remember a time or two when we experienced an annoying sales presentation. Perhaps one of the more annoying scenarios is the salesperson who is racing through a product presentation, covering every benefit and feature, without ever checking to see if the prospective buyers have any desire for such a product and, if they do, why they would want it. One person may buy the product to meet a practical need and another may buy the same product to meet an emotional need. We make this point because every sales presentation purports to have the answers, but having the answers assumes that we know the questions—and these questions differ from client to client.

Before walking clients through a list of features or benefits, ask a question that clarifies their interest. Here are some examples. "Do you feel a need to lower your taxable income?" "Are you interested in setting up a college savings program?" "Are you planning on retiring at age 62—or at any age?" "Are you concerned about providing ongoing financial support for anyone else?" "Do you feel inclined to use some of your wealth for charitable purposes?"

These and other questions should be asked rather than assumed. To assume that anyone's concerns are the same as yours, or that their concerns will be what you think they should be, is foolish in this day and age. Not every person is concerned about taxes—some feel it's their patriotic duty. Not every person is concerned about saving for college—some feel their kids need to earn it the old-fashioned way. Not every person wants to retire (80 percent of baby boomers say they have no intention of ever fully retiring)—some want to work until their dying day. Not every person wants to give any of their money away—some want to spend every penny and have the check to the undertaker bounce.

The bottom line is this: to avoid the common pitfalls, design your presentations to pinpoint exactly what your clients' needs are—and their reasons behind those needs—and then align your products/services to meet those needs.

PRESENTATION PRINCIPLE #3: SIMPLIFY THEIR LIFE

People today are busy, and generally speaking, their lives are cluttered. Almost everyone is looking for some breathing room. They will readily receive any move to sim-

plify their financial life and life in general. Therefore, drawing a direct correlation between the product and service you are selling and how it will make their life easier is
important.

Life is frittered away with detail—simplify, simplify.

—Henry Wadsworth Longfellow

Because most people don't take the time to organize their financial affairs—and because they don't often have a clue as to what their financial affairs would look like if
they were organized—they live life with a little black cloud of financial or investment
stress following them around. The wise financial professional will address this issue
in his presentation so that the client gets the feeling that they will have less anxiety,
regret, and confusion by virtue of partnering with that financial professional.

My mother and I went to see an advisor because her finances were spread all
over the place and she was having trouble seeing the forest because of all the trees.
She really wanted to close her business and take some time off before starting on a
new venture, but she didn't have the foggiest clue as to when and if that would be
possible because of the way her investments were spread out. So she took her folder
full of investment statements into an advisor's office and laid it out on the table. The
advisor began looking at each account statement and making comments like, "We
can do better than that for you" and "I don't know if you want to be in this." He
went through piece by piece and told of a better option he could provide and how
he would go about it.

By the end of this session I could tell my mother was extremely agitated. Afterward she told me, "I'm more frustrated now than when I came in. If I do what he's
saying, I'm going to have to pay taxes as well as a penalty on one investment because I'm exiting early. He seems to have an option for everything, but I still don't
know when I can close my business. All I really want to know is when I can do what
I want."

—Ed B., age 39

A large question like, "When can I do what I want to?" looms in the back of every
client's mind. Clients want *that* question answered. You can answer a million other
questions, but if you leave that key question hanging, they will be unsatisfied with
your presentation.

Here are some guidelines for helping your clients simplify their lives.

- Help them to see the big picture.
- Help them to figure out how long it will take to reach their goals.
- Help them to gather their information and then categorize and summarize this information in the simplest terms possible.
- Ask them how you can help to remove stress from their financial lives.

Just as Vince Lombardi would start every training camp with the words, "This is a football . . . ," so the effective financial professional should stress the financial basics. Most clients don't want to know all the details, the jargon, or the ins and outs of every investment choice. They do, however, need to know if their current situation is a good portrait of wise financial management. They need a simple overview of what they must do to reach their goals. Paul Hornung, the legendary Green Bay Packers running back, was stunned when he came to the Packers to find a thin playbook with about a fourth of the number of plays in it that the average NFL team had. When he asked Lombardi about this, he was told, "We just need to do a few things better than anyone else. You may only have a few running plays, but you have a world of options while you're running those plays. You just have to be able to react to what is happening."

The playbook we give our clients should be like Lombardi's playbook—simple to understand and having the flexibility to respond to what is happening in the markets. The financial professional who speaks in simple, understandable terms and who can help the client see the forest in spite of the trees will never lack for an audience.

PRESENTATION PRINCIPLE #4: BECOME THE BRIDGE BETWEEN WHERE THEY ARE AND WHERE THEY WANT TO GO

I like to position myself with my clients as a bridge builder between current financial reality and desired financial status. I see myself as being both a visionary and an artisan. I have to help them articulate a vision of where they want to go—because if they're not headed anywhere in particular, there is no need for my involvement. There is no point in building a bridge with your clients if you don't know where that bridge leads you. I am an artisan from the standpoint that I can help to procure the most ideal materials for constructing their bridge. Every client's vision is different, and the materials needed vary as well. I like the idea of being the force that helps transport them from where they are to where they want to be.

—Randa P., financial professional

To convince your clients of your worth, your presentations must accomplish the following:

- Find out specifically where they want to be and at what age they want to get there.
- Show them where they are right now.
- Demonstrate how you can bridge the gap between where they want to be and where they are.

Clients want to know what you bring to the table that would make them want to turn over their assets to your management. Is it your ability to purchase stocks, mutual funds, bonds, annuities, and/or insurance policies? What can you do for your clients that they cannot do by themselves—or with the other 500,000 financial professionals who are licensed to sell?

What do you bring to the table in your presentation that compels clients to do business with you? Is it the fact that you will offer a diversified portfolio and spread their money out in a number of asset classes? While these are prudent moves, they are not unique services. "Well," some financial professionals might object at this point, "selling investments and diversifying risk are core functions of my business." Our point is that these are core functions of almost every other professional's business, but they should be peripheral functions of your business when you present it. Your core business is what you can do to help take clients from where they are to where they want to be. Once you establish this core, you give your clients a solid sense of context for the products that will facilitate the plan they need.

Find Out Specifically Where They Want to Be and at What Age They Want to Get There

George Burns was asked what he wanted for his 87th birthday. He replied, "A paternity suit."

Discover what your clients really want and why. Are they looking for financial emancipation? Are they desiring security in case of job loss or disability? Are they striving to ensure the financial independence of parents or children? Or are they looking to free up their lives to live a more balanced existence? Once you discover this big issue in each client's life, it becomes the shining North Star in your presentation. Everything you do and say is directed toward helping your clients reach this place.

Once your clients have articulated the big goal(s) in their life, you need to try to get them to place a time constraint on reaching that goal. Without a deadline, goals have little more guiding power than a New Year's resolution. However, when you can get a client to say, "I want to be financially emancipated to pursue my dream agenda by the age of 50," you now have the foundation for the bridge you will build. Immediacy now enters the picture. Once the question of when is answered, you have a perfect segue for step two in the bridge-building process—show them where they are right now.

Show Them Where They Are Right Now

Don't be remiss about giving people a good reality check, for often their goals are unrealistic. Take, for example, the 44-year-old client who wants to retire at 55, is earning $60,000, and has $45,000 in investable assets. He needs a more realistic picture of what and how long reaching this goal will take. A more realistic goal for this client might be to find a way to segue into the kind of work he could do for many more years, and enjoy, to prolong his earning days. Many of your clients may not have a clear picture as to where they are in relationship to their goals. They often don't know how to sit down and figure out what getting there will take—much less how long it will take.

In this step of the presentation process, you are going to give a view of their financial life from 10,000 feet. Your presentation language at this point should sound something like this:

"If I understand you correctly, your desire is to be in a position to do X, and you would like to be in this position within X years, if possible. After looking at your current financial situation and comparing it with what it will take to accomplish your goal, my estimate is that it will take somewhere between X and X years depending on how aggressive a path you are comfortable taking. I've seen this scenario before, and the good news is that I know it is possible if we make a plan and stick to it."

You have now laid the groundwork for:

- Developing a plan to help them reach their goal
- Exercising the discipline to follow that plan
- Establishing a time line

If the client shows interest at this pivotal point in the presentation, all you have to do is present the materials you will use to build the bridge—for they already have, in effect, agreed to the architectural drawings.

Demonstrate How You Can Bridge the Gap between Where They Are and Where They Want to Be

Just as a specific set of materials will be needed to build a bridge, funds, insurance policies, and various investment tools are needed to build the financial bridge. After you discover the core goals—where your clients want this bridge to end—you need to find out what materials are best to complete the process. Few people have or want to take the time to keep up with which funds are performing well, staying true to their discipline, and being managed consistently well. Nor do people today have the time to sift through volumes of financial information and propaganda to figure out what information is reliable and which is creative manipulation for the profit of a few. Few people want to do all the homework necessary to balance, constantly monitor, and rebalance their financial picture. This is where you are worth your weight in gold. You will do the dirty work, stay on top of the performance and integrity ratings, sift out relevant information from the propaganda, and stay on top of how their investments are progressing in relationship to their goals.

Your job is not only to present the best materials (investment vehicles) to the client, but also to show the criteria you use in determining what are the best materials. We have a financial professional friend who likes to do this only with independent research on the investments he offers, and his favorite is *Forbes*'s "report card" on mutual funds in up and down markets. He says that report cards intuitively resonate with clients who want to know how a company performs in good and inclement market conditions. They don't want a genius fund in bull markets and then get stuck with a dropout in bear markets. As a financial professional, you build client confidence by presenting both the materials and the rationale you use for selecting those materials.

Effective presentations hinge on meeting the felt needs of the client. Their agenda must be your agenda as you present. Few clients will walk away from an individual who can expedite the journey between the reality they are currently disappointed with and the place they have always dreamed of being. This partnership becomes all the more attractive when your clients hear you articulating exactly what they want inside and then showing a clear path for getting it. Presenters who use a human connection approach are the ones who not only understand what their clients want, but can clearly articulate how to get it and, most important, demonstrate their indispensable role in the process.

CHAPTER 13

Act III
Resolving the Conflicts

Moving from Agreement to Action

The issues your clients face are not resolved until you help them to act on their own behalf. Discovery and presentation are wasted if they do not advance to action. In this chapter, we will illustrate how you can help your clients find a reason to act and the motivation needed to move.

Years ago, so the story goes, the world's greatest tightrope walker was about to embark on a walk across the Niagara Falls. The wind was blowing enough to cause great excitement with the large crowd that had gathered. Hearing the boiling murmur, the showman asked the gathering, "Do you believe that I can walk across the Falls on this rope, in spite of this great crosswind?"

"You can do it!" the crowd urged.

Wanting to raise the ante, the tightrope walker asked further, "What if I were to roll a wheelbarrow out in front of me, do you still think I could do it?"

"You can do it, you're the best there is!" they yelled with greater fervor.

Sensing the imploding anticipation he taunted further, "Finally, I will present you with the ultimate scenario. Do you believe I can put a fellow human being in this wheelbarrow and roll it across the rope while battered about by this disturbing breeze?"

Ecstatic with the possibility of such a spectacle the crowd exploded in encouragement, "You're the best that ever was! If anyone can do it, you can!"

"Fine," he answered, "I will take you up on the challenge. Now, who would like to ride in the wheelbarrow?"

As every person who has made a living in this industry knows, a long distance lies between agreement and action. Exactly how far that distance is, nobody knows, but our guess is that the distance is approximately 18 inches—the distance from the head to the heart. People do not make decisions to spend or invest without running that decision through an emotional filter. In fact, neuroscience tells us that when people are processing information, the flow of that information in the brain registers in the limbic center (the seat of emotion) *before* it registers in the cerebral center (the seat of rationality). Simply put, when you are conversing, people are feeling first and rationalizing second. You must get past the gate of emotions before you will be able to tap in to the logic. Deal improperly with the emotions, and your conversation is over or seriously set back. Some of what you read in this chapter will debunk what you've been taught about closing sales. If you are failing to close, it is usually because you have failed to make a connection. What is the point of using presentation material that doesn't connect and then asking for their business?

This is exactly where so many professionals err in their attempts at persuasion—they do not understand the role of emotion in the decision-making process. Consequently, they neglect key emotional issues with fact-laden, dull presentations or by trying to overpower clients intellectually. The skilled financial professional understands the pivotal role of emotion in the decision process. Getting your client to nod in agreement with what you are saying is one thing, but it is altogether another matter to get them to act on that information. If they don't jump in the wheelbarrow, you have failed to make a human connection.

IN THIS CORNER . . .

When you talk to clients or potential clients, a wrestling match is going on within their brain. One side of their brain is asking, "Does this make sense?" while the other side is asking, "Does this feel right?" Which side of the head wins this argument 99 percent of the time? "Does this feel right?" will prevail even in the face of overwhelming evidence to the contrary. All of us can tell a story of a decision we made or a choice we passed on where rationality seemed to point in one direction and our emotional radar pointed another way. Although we may not be able to articulate why we don't feel right about the decision, we just know that it doesn't feel quite right. Consequently, we do not act.

The wrestling match is between rationale and emotion. Facts, statistics, rankings, charts, and histories can appease the rational side of the brain but not necessarily the feeling side of the brain. The feeling side of our brain has its antenna up for sincerity, credibility, likability, ease of communication, understandability, and values matching—to name just a few. If any of these areas do not feel right to your clients, they will pass on working with you or pass on what you are offering. To make a decision, people must first feel comfortable with you, your company, your ideas, and your level of experience. When these feelings are not comforted, people begin to make excuses such as needing more time or more information. When the time comes that they feel comfortable, they are more likely to make the decision you are trying to encourage them to make.

Have you ever made what you thought was a great presentation to an individual or a group and ended up with a zero? They nodded like they agreed, but they didn't sign on the dotted line. Having this experience too often will cause many financial professionals to become reticent to close with their prospects. When this happens, chances are that you missed the emotional target. You have to stop and ask yourself, "Why would they make such a decision? Would it be to feel secure? Maybe to get a sense of hope for the future? Perhaps to look good and be able to brag to their brother-in-law?" People have an emotional agenda that must be met if you hope to convince them. If you are not sure of the emotional target, you can do no better than grope in the dark with your presentations. We must never take our eyes off of the first principle of making effective client connections: *Feeling trumps logic in the decision-making process.*

"I had put a lot of work into my client presentations. I had organized my materials, had nice-looking materials, and could give a clear, articulate presentation of those ideas. There was only one problem—they weren't buying. I felt like I was shooting arrows in the dark. I was frustrated. I thought I was giving professional-quality presentations, and I was getting amateurish results. This continued until I shifted my emphasis from myself and my own ideas to my clients and their ideas. Instead of trying to impress them with my knowledge and experience, I sought to understand their knowledge and experience. While I was inquiring about their life and ideas, there would be emotional concerns that would arise. I began to put my focus on resolving those issues instead of pushing my ideas. It was at this point of progress that I felt I had moved [away] from being a seller."

—Troy L., financial professional

This financial professional came to a number of realizations that are fundamental to becoming skilled at making connections with clients. Financial professionals who go through Speak Performance Training quickly learn the following principles:

- *This is not about you, it's about them.* Are you more concerned with helping them or impressing them?
- *Even skilled marksmen will fail if they are pointed at the wrong target.* Without knowing what issues weigh heaviest with the client, presentations are a roll of the dice.

How emotionally on target are your presentations? There is only one way to tell, and that is, simply, are you getting decisions? If you are and they are staying with you, then you are on target. If you are not getting decisions, even with what you feel are good presentations, then chances are that you are missing the emotional target. Decisions are rooted in emotional comfort levels. Put another way: Emotion is the engine that pulls the decision train; logic fills the boxcars behind. To succeed in this business, you must do a gut-check to make sure that you, your ideas, and your manner are giving people the right feeling.

THE LINEAR LOGIC-JAM

No one is thinking, if everyone is thinking alike.

—Benjamin Franklin

Next, we would like to discuss why so many of our presentations fail to hit the target and result in indecision and procrastination on the part of the clients. Their indecision leads to failure to advance the sales process, and thus stunts the growth of the business. We feel that the blame falls on the way most of us were trained to sell in the first place. The standard approach to selling has been characterized by using linear logic to reach an emotional end. It does not always work well because our linear presentation often misses the key emotional needs the client feels, and that leads to indecision. Figure 13.1 is an example of how this linear approach is used in most sales presentations.

The classic sales presentation goes something like this:

The financial professional begins by telling some of the features of his fine product (A) and some of the reasons why Ms. Client would want to buy this product (B). About this time in the presentation, after being overwhelmed with the reasons why she ought to do something, the client's defenses begin to surface and she begins to raise objections. The financial professional tries to answer those objections with closing statements (C) and then attempts to secure a decision (D).

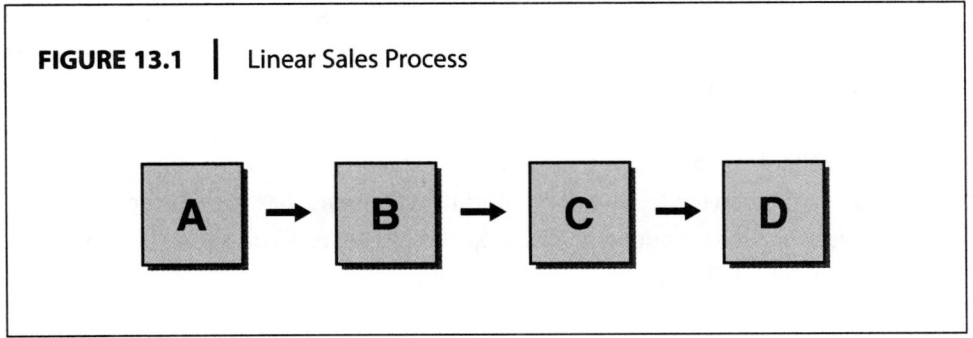

FIGURE 13.1 | Linear Sales Process

This is the linear logic that most sales professionals have been taught. However, the logic is philosophically flawed. It is flawed because of the failure to recognize how the human brain works as well as the failure to recognize the client's most crucial need in the decision-making process. We submit that the reason we encounter so many objections is that we are using objectionable material. The brain has two sides with two separate functions. The left side of the brain is for counting, comparing, rationalizing, and analyzing. The right side of the brain is for sensing, feeling, understanding context, and relating. The right side is where the more intuitive functions take place and is also where the decision trigger seems to be housed. Decisions such as "Go or don't go" or "Risk or don't risk" are matters that must be settled in the sensing side of the brain before the rationalizing side of the brain will allow a hand to sign a dotted line.

When using exclusively left-brain logic to reach a decision point, we ignore the design of the human brain. The brain must be emotionally satisfied that this decision is best before allowing action to take place. The more information you feed to the left side of the brain (charts, statistics, etc.), the more it will analyze, rationalize, and procrastinate. Most financial professionals we have seen use far too much left-brained material because they see financial planning as a largely left-brained proposition (numbers, percentages, facts, and histories). But the fact is that people are more likely to be convinced because they feel comfortable with you and your style than they are on account of your prowess with numbers and charts. Understand this second principle if you hope to succeed: *More information does not lead to a faster decision.*

Because of the nature of the rationalizing side of the brain, the more information and proof you feed it, the more the defense mechanisms get aroused. Very often the introduction of more information simply leads to paralysis by analysis. As a case in point, when a financial professional says to a client, "This fund is ranked 21st out of 189 similar funds," the rational side of the brain is jousting with that fact and "Why wouldn't I just buy the number one ranked fund?" Try to sell that same client the number one fund by saying, "This fund is ranked number one in its category," and the rational defense switches to, "Well it can't be on top forever; as soon as I invest, it will start coming back to the pack."

This sort of rational jostling will go on ad infinitum until the emotional target is identified and hit. Once that happens, suddenly all such rationale is silenced and takes a back seat to the feeling of comfort the client now has with the decision. How do you overcome the emotional hurdle that stands between you and a decision? By changing to a method of presentation that recognizes the client's need for emotional satisfaction first and rationality second.

THE INTUITIVE LEAP

Instead of taking the client on a statistical tour, your first job is to find out what will make the client comfortable with this buying decision. Much of this reconnaissance is done in the discovery stage, which we discuss in greater detail in Chapter 11, "Revealing the Characters and Dramas." Another means to identifying your emotional target is by asking a question that cuts to the quick of the client's comfort zone. We offer the following example that we saw one financial professional using to great success. Rather than boring his clients with excruciating details about the products he offered, he would offer this scenario:

"Mrs. and Mr. Client, for the purpose of better understanding what types of investments you are going to be most comfortable with, let me present you with a scenario. Let's say you wanted to move to a beautiful condominium on the lakefront and you

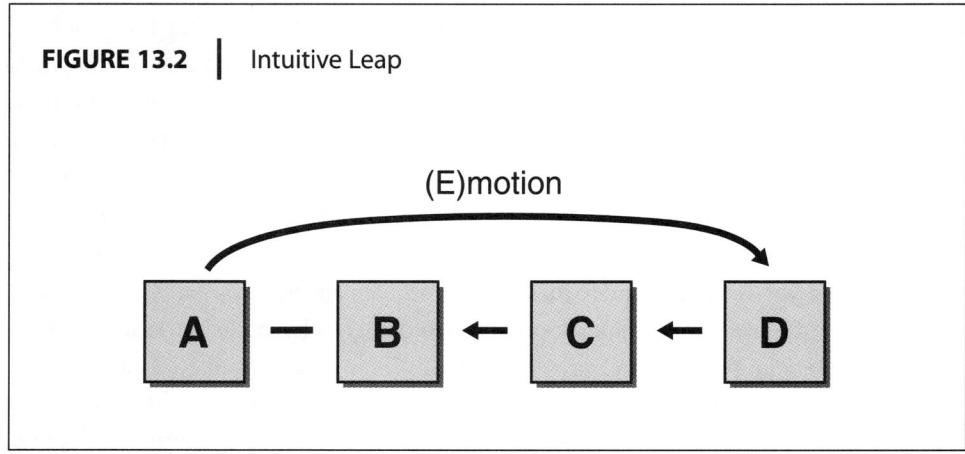

FIGURE 13.2 │ Intuitive Leap

(E)motion

A — B ← C ← D

found out there were three types of places available. Would you prefer the condo on the top level with a panoramic view, a condo on the bottom floor so you could get out quickly in case of an emergency, or one in the middle where you could get a little of both advantages?"

Clients would then tell this financial professional which type of condo they would prefer, and the financial professional would segue with, "That helps me understand what level of risk you are going to be comfortable with. What I will show you now are the funds and strategies that are in that comfort zone. It's not only important to be invested well, but it's also important to be able to sleep at night." This wise financial professional would then make his recommendations and was rarely met with objections. He had found his emotional target first (risk tolerance) and the rest of the process was simply aligning the product that matched the emotion. By taking such an approach, the financial professional has achieved an intuitive leap in two respects:

1. The clients now understand they must use products that fit their emotional comfort zone.
2. The financial professional is now on the same side of the table regarding the emotion that drives the clients' decision-making process.

Another great example of how to make this intuitive leap with clients was offered to us by our friend Tom, who sold 401(k) plans to employees at factories throughout the Midwest. Talk about a presentation nightmare, Tom said:

"I used to go into these places and explain what a 401(k) was—all the options within the plan and how each one worked and the contribution parameters—all in the space of 20 minutes. The only way to describe the look on their faces was 'compounded disinterest.' Needless to say, I wasn't getting the best results.

One day, I hit on the idea of simplifying my presentation into easy-to-understand terms that would engage their interest. I said to the first person I met with, 'I want to ask you two questions. First, if I told you that I was going to meet you here every Friday afternoon and I was going to give you a dollar for every dollar you laid on the table every week, how much would or could you bring?'

This question would get the conversation moving as I informed them of exactly what their company was offering. They realized how foolish it would be to pass up free money. They began mulling over a reasonable amount they could allocate for the imagined Friday meeting.

Then I would ask, 'Do you remember when the speed limit was 55? When it was 55, were you the type of driver that drove 55 because that was the law, or did you drive 62 because you knew that's where the risk really began? Did you turn on the radar detector and put the pedal to the metal?'

Their answers would indicate their risk tolerance, and I would then point to an investment option that matched their level of tolerance. For example, I explained, "This fund here would be the driving 62 fund because it takes moderate levels of risk but gets you where you want to go a little quicker than driving 55." They loved this presentation because they could get their arms around it. I loved it because it got results. I jumped to about a 95 percent enrollment rate from less than 50 percent, and almost every participant was maxing out their contributions."

This story is a perfect example of the third and final principle of making that human/ emotional connection: *The decision gets made when the right emotional chord gets played.* Tom simplified his presentation, shifted his target from the intellectual to the emotional, and got stunning results. When Tom was approaching the presentation from a strictly rational approach, he couldn't get action. When he went after the emotional targets of "Only a fool passes up free money" and "How much risk can you live with?" he obtained immediate buy-in. All of a sudden, everything he said had rational appeal.

Until you get emotional buy-in, people will argue with your rationale. But after you get emotional buy-in, they will begin to rationalize the decision on their own. Every master of persuasion knows that having clients talking themselves into a decision is far more preferable than to be talked into it by another. All human beings have emotional similarities. We don't want to lose what we have. We don't want to pass up a good opportunity. We don't want to look a gift-horse in the mouth. We do want to rest easy at night. We don't want to be old and poor. The wise financial professional understands that until the right emotional chord gets struck, no agreement will occur.

Sales presentations are not necessarily closed, in the client's mind, at the end of your presentation. They are closed when you strike a relevant emotional chord or theme in the mind of your client. That may happen in the first two minutes or the last two minutes. Whenever it happens, then the deal is done in the client's mind.

Financial professionals often ask for the client's business before they make this crucial emotional connection and are rejected. Your presentation should reveal specific needs, offer specific solutions, and end with you asking the client to do something specific. You will be safe asking them to do something specific, or closing, only when you have made the emotional connection. If you have done your discovery and presented properly, asking for the order will be seamless and easy.

If you want to move clients from agreement to action, you'll have to begin offering presentations that have as much emotional appeal as rational appeal.

CHAPTER 14

The Power of a Story

Thirty years ago, Nobel Prize–winning brain researcher Roger Sperry, with his associates, conducted split-brain research on patients who had been having epileptic seizures. The scientists severed the corpus callosum, which connects the left and right sides of the brain. As a result, the two sides of the brain were incapable of communicating with each other and provided a rare research opportunity to observe the various functions of the two sides of the brain. In one set of experiments, they hooked each side of the brain up to an electroencephalogram (EEG) and studied the left and right brain responses to various stimuli. When the subjects heard statistics and facts, the left side stirred with electrical activity, but the right side of the brain literally went to sleep or was idle. Researchers then told subjects a story, and immediately the right side of the brain was fully engaged and the left side continued its interest.

When we are attempting to connect with clients using charts, facts, and statistics as primary tools of the trade, we are taking a half-brained approach to the task. Sperry's split-brain experiments demonstrated a potent point regarding attempts at getting a listener's interest level. When material is statistical, factual, and numerical, you're only engaging one side of the brain. That's why an audience has that glazed-over look in their eyes—ready to enter into a deep coma—if the presentation goes on much longer. When presenting only this way with data, statistics, long lists of facts, etc., we are literally putting half of the client's or audience's brain to sleep. This is not the way to commence the process of connecting with your audience.

When Sperry's research team said the words, "We want to tell you a story," suddenly both sides of the brain were engaged. These are magic words: "I want to tell you a story." We teach people to start their presentations with those magic words. Even if they desire to start their talk with a stirring statistic, we advise them to say, "I want to tell you a story about this number." Why? Because leading others to action without engaging both sides of their brain in the process is very difficult. It's a matter of brain circuitry and how the brain gets engaged. If you want to try to connect with an individual, it just makes sense to start by aligning yourself with physiological law. Another reason you want to learn to use stories better in your presentations is because your business depends on your ability to connect with the right side of your clients' brains.

RISKY BUSINESS

We want clients to measure risk, to look into the future, and to visualize how today's decision will affect them 20 years from now. They possess these abilities in the right side of their head, and we simply need to learn the language that will trigger those abilities.

Typically, when we sell financial products, we speak the language of the rational side of the brain (Lippers charts, Morningstar rankings, etc.), which is fine to a point. The left side of the brain that does all that rationalizing, however, will not decide on anything until the right emotional chord gets struck. The left side of the brain will analyze from here to eternity. The more information you give the left brain to analyze, the more it will procrastinate. Left brain–dominant people are those who can't get enough information and have a terrible time making decisions. They analyze, criticize, and agonize over a decision, but they cannot decide. The right side puts all the pieces together into a whole and forms a picture. The right side gets a gut feeling about the idea and then gives permission to take the leap. Once this emotive decision has been made, the left side kicks back in and wants to get it done with planning and organizing.

What this should teach us is that we need to be able to speak the languages of both the left and right sides of the brain—the language of the left side for working with numbers and organizing a plan, and the language of the right for establishing context, stirring imagination, and connecting emotionally. The financial services industry is notoriously poor at speaking the language of the right brain. Its professionals would do well to study the language of marketers and ad people who have a firm grasp of the concept of communicating both fact and feeling. Once you understand that decision making and risk taking are largely right brain functions, you will immediately see the relevance of learning to speak the language of the right brain—which is found in stories, illustrations, metaphors, and the ability to paint the big picture. Your ability or inability to master these tools can greatly affect your livelihood.

Not only are these tools of language necessary for capturing a client's attention, they are also crucial for the purposes of enlightenment. It is important to be able to explain the products and services we sell in clear and simple terms. By failing to do this, we leave clients and audiences confused—and such confusion surely leads to procrastination and regret. A study by the Securities and Exchange Commission (SEC) showed that 33 percent of clients felt they were pressured to buy something they weren't sure about, and 25 percent said they didn't understand what the financial professional was talking about. If you want to succeed in the business of connecting with your clients, you are not going to do it by speaking cryptic industry lingo and by talking over people's heads. One of the sure signs of genius is the ability to reduce complex ideas into clear and understandable terms.

WHAT'S YOUR STORY?

Take a look at your presentations, both one-on-one and to larger audiences. Are you just throwing out facts and figures, or are you engaging people with relevant illustrations and stories? Do you use material that feeds the imagination as well as the intellect? Does your presentation fuel the emotional trigger as well as the rational computer?

One of the exercises we like to use to help people unleash their storytelling ability is to have them fill out a short, autobiographical questionnaire designed to prod their memory for facets of their experience that might transfer successfully as an analogy to the world of financial services. We have been astonished to see the difference this exercise has made for some people in the quality level of their presentations.

The following story is an excellent example of how using connective skills can significantly increase using stories to complement facts and figures. Gary met Jack, a financial professional, in one of his speaker training sessions. One of the techniques employed in the training is to have participants get up and give a short presentation on a financial services theme at the beginning of the session. They then present on the same topic at the end of the session—integrating the many techniques they have learned. The difference the experiential archeology exercise made in Jack's presentation had a stunning effect on the group.

Jack's initial presentation was on the importance of asset allocation. He gave the run-of-the-mill patter about the different asset classes, and suggested allocations depending on risk tolerance, etc. Nothing was particularly wrong with Jack's presentation; it just lacked vitality and sounded like a presentation that would and could be given by any one of a million other financial professionals. Jack's presentation is not unlike the thousands of presentations that go on each day. The more stories you can use to complement all the facts and figures you have, the more effective your presentation will be. Why? Because it engages the whole brain and, consequently, their attention capacity.

Your next logical question might be, where do you get all of these questions? We recommend a proven training concept called *mining your life*—digging deep into your past to look for life experiences that could help to illustrate your point. We know that people love to listen to stories. The time you spend developing your skills at storytelling will pay off handsomely with more attentive clients.

In our training session, each of the participants filled out the Mining Your Life questionnaire. After completing the questionnaire, the participants give a presentation about interesting, unknown, and unusual aspects of their lives. The story Jack told was of his fascinating and challenging experience as a fighter pilot. He told about close calls and brushes with death and included aspects of his training as a pilot that had prepared him for such eventualities. The workshop participants were spellbound by his story.

Gary then challenged Jack to find analogies and integrate aspects of his unique story into the later version of his presentation on asset allocation. That adjustment alone made a remarkable difference in both the presentation and the presenter. The next time Jack stood up to talk to the group, he told his story and expertly weaved in parallels to his topic. Jack talked about how the plane he flew was equipped to fly fast, but he also had systems on board in case things didn't go well, including a parachute. He talked about being equipped and trained to fly in all sorts of conditions and related it to having a portfolio that could navigate through any manner of market condition. The presentation went from rote and mundane in the morning to creative and engaging in the afternoon—simply by taking a storytelling approach and tying that story to the idea he was selling.

Not only did the group see a dynamic shift in the quality of the presentation but also in the demeanor and confidence level of the presenter. Instead of reiterating generic facts, he was telling *his* story. His style was more inspired, and his words carried more conviction. Jack made this presentation more personal. This shift alone can have a magnetic effect on an audience, be it one or one thousand. People love to hear a good story, especially if they can find parallels between that story and their life.

What stories could you begin integrating into your presentations to make them more dynamic? Take a little time to fill out the Mining Your Life form in Figure 14.1 and start mining your life for material that can provide insight and enlightenment to your clients.

Make your story a chief aspect of your competitive advantage. Nobody else can tell your story. Look at your answers on the chart and look for parallels in the world of

---

FIGURE 14.1 | Mining Your Life Questionnaire

1. List the different kinds of jobs you have held in your lifetime and an insight or two that you gained from each of those experiences.

JOB	INSIGHT
•	
•	
•	
•	
•	

2. Tell something unusual or interesting you have done that others might not know about.

3. Tell of a key value that you were taught growing up. Write a story that illustrates this value.

4. Tell about the best and/or worst money decision you have ever made.

---

financial services. How can you translate your experiences into more dynamic presentations before a single client or a room full of people? Your personal stories can be the critical aspect that differentiates you from every other financial professional out there.

From Knowledge to Wisdom

One of the great benefits of using stories as a means of making connections is that stories translate something greater than statistics. Statistics and facts transfer knowledge, but stories transfer wisdom. The financial services world today is facing unprecedented levels of competition, in part because of the abundance of information available to clients. Many potential clients rationalize that they have access to the same information that you do, so why do they need you? They get company and fund research for free. They can download advice from A to Z from online financial professionals. Financial professionals of the future are not going to position themselves as sources for information but rather as sources for discernment and wisdom.

Telling your story is a means of unveiling your experience level. Clients want to entrust their money to a professional who communicates experience. None of us wants to be someone else's guinea pig. When we hear a story from someone who has endured ups and downs and weathered many storms, we are more likely to place trust in that individual. We trust that this individual has learned from those experiences and hope that we can benefit from those lessons. Your stories need to communicate this feeling to the client. Experience is at a premium in a marketplace that is overwhelmed with contradictory information.

Knowledge in any form or in any volume cannot replace the lessons of experience that are commonly called wisdom. When you begin to integrate the stories of your experiences into your presentations, people will begin to look to you as a source for financial wisdom. You've been down a path they have yet to travel. You can save them some flat tires, accidents, and fatal crashes with the lessons you offer.

Wisdom is the faculty of making the use of knowledge a combination of discernment, judgment, and sagacity. Knowledge is the accumulation of facts, intelligence is the development of reason, and wisdom is the seasoned discernment. Wisdom is insight into the heart of things. Wisdom is in knowing not just the subtleties of the market but of people as well. Superior to knowledge, wisdom is the right application of knowledge in handling dilemmas and negotiating complex situations.

Knowledge and wisdom, far from being one
    Have ofttimes no connection. Knowledge dwells
    In heads replete with thoughts of other men;
    Wisdom, in minds attentive to their own. . . .
    Knowledge is proud that he has learned so much;
    Wisdom is humble that he knows no more.

                      —William Cowper

Teddy Roosevelt said, "Wisdom is nine-tenths a matter of being wise in time." Most of us are too often wise after the event. But if wisdom surfaces after the event, then it is important to look back at some of the events and experiences in our lives and see what wisdom can be mined and culled. Those stories—that are your stories alone—

can be viewed as sources of insight. Every client and audience will appreciate hearing the story that helps them to walk away wiser.

YOUR CLIENT'S STORY

In Chapter 11, "Revealing the Characters and Dramas," we discussed the importance of drawing out your client's story. Before attempting to persuade a client, you must know where they have been. What types of experiences have they had in life? In their career? What sort of experiences have they had with money? With other financial services companies and professionals?

Too many financial professionals fly right past this side of the discovery process and do so at their own peril. What you do not know about a client's history and experience can come back to bite you. We call negative experiences *land mines*, and part of your job is to sweep for these experiential land mines before you start making recommendations. The risk you take by not getting your clients' stories first is saying something that reminds them of a negative experience in their past. Suddenly, because you did not think to inquire of their story, you are associated with someone or some company they do not care for, and you are relegated to the trashcan in their emotional hard drive.

We have heard countless stories from financial professionals who have unwittingly run into these land mines and learned their lessons the hard way. They recommended stocks of companies that these clients had been burned by. They used an approach that had failed for this person in the past. They recommended funds in parts of the world where the client had lost a loved one in war. They said something that reminded the clients of the financial professionals they had just left. All these land mines can and should be avoided by being competent in the discovery process. In making a client connection, equal in importance to knowing where to go is knowing where not to go. The way to discover where not to go is to get your client's story.

CRYSTAL-CLEAR COMMUNICATION

The way top financial professionals connect is by simplifying matters, not complicating them. We have met many financial professionals who purposely add complexity to their presentations, thinking it raises their stature and indispensability in the eyes of their clients. This complicated approach, however, works against, not for, the financial professional. The top producers we have found in this business do just the opposite.

By using simple illustrations, anecdotes, and metaphors, they bring themselves and their ideas into the mental grasp of every client and audience. Consequently, clients love talking to them, and audiences love listening to them.

A proven psychological fact is that storytelling techniques put the mind in a light, trancelike state and make people more susceptible to influence. Everyone loves a good story, an illuminating analogy or metaphor, and an understandable illustration. Those who have discovered the secrets of influencing others make sure their connection process fully utilizes these communication tools.

If you wish to animate your presentation, you need to make use of these dynamic tools of speech: the illustration, the metaphor, the humorous anecdote, and the analogy. Following are descriptions and examples of each.

The Illustration

Il•lus•tra'tion: an example or instance that helps to make something clear.

Financial advisor Allyson Lewis, author *of The Million Dollar Car and $250,000 Pizza,* has done an excellent job of illustrating how great an impact choices we make in our weekly spending habits can have upon our eventual retirement nest egg. Much like the Fund Company TV ads that show how much your savings would grow if you were to put off a large ticket purchase of a car, ring, or a watch, Allyson has illustrated this principle with our smaller but consistent spending habits.

As Figure 14.2 shows, little purchases such as excess shoes, lottery tickets, and soda pop can add up over the long run. She illustrates how the money could be used either for retirement savings or for some other form of larger enjoyment. The purpose of Allyson's illustration is not to imply we shouldn't enjoy the little pleasures of life but more to prove that, with a little scrutiny and discipline, we can all save for our future. Every financial professional tries to communicate this, but Allyson's illustration brings the concept alive and makes a more meaningful impression.

Metaphorically Speaking

The greatest thing by far is to be the master of the metaphor.

—Aristotle

Warren Buffett, a virtual master of the fiscal metaphor, was once asked about investing in a bull market. His reply was, "A rising tide lifts all boats. It's not until the tide goes out that you realize who's swimming naked." Now you could try to communicate

FIGURE 14.2 | Small Change Is Big Money

ITEM	COST	ANNUAL COST	YOU COULD'VE USED IT FOR . . .	IF YOU INVESTED IT IN A 401(K), IN 2020 IT'D BE WORTH . . .
ATM FEES	$2.50 per week (didn't use your own bank)	$130	Session with a financial planner	$7,280
SODA	$.75 per can, five times per week	$195	Limousine tour of Napa wineries	$10,192
PEDICURE	$35 per session, four times per year	$210	Donation to Habitat for Humanity	$11,595
LOTTERY TICKETS	$1 per ticket, five times per week	$260	Springsteen tickets (four)	$13,302
FROZEN YOGURT	$3 for a large (with sprinkles), two times per week	$312	Spring ski weekend at Vail	$15,962
CIGARS	$5 per stogie (box of 25), four boxes per year	$500	Autographed photo of Humphrey Bogart	$25,580
MOCHA LATTE	$3 per grande, five times per week	$780	30-exercise multistation gym	$43,682
MOVIE TICKETS	$20 per week (two tickets, popcorn, soda)	$1,040	46-inch projection TV with universal remote	$53,207
WOMEN'S SHOES	$70 per pair, 15 times per year	$1,050	Fantasy cruise in the Caribbean	$53,718
DINNER FOR TWO (OUT)	$50 per dinner, two times per week	$5,200	2,300 shares of Jenny Craig, Inc.	$291,214

this same concept in literal terms, but it wouldn't have the same impact. Trying to communicate this concept by virtue of explanation would strip the idea of its humor and ability to stir imagination. By relating one concept to another unrelated concept, you create a metaphor. People may not fully understand financial concepts, but they do understand rising tides and swimming naked.

The secret of making great human or people connections in every realm is the ability to bring understanding and clarity through the application of the appropriate metaphor. Benjamin Franklin did it. Jesus rarely communicated without a metaphor or parable. Martin Luther King, Jr. was a master of it. Those in history with the greatest reputation for connecting with others had a great affinity for the metaphor. Maybe we need to learn something from them.

A metaphor is a translation from one mental language to another, from the literal to the analogic. Its power is the instant understanding it brings by reason of the translation. With understanding there will be a direct hit.

—Ned Hermann

Following is one of the classic financial metaphors, Mr. Market. Warren Buffett's mentor, Ben Graham, taught him the Mr. Market metaphor. It is timeless and highly understandable to clients. Every financial professional, in our opinion, should have it on their wall or have copies available for clients. Every client can relate to dealing with foolish and manic personalities. The Mr. Market metaphor helps clients see market gyrations in a brand-new light. The very factors that once kept clients awake with stress may now keep them awake with anticipation.

You should imagine stock quotes as coming from a remarkably accommodating fellow named Mr. Market, who is your partner in a private business. Without fail, Mr. Market appears daily and names a price at which he will either buy your stock or sell you his.

Even though the business that the two of you own may have economic characteristics that are stable, Mr. Market's quotations will be anything but. For, sad to say, the poor fellow has incurable emotional problems.

But like Cinderella at the ball, you must heed one warning or everything will turn into pumpkins and mice: Mr. Market is there to serve you, not to guide you. It is his pocketbook, not his wisdom, that you will find useful. If he shows up someday in a particularly foolish mood, you are free either to ignore him or to take advantage of him, but it will be disastrous if you fall under his influence.

At times, he waxes euphoric and can only see the favorable factors affecting the business. When in that mood, he names a very high price because he fears that you will snap up his interest and rob him of imminent gains.

At other times, he is depressed and can see nothing but trouble ahead for both the business and the world. On these occasions, he will name a very low price, because he is terrified that you will unload your interest on him. Under these conditions, the more manic-depressive his behavior, the better for you.

One other fella we might mention here is Mr. Market's best friend, Mr. Media. Mr. Media loves to take his cues from Mr. Market and shout them in the streets and over the airwaves.

One day it is, "The market is up 100 points—buy everything!" The very next day Mr. Media shouts, "The market is down 100 points—run for the hills!"

Sometimes a metaphor speaks volumes beyond what facts and statistics can do.

Humorous Anecdotes

Don't gamble! Take all your savings and buy some good stock and hold
it till it goes up, then sell it. If it doesn't go up, don't buy it.

—Will Rogers

A nickel ain't worth a dime anymore.

—Yogi Berra

Perhaps nothing gets and maintains a person's (or audience's) attention like the humorous story or statement. Once people laugh, their receptivity leaps exponentially. Humor has a way of breaking down defenses and tension and puts people in a more liberal state of mind. In your public presentations, the best way to break the ice with your audience is by telling a funny story—about yourself.

People quickly warm to those individuals who can laugh at their own failings and mistakes. The best sense of humor is possessed by those who can laugh at themselves. It has been said that humor is truth in intoxicated form. Our experience in close to 20 years of public speaking proves this idea. Once the crowd begins laughing, you are well on your way to winning converts to your ideas. It is as if a dam breaks and the walls of skepticism are removed. The first and greatest advantage of a keen wit and a self-deprecating approach is that it helps to relax the client. A relaxed client is a receptive client. A tense client is in a defensive state. Humor is unmatched in its ability to topple defenses.

You don't have to be a great joke teller to be funny. All you have to be able to do is poke a little fun at yourself. We have noted this chief feature in successful financial professionals and the best presenters—they are quick to have a laugh at their own expense. Only secure and self-confident types can laugh at themselves. Therefore, people prefer to work with this type of individual. You could almost say that the more seriously individuals take themselves, the less seriously others take them.

Self-confident and secure people:

- Are not defensive
- Admit their mistakes quickly
- Don't pretend to know things they don't
- Don't expect presentations to go perfectly and flow with them when they don't
- Learn from mistakes rather than make excuses
- Laugh easily at their mistakes

The above traits are important for presenting to any size audience to win their trust. When it comes to managing money, how many clients want to work with an insecure financial professional who lacks confidence? At this juncture, the point we most want to make is this: when you tell your story, tell it in a way that warms the audience to you. Nothing accomplishes this like a good sense of humor and a tale told on oneself.

The Analogy

A•nal•o•gy: a resemblance in some particulars between things otherwise unalike.

One financial professional we know loves to use a good analogy to instruct his clients. When clients called wanting him to chase dot-com stocks with stratospheric valuations, he would share the following analogy:

Financial Professional: "Do you ever play blackjack?"

Client: "Sure, once in awhile."

Financial Professional: "Well, I want to share a little story with you. A guy I know who's been playing for years was sitting at a table one night for a couple of hours and was probably about even at that point. About midnight, some hillbilly in a muscle shirt who looks like he's working on his 15th drink sits down to his right. The dealer throws this guy a 17 and the dealer is showing a 9. The guy says, 'Hit me,' and gets a 3 and wins the hand. My friend can't believe it. He always plays by the rules—hit on 16, hold on 17. A couple of hands later this fella gets an 18 and says 'Hit me,' and gets another 3 and wins again. He picks up his pile of chips and leaves the table. My friend thinks to himself, 'I play by the rules and I have nothing to show for it,' so the next time he gets dealt a 17 and says, 'Hit me,' and gets a queen."

This financial professional then informs his client that some people will get away with playing the game against the rules—like buying companies with no earnings and no prospects of earnings—but the majority will get burned if they try to play fast and loose with the rules of prudent investing.

Analogies work their magic by taking a truth that people may be familiar with in one realm and showing how that same truth applies to their wealth-building process. Analogies are especially effective when the client or audience is totally uninitiated in the topic you're going to discuss. The simple phrase, "It's kind of like . . ." will open the windows of comprehension and ultimately lead toward more effective presentations.

Another example of analogic creativity a financial professional shared with us was his approach to selling annuities. His presentation goes like this:

Financial Professional: "May I ask if you own your own home?"

Client: "Yes, I do."

Financial Professional: "There are two questions I'd like to ask you. First, how much did the home cost, and secondly, how much do you pay for insurance each year on the home?"

In a modest example the client says $200,000 was paid for the home and $800 paid per year in insurance for the home.

Financial Professional: "When you bought your house did the bank require you to get insurance?"

Client: "Of course."

Financial Professional: "Naturally the banker insisted on insurance because it was largely his money at risk. The reason I bring this up is because there is a parallel between that scenario and the annuity I want to talk to you about. You see, the annuity is the only investment I can offer that is insured. You can select an annuity that will pay you a guaranteed percentage, even if the market loses ground. Of course you pay a small fee for that insurance just like you do with your home. The one major difference, however, between the home scenario and this one is that, in this scenario, you are the banker—it's your money that is at risk."

This sort of analogy suddenly puts an annuity in a never-before considered frame of reference. It sheds new light and causes understanding to reign where confusion once dwelled. When you speak, make good use of analogies to help engage your clients' interest and raise their comprehension. If you are short on analogies, metaphors, and illustrations for financial services settings, you may want to pick up a copy of *Storyselling for Financial Advisors,* written by Scott West and Mitch Anthony. This book is replete with scores of analogies that you can instantly integrate into your presentations.

Connecting with Dynamic Presentations

Cornerstone #1 of Dynamic Presenting

Convicted and Convincing

Enthusiasm is at the bottom of all progress. With it there is accomplishment. Without it there are only alibis.

—Henry Ford

Find purpose in life so big it will challenge every capacity to be at your best.

—David O. McKay

If you are in the financial services business a long time, one thing you will see is a variety of speakers. I have been attending and speaking at national sales conferences for more than two decades and have seen the best and the worst speakers have to offer.

As I designed my own speaking skills training, I started my blueprint by asking what separated the small group of impactful speakers from the average speaker. From personal observations and surveying many of my speaking colleagues, I found that there are four main attributes that the best seem to have. These are the cornerstones on which great speakers build their speaking careers. As you read these next four chapters, ask yourself how you personally measure up in the areas of conviction, preparation, structure, and delivery skills.

The first cornerstone of the connection process is this: *our power to persuade is greatly influenced by the sense of personal conviction we translate to our audience.* People are more likely to believe and feel more assured with the choices we are asking them to make if they see the fires of conviction burning in our speech and action.

The Oxford Dictionary definition of persuasion is "to cause to believe." We believe the first cornerstone for any effective presentation—in front of one person or a thousand people—is the degree of conviction you bring to the table. Conviction about a topic translates into *convincing* for the audience. Webster's definition of convince, "to make feel sure," adds additional light to this matter of conviction. Pure eloquence will not suffice. The petals quickly wilt from flowery speech that is not rooted in a sense of personal conviction.

A story is told of an acquaintance of Abe Lincoln's who took him to a church to hear a preacher renowned throughout the world for his eloquence. The clergyman delivered what Lincoln's friend thought was a beautiful sermon. After the service, as they were walking back to their homes, he asked Lincoln if he was impressed with the preacher's oratory. "Not really," Abe replied. "He didn't ask me to do anything great."

A sense of purpose and passion permeates the psyche and soul of the audience when the speaker speaks with conviction. People want to hear the call to higher ground, better lives, and purposeful living. The truly convincing financial professional knows how to tie his or her products and services to that greater sense of life fulfillment. Your audience needs to see that you are personally involved, that you speak with conviction.

True conviction is important not only in our talking, but also in our walking. In a skeptical society that has been jaded by empty and whimsical promises of customer satisfaction and satisfaction guaranteed, more than convincing speech is needed to sell your passion. People have learned to watch and wait. Nonetheless, whether it comes by word and action, true conviction is what the client is spying out. Because your clients are all unique individuals, they don't want cookie-cutter answers to their problems. They don't want help from someone who is just doing a job—because their hard-earned money is at stake. Your clients want to deal with someone who is guided by a sense of calling or feels they are serving a noble purpose by serving their clients.

THE SPINAL COLUMN OF CONVICTION

"Years ago when I was young in the business, I had an appointment with a successful gentleman who had just sold a business. One of his relatives, who was a client of mine, had referred him to me. I was well prepared for this presentation as this would have been the biggest account I had ever landed if I got it. After the small talk, I went into the specifics of what I would recommend he should do with his money. When I was finished he said, 'Which of the products that you just recommended to me do you own yourself?' It was a matter of pure luck that I owned one of the funds and one of the stocks that I had recommended to him. So, I pulled out my statement to show him—and that settled matters for him. He was looking for a disconnect between what I was selling and doing for myself. At that point, he agreed to work with me. He later told me that he had spent many years in sales and never sold any products that he didn't own himself—because of the conviction he conferred to his clients.

This experience caused me to take a searching inspection into the areas of my business where I was vulnerable to duplicity. I stopped selling products that I was lukewarm, apprehensive, or negative about, and I felt better about myself for it. There is no question in my mind that my clients sensed my convictions—which, in turn, increased their confidence in me and bolstered my reputation."

—Fred B., financial consultant

Financial professionals find that a sense of purpose fuels their passion and, consequently, their efforts in front of the client. David Bach, a highly successful financial advisor and author of the best-selling book, *Smart Women Finish Rich,* describes the energy that has guided his career success as "a burning passion regarding making wrongs right." Bach discovered, through observation and through the inculcation of a wise grandmother, that wealth ends up eventually in the hands of women. Women generally outlive men and yet, until recently, have had very little exposure to investment matters.

Bach saw an opportunity in this unjust and inequitable situation that he translated into a noble career of educating women on how to take charge of their financial lives. When Bach first presented his ideas to the industry, there were many doubters and naysayers. David's passion and drive on the topic quickly silenced these doubters. Bach's passion to empower women in the fiscal arena is palpable in his presentations, and women respond enthusiastically to those presentations. Their conviction has made David a top producer. We have heard other people talk about the women's marketplace and how to serve it, but the presentation's effectiveness is diminished when compared to David Bach's message. The difference is passion and conviction—the spinal column of all persuasive presenting, regardless of audience size.

Our advice to those who want to be more powerful persuaders is this: If you are not moved by a topic just *thinking* about it, then your audience isn't going to be moved when you're *talking* about it.

SUCCESS STORIES

The financial services world is full of stories of people who found a glaring need and passionately pursued meeting that need. These people discovered that when their story was anchored to a passionate story line, the industry professionals and clients wanted to be a part of that story.

Years ago, Edward D. Jones saw an injustice that held the seeds of great opportunity. The company developed a strong business connection that still exists today. Why shouldn't any man or woman living in a small town 2,000 miles from Wall Street have the same investment opportunities offered in metropolitan America? Jones decided to take the investment business to the highways and byways of this nation. He established offices where no other firms had dreamed of locating, because in their mind, the opportunity for profit was not great enough. Jones's idea was to offer investment services with a personal touch, and the idea worked. Today, you will find Edward Jones offices in every major city in America, and you will also find them in every outpost. They established their business in places where everyone is a neighbor and where family connections go back for generations.

If you were driving on Highway 16 in south central Texas and happened into Bandera, population 877, you would not expect to find a brokerage firm. You might expect to find a gas station, a couple of bars, and a church or two. But in Bandera, the Cowboy Capital of the World, you would also find Lamar Seale III, whose Edward Jones office is prospering by meeting the investment needs of ranchers and tourist industry (dude ranch) entrepreneurs. Lamar Seale, a lover of the outdoor life, decided to move to the Texas hill country. He found plenteous opportunity as a financial professional in spite of the sparse population. Edward Jones requires a minimum level of assets before locating in any area; to their surprise, they found three times that minimum in this little Texas town with no industry to speak of.

No other firm would have even considered opening a branch in such a miniscule population center, but the Edward Jones story is about discovering opportunity in places that others consider fly-over zones. Edward D. Jones did some homework, found a widespread need, and pursued his story with passion. The pattern of a successful business is telling a story that captures the interest and imagination of the clients and the people who serve them.

Gary's firm is another success story with the same sort of underpinnings. The founder of the firm, Bob Van Kampen, was selling Unit Investment Trusts (UITs) to a customer when the customer said that he would buy the trust if it had insurance on it. Van Kampen searched across the financial services landscape for this product, but to no avail. He decided that if this customer was searching for such a product, then others in similar circumstances would be as well. He began to interview investment professionals about the idea of providing such a product and was greeted with much enthusiasm. They assured him that his idea was a product story that would translate well to their clients.

Bob Van Kampen began his company with the conviction that the insured UIT product fit a client need in the market. He quickly built a reputation within the industry. He spoke passionately to other professionals about the need for this kind of specialized investment vehicle, and the word got around. Soon his firm was adding other specialized products to meet the needs that would turn up in industry research. Today, Van Kampen Investments is a highly regarded investment firm, with over $83 billion under management and supervision at the time of this writing. Gary has seen two keys to the growth he has witnessed in his 23 years at the firm, products that meet real needs and people who tell those product stories with passion.

I COULDN'T HELP BUT BUY

Enthusiasm is contagious—so is the lack of it.

—Anonymous

Conviction and passion are the two key elements—the sand and water that you must have—to form the first cornerstone of your persuasive efforts. One without the other will not work, because conviction is based on knowing or, at the very least, believing that you have the answer they need. One investment wholesaler told us about how a financial professional once told him, "I can't help but say 'yes,' you are so evangelistic about what you sell." This advisor saw an enthusiasm that spoke of a strong sense of conviction under the surface.

Do you believe in what you are selling? The acid test is the sense of enthusiasm you feel when you are talking about it. Not that you have to be jumping out of your skin with excitement, but you do need to convey a resolute belief in what you are doing. Your clients will quickly read your nonverbal signals if your eyes are backtracking while your mouth is moving. They can hear the disconnect in your tone of voice that seems to have told the same old story too many times. These signals do not attract client interest—they repel it. Given the choice, people will always choose to work with those who are passionate about what they do. They begin to feel like they have a crusader on their side. They feel that they are partnering with someone who will not lose interest in them or the task at hand.

What are the philosophies that you follow with money and with people? These philosophies, once articulated, are important planks in the platform of belief and conviction that you communicate to your clients. People want to get a sense of their financial professional's philosophical approach to ensure that they have a values match.

We have met financial professionals who begin their presentation by saying something akin to, "This is what I believe about money . . ." and "This is what I believe about people's tendencies with money . . ." Once a client senses a philosophical link, the rest is just a matter of working through the processes.

A PASSION FOR SOLVING PEOPLE'S PROBLEMS

Nothing motivates humans quite like the process of solving their problems. It has been accurately stated that people are most motivated to buy for the simple purpose of solving problems. People come to financial professionals because they have a problem or see a problem coming. The financial professional who has a passion for solving people's problems and the insight to deliver that solution will never lack for clients. Remember, even if people will not readily admit a problem, one is lurking under the surface. If there wasn't a problem, they probably wouldn't have been motivated enough to sit down and talk to you.

Years ago during the farm crisis of the early 1980s, after reading each day in the newspaper of suicides, Mitch directed an effort to establish a national suicide help line. He worked on a suicide help line himself for many months to get a feel for the mindset of the people who were calling. He made some important discoveries about human nature, problem solving, and ways to best utilize the powers of human connection.

It was quite common while answering this help line to have a caller say, "I want to die. In fact, I've got a loaded gun in my hand and I'm ready to pull the trigger."

Mitch would answer such a statement with, "I only believe half of what you just told me. I believe the part about the gun; it's the part about wanting to die that I'm not sure of."

The caller would object, saying, "I'm serious about this, like I told you I've got a gun in my hand." Some would even threaten to pull the trigger with him still on the line.

Mitch's standard answer at this point was, "If you really wanted to die, you wouldn't have made this phone call. The fact that you found the resolve and courage to dial this number tells me that what you really want is to live."

This retort never failed to help the caller make the turn into a more constructive thought process and conversation. Mitch's research into the topic had taught him that suicidal people didn't want to die as much as they were afraid of living. He would tell them this and challenge them with the idea that what they needed to do was find a way to live. The lessons regarding conviction and connecting that Mitch learned in these sessions were manifold and profound. As he has said many times, "After phone calls like that, public speeches and sales presentations feel like child's play."

The first lesson pertaining to connection and conviction is that people sometimes need help in figuring out what they really want. They feel they need some help but can't always specifically articulate what they need. Your conviction and passion can help to move your clients in the direction they need to go. Just like an engaging counselor, an effective financial professional can help clients sort out their true objectives from the sometimes frustrating tangle of their financial lives. The more willing you are to confront the real issues, the more likely it is that clients will trust you to help fix their financial problems.

The second lesson for gaining conviction is to do your homework. You need to know more than your clients about the path to more desirable circumstances; otherwise, you have no business being in the advisory position. Giving the same answers to every individual is not advice—it is elementary-level sales. Professionals who take the time to study the problems their clients face and the answers they need will stand head and shoulders above their peers. Our next chapter on the connectivity cornerstone of preparation will deal more thoroughly with the importance of research and rehearsal.

The final lesson that Mitch took from the world of crisis counseling that applies to any financial professional is that people are swayed by the level of confidence you display in yourself. You can make the unusual, attention-grabbing statement when you believe that you know what you're doing. Your conviction and passion about what you do will come shining through. This point must follow the point of preparedness, because posturing as a confident financial professional without doing your homework is nothing but superfluous arrogance—the insightful client will see through your veneer. People who lack knowledge or wisdom want to lean on someone who has a resoluteness, an assuredness, and a demeanor of calm confidence about them. To make that human connection, you must be able to look your client or audience in the eye with an unblinking faith. You must be able to convey that you've done your homework, and that you know the answer because you've seen it work. This kind of confidence helps to allay your investors' fears and lets them sleep at night.

KNOW THYSELF

Take a few minutes to evaluate your conviction levels in the following areas: your personal skills, your company, your investment philosophy, and the products you offer.

- Describe what purpose you feel you serve as a financial professional.
- Describe your philosophy regarding the management of money or wealth.
- What are my strengths and abilities I have to offer my client?

- Why is my company one that I can recommend with confidence?
- Why do I believe my investment philosophies are best for my clients?
- Why are the products and services I use the best for my clients?

These are the six basic areas that top producers speak of with great confidence in their dealing with clients.

Your conviction level as a financial professional will either be emboldened or challenged by the set of questions. If your efforts lack conviction, these questions will reveal it. If your efforts at connecting are rooted in a noble sense of purpose and well-thought-out values, this will be revealed as well.

Lead with Conviction

Gary loves to tell the story about his first public-speaking assignment as a sales manager for Procter & Gamble (P&G). Gary was promoted at 23 years of age to sales manager and asked to lead a group of 60 salespeople whose average age was 45 years. Needless to say, not all the members of that sales group were thrilled with the fact that Gary had a management role at such a young age. It also didn't help that Gary looked like he was only 16.

His first speaking assignment as sales manager was to go to the regional sales meeting and stir up the sales force to sell more Lava soap. They didn't give this greenhorn manager the worst-selling product in their lineup by accident. At the time, Lava was a bottom-shelf soap in the grocery store and an under-the-sink soap in the home or workplace. A product sitting on the bottom shelf of a grocery store doesn't sell well simply because nobody can see it. The problem with a soap being under the sink is that it doesn't get used much and gets replaced about every two years, which is why it inhabited the bottom shelf of the store.

Gary decided to do some research. He figured he was going to have to dig long and hard to find some good reasons to give his jaded sales staff even a hint of motivation to go out and sell Lava soap. In doing his homework, Gary found out that the P&G brand group did their normal excellent job of building a case for their product. He learned that Lava at one time was the best-selling soap in America. But this was in the days when Americans were working primarily in industrial and agricultural jobs. Their hands were being soiled with grease and grime, and Lava could cut through it. As America moved from a predominantly blue- to white-collar nation, Lava soap got transferred from the soap basin on top of the sink to its early grave under the sink.

Procter & Gamble's research into the reasons for declining sales revealed that people didn't like the soap sitting on top of the sink because the white bar always looked dirty. To solve this dilemma, P&G changed the soap color to a green that veiled the dirt. With this information, Gary felt he had the ammo he needed to mount some momentum for selling the "new and improved green Lava."

Gary was the last to present at that conference. The other three managers were given the choice products to present, and Gary brought up the caboose with his presentation on Lava soap. The crowd was expecting a sleeper and got a wake-up call instead. From his research, Gary had gained a sense of conviction and confidence that the new color could get Lava moved back on top of the sink and up to higher shelving in the grocery stores. He presented this message and mission to his sales force. That sense of unbridled enthusiasm and conviction transferred into sales energy, and the team went out and sold more Lava soap than had been sold in years.

If a green sales manager can muster conviction over a green bar of soap, what sort of conviction do you suppose you can evoke with the products and services you sell?

One final thought on conviction is that it lays the groundwork for a spinal-column quality that all top producers have—perseverance. Over time, markets, clients, and problems will constantly test your emotional endurance in this business. Having a solid conviction about you, your company, your investment philosophy, and the products and services you use will be the rudders of stability for your success.

Once you've clarified and articulated exactly what it is you believe, it is then time to begin work on the second cornerstone—preparation.

The definition of luck is when preparation meets opportunity.

—Anonymous

By displaying enthusiasm, passion, and conviction, you will draw people to you, but you will experience a quick exodus as well if you do not have a firm grasp on your topic and on your audience. Preparation is a powerful complement to passion. Passion and conviction are about working up the resolve to run in the race; preparation is going into training so you can win. Conviction is the work of the soul and emotion; preparation is the work of intellect. Running this race with conviction will guarantee that you will lap at least half of your competition.

CHAPTER 16

Cornerstone #2 of Dynamic Presenting

Prepared for Battle

Steve Mikez, a public-speaking coach to financial professionals, loves to tell about the difference preparing for a public speech made in the life of Abraham Lincoln and in the fate of our nation. Steve comments that if you ask the casual observer of history what was the most powerful or influential speech Lincoln ever gave, they would most likely say the Gettysburg Address. But in terms of Lincoln's career and the fate of the nation, his most pivotal speech was given in a debate in the winter of 1860 at the Cooper Institute in New York City.

In spite of harsh criticism of his earlier attempts at elocution, Abe Lincoln decided that he could further his career greatly by becoming a better public speaker. As a platform for this development, he often took appeals to the Illinois Supreme Court. (To this day Lincoln holds the record for any attorney for number of appearances before this court.)

Lincoln's opponent in the debate at the Cooper Institute was the same as his opponent in the presidential election, Stephen Douglas. Douglas had a reputation as an eloquent and polished public speaker. This was in sharp contrast to Lincoln, who was awkward, gangly, and homely in appearance and was considered a country bumpkin by Easterners. In fact, a large contingency of the press turned out just salivating to see Douglas grind Lincoln to dust in a highly publicized event.

Lincoln first received notice of this debate in the November of 1859. The debate was to take place just over three months later. During this time, Eastern scribes did a great amount of speculating on the embarrassment that Lincoln would bring upon himself in debating someone as skilled at oration and dialectic as Douglas. These prognosticators, however, did not know the dedication that Lincoln had for conquering the public-speaking platform. He labored over every word and nuance of speech during those three months. Lincoln had little doubt regarding the significance of this event. He knew that the result would be widely reported and would prove pivotal in his career.

He came to the Cooper Institute regarded as a country hick and left as a conquering hero. One influential reporter wrote that he and many of his peers had come to see Lincoln for amusement purposes and left with unrestrained admiration for the man. Honest Abe gave such a stirring discourse on the subject of slavery reform that one of the writers who came to be "amused" suddenly found himself "yelling like an Indian" in favor of Lincoln. The crowd was stunned into a state of approbation by Lincoln's well-prepared and dramatically delivered oratory.

Steve Mikez likes to remind his public-speaking students that if preparation for a public speech can change the course of one presidential candidate and, consequently, the fate of a nation, then this skill has a good chance of doing something for their career as well. In the same breath, Steve reminds these financial professionals that it was preparation that made the difference for Lincoln, not raw talent. In 1860, no one doubted that Stephen Douglas was the more skilled orator of the two, but history remembers the one who was better prepared.

STEPS TO PREPAREDNESS

Successful salesmanship is 90 percent preparation and 10 percent
    presentation.

                                        —Bertrand R. Canfield

Being prepared to deliver a powerful speech requires three distinct but related steps. These steps are:

1. Get into the material.
2. Get the material into you.
3. Get the material into your audience.

You must know more than your audience on the topic you want to address—much more. This is the reason you get into your material in more than a superficial way. You want people to recognize you as a fountain of knowledge and wisdom on the topic you're addressing. If they can hear what you're saying from a hundred other people, chances are that they'll tune you out early. This is why you get into the material.

You must personally own the material you speak about. A bridge spans the distance between knowing something and *knowing* something. When Genesis 4:1 says that Adam *knew* Eve, we don't think it meant he could quote statistics about her. Too many speakers spew out facts, information, and statistics but fail to personalize the impact or importance of those pieces of knowledge. Consequently, the audience, sensing the speaker is just reiterating rote material, emotionally disengages from the presentation. This is why you must get the material into you.

If you deliver a speech that harvests neither agreement nor action, you have wasted your audience's time, as well as all your preparation and delivery. So often we do not get agreement or action because we do not understand our audience—their goals and desires, their experiences, their biases and attitudes, their needs, their capabilities, and the language they like to speak. Precisely this ignorance drowns many a speaker just as they begin to launch their speech. The audience, sensing that the speaker is trying to bring a generic solution to a specific need, quickly throws the errant orator overboard. This is why you must learn how to get the material into your audience. We will deal more extensively with this topic in Chapter 19, "Know Thy Audience."

The will to win is worthless, if you do not have the will to prepare.

—Thane Yost

All of these skills are the result of preparation. Take the time to prepare, and you will master the material, the environment, yourself, and the audience—in that order. If you are not willing to do the digging and sleuthing necessary for preparation, don't even bother, because no one is going to listen anyway.

We find that many times the people with the most potential to become a powerful speaker never realize their full potential because they rely on natural abilities instead of a disciplined approach to preparation. My question to the gifted presenter is how much better could you really be if you spent time properly preparing. It is a waste of talent to underprepare for important connection opportunities.

GET INTO THE MATERIAL

A story is told about a research assistant who had the responsibility of gathering background for a speech to be given by Henry Kissinger (Michael M. Klepper, *I'd Rather Die Than Give a Speech*). The assistant spent a week slaving over the research and delivered it to Dr. Kissinger. Less than an hour later, it was returned with a note that

Kissinger thought he could do better. The assistant redoubled his efforts, and after another week of burning the midnight oil, he resubmitted the research. Again, it was returned hastily with a note that stated the speech needed more refining. After spending a third week sweating blood on the report, he asked to personally deliver it to Dr. Kissinger. He informed Dr. Kissinger that he had spent three sleepless weeks on the report and could produce no better.

"Very good," Kissinger replied. "Now I'll read it."

How much more about this particular topic do you know than your audience? Could you talk for hours about it? Please don't talk for hours, but do learn enough so that you could. As one of Mitch's Australian friends likes to say, "You want to listen to speakers who have more under their bonnet than what they are telling. You get a sense that there's a lot more that they could tell." The Aussie uses the word *bonnet* for the hood of the car. This word serves as a worthy metaphor for the point we are trying to make. Do the words you are going to speak represent the sum of your knowledge? Are you using all your horsepower? If you are, you're taking a tremendous risk that the mind of the audience may race right past you. You have to give the impression that you have a lot more horsepower under the hood. In other words, you have a lot more you're not telling, but could tell later, if they are interested in hearing it. The only safe way to give this impression is to make it a reality. Master the topic long before you attempt to master an audience.

Steve Mikez advises that you only deliver a public speech on a topic that you have a sincere and genuine interest in. Your job is not to transfer information to your audience; it is to transfer energy. That is why we offered conviction as the first and foremost cornerstone of effective presenting. You can go about getting the material into you in a number of ways.

- Read everything you can on the topic.
- Interview someone who understands the topic better than you do.
- Listen to other speakers talk about the same topic.
- Go hear what your competitors are saying on the topic.

We have heard that if you apply yourself diligently to any one specific topic, you can surpass 99 percent of the world in the knowledge of that topic by studying it for 15 minutes a day for two years. We don't know where that statistic came from, but we are inclined to believe it. We have met many financial professionals who have created great businesses by building highly specialized knowledge bases. The riches are in the niches in today's marketplace.

If you truly apply yourself to continue learning on any specialty for which you think there is a market, you will rise from student to practitioner to guru much faster than you thought imaginable. Not many people out there have both the desire and the discipline to apply themselves studiously to the task. If you are one, you've cleared the first hurdle of preparation—getting into the material.

GETTING THE MATERIAL INTO YOU

The late, great musician Louis Armstrong was once stopped on the streets by a fan in Manhattan. After blubbering for a moment, the fan asked Satchmo if he was playing in New York City.

"Yes," Armstrong replied. "Tonight at Carnegie Hall."

"Great," replied the fan. "How do I get to Carnegie Hall?"

"Practice, baby, practice," was Armstrong's answer.

Practice, Baby, Practice

For you to make a good showing before your audience, you have to practice. Practice until the material becomes as natural as breathing to you. We tell our students to remember the "Rule of Seven"—practice your speech at least seven full times before actual delivery. Practice is especially critical should you have some type of presenting tool failure. Once, at a public seminar, Gary's laptop froze up and he had to deliver the presentation strictly from some sparse notes and memory. Because he knew the material cold through his practice routine, the presentation came off as if it were planned to be done without slides.

In the next chapter on "Having a Flight Plan," we will offer insights on how to deliver a focused and cohesive presentation. What we want to do here in the preparation phase is give you the structure for building your presentation. The first step in getting the material into you is to organize all your information into a nice, neat, presentable format, and then practice your presentation until you've got it down cold.

GETTING THE MATERIAL INTO YOUR AUDIENCE

Below is a suggested bone structure on which you can hang the meat and muscle of your presentation. These preparation points are critical for any presentation. They will help ensure your presentation has the greatest impact on getting your message into your audience.

- *Theme.* A succinct description that captures the essence of your message
- *Open.* An attention-grabbing introduction to your message
- *Body of Message.* Two or three points, analogies, stories, or metaphors supporting each point
- *Close.* An attention-grabbing summary that reinforces everything they just learned in the course of the talk

Building a Theme

You must be able to articulate your theme succinctly and with enough visceral effect to whet the appetite of your audience. If you are speaking at a conference and people can attend other electives, this theme line will make or break you. Our advice is to make it simple and make sure it arouses curiosity. If you were to say, "Understanding the corollary roles of alpha and beta measurement in diversification," you might attract a couple of analysts with titanium pocket protectors, but you probably won't fill the room with the kind of audience you want. If you want to attract interest from potential clients or peers, you might opt for, "How to keep from grumbling when the markets start tumbling."

Some samples of well-developed and intriguing themes, expounded over the space of 250 pages, can be found in some popular, modern book titles. Some examples include:

- *The Roaring 2000s* and *The Great Boom Ahead* by Harry Dent
- *The One-Minute Manager* by Ken Blanchard
- *Mastering the Short Game* by Dave Pelz
- *Smart Women Finish Rich* by David Bach

What these titles have in common is that they crystallize the message and intrigue the potential audience in just three or four words. Developing a good theme line is just like developing a good title to a book—it has to make the listener want to hear what is on the next page.

Steve Mikez offers a few suggestions of seminar titles that illustrate creative titling:

- Pay Yourself First
- Going Broke Safely
- Keys to Building Generational Wealth

- The Seven Great RetireMyths (borrowed from Mitch's book, *The New Retirementality*)

Look for some imaginative input when developing a theme line. After all, if nobody comes to hear you, how good your speech is won't matter.

The Opener

There are many ways to grab your audience's attention and magnetize their interest level. You can use a short quiz or self-assessment, a pithy quote, humor, a story, or a provocative question or fact. We think the important thing here is to make sure the opener is relevant and an eye-opener to some degree. You must "disturb" them and make them a little uncomfortable with their current situation. The first step in creating any true behavioral change is to create some awareness that the audience needs to change, so this is a critical part of any speech. Chapter 21, "Setting the Hook," deals with this topic extensively. Remember, your opener is the lure to get people into your boat for the next 30 to 60 minutes. You can't afford to float a lure that doesn't shine or stir the waters.

One of the weak techniques we often see is for the speaker to stand up and try to play the comedian with a joke, or what was previously known as a joke before they told it—and which is totally irrelevant to their presentation. Their reasoning for this approach is most likely based on someone telling them that if they can get their audience laughing and relaxed, they'll have smooth sailing. This fact is true, but this terrain belongs to those who have material that has a track record for getting those laughs and can be tied directly to the theme. How many times have you seen a presentation start with a "groaner," a joke that falls flat on the floor? Someone should have warned the speaker what would happen if the audience *didn't* laugh.

If you're not a practiced comedian or joke teller, open with a passionate statement as to why you are there and why you want to talk about the topic at hand. People would rather witness a sincere statement of passion for the topic than an awkward effort at comedy. For further tutoring on delivering an opener that lures rather than obscures, see Chapter 21. Think of your opener as a sneak preview—if they don't like the preview, they won't rent the movie.

The Body

Your job in the body of the speech is to build the most compelling case you can in a progressive manner, both intellectually and emotionally. Distill the three most compelling points you can from the material you have gathered. Develop two or three stories, analogies, examples, or illustrations to bolster those points, and do this for all three points of your speech.

Your mission is to organize the three segments of your speech in a way that gives the impression of a growing revelation, like watching a flower open as the sun shines upon it. Steve Mikez suggests giving each piece of material you're thinking of using the BIT test. Filter the material, story, or illustration through the following three questions:

1. *Is it benefit driven?* Can the audience derive some benefit by hearing it?
2. *Is it independent?* Would it make for good material standing on its own?
3. *Is it theme building?* Does it relate well to the entire mission of the speech?

If it doesn't pass the three filters of the BIT test, throw it out and find material that does.

Another consideration for the body of your speech is the progression of your three-point approach. Each layer should build and progress upon the other. Too many speeches are disjointed, lacking cohesiveness because the developer did not understand the art of progressive revelation in speech making. A good speech is one that leaves the audience wanting more, not begging for less. We offer the following three-part outline for building progressive revelation:

1. Explain and illustrate why we need these ideas.
2. Explain and illustrate the ideas.
3. Explain and illustrate how to make these ideas work for you.

We suggest that you review Chapter 14 before you commence this part of your outline. Remember facts have no life without stories. You may have the facts, but those facts will not come to life until filtered through your experience and the stories of others' experiences.

Mining Your Life

One of the most instructive and revelational exercises we take financial professionals through in preparing for a public speech is an exercise we call "experiential archeology." In this process, we ask participants to mine their lives for experiences that are relevant to and illustrative toward their chosen speech topic. A main part of any preparation process has to include the stories or illustrations you will use in the presentation. People in audiences love to listen to stories and illustrations rather than a long list of boring facts and figures, which is so prevalent in our business. Remember, the facts/figures and your stories must balance each other. You don't want this to come off as "financial lite" with too many stories and not enough facts. The proper balance will empower each point that you bring to your audience. For every main point you make in a presentation, you should deliver a corresponding story that crystallizes it.

One of the best sources for stories is you. We recommend that you mine your life for experiences and situations that you can tell with passion and are relevant to the point you are trying to make. The process of mining your life requires that you take some time to recall major accomplishments, disappointments, struggles, and victories you have had and include them where appropriate. People love to hear personal stories about other people—it helps an audience relate to the speaker. Our major point here is to take time to prepare your stories and illustrations. It may make or break your presentation.

You can exponentially increase the impact of your speech by this personalization process and will be better able to make that human connection. By taking your outline through this process, you bring visceral impact to your presentation. Your speech is no longer about far-removed facts and unproven theories; it is now about ideas affirmed by life experience.

To illustrate this marked difference, we ask our workshop participants to present an idea in two distinct manners. Here is how it works. We provide a topic title such as "Land Mines and Gold Mines in the Selling Process" and in the first go-round ask participants to share a list of dos and don'ts on this topic. In the second go-round, we ask the participants to tell a personal story about wanting to make a purchase when the person selling did all the right things or all the wrong things. We give participants some time to do the necessary experiential archeology and then invite them to stand up and deliver their second presentation on the same topic.

What an amazing transformation takes place for both the presenter and the audience! It is the difference between watching the movie and reading the credits. Audiences are much more engaged by real-life experiences than they are by a laundry list of ideas. The story brings the point to life. As obvious as this point seems, we still marvel at the number of people we watch who stand up to speak in public and don't illustrate and animate their points. They end up gorging their audience with idea soup instead of satisfying them with one tasty and well-prepared dish. Another great aspect about telling stories from your life is that you don't have to worry about memorizing a script—it's coming straight from your life.

The Close

Have you ever listened to a speech that only ended because the material simply breathed its last desperate, dying breath? Have you ever given a presentation that just seemed to sputter out at the end? Anyone who has dared to speak in public knows this feeling. It is the anticlimactic ending, a disappointment to both the hearers and the speaker. How do you avoid it? You don't spend all this time preparing and rehearsing just to hear the firecracker fizzle at the end. The rule of thumb we offer for scripting your close is, "Offer the audience a specific way to act on the ideas you share."

Most presenters we see do not offer up a specific close. They don't recommend to an audience the specific next steps. Too many times we hear, "I hope you enjoyed tonight's presentation. I will be around afterwards to answer any questions you might have." Hello! You have just spent hours and hours of preparation—not to mention the emotional energy spent on worrying about the presentation—and you don't even ask them to do anything? Our point is to lead them at the end. If you have executed on the four cornerstones of a great presentation, then you will have a good portion of that audience ready to go. Whether or not the audience finds your presentation interesting hinges largely on whether or not they can *act* on that information. If they cannot, they will mentally file it away in the I file for Irrelevant.

We pay close attention to the topics of conversation among participants in the first 15 to 30 minutes after the talk. Even if they are saying things like, "She was a good speaker," you still may have missed your mark. The idea was not to get them excited about your oratory ability—the goal was to get them excited about your ideas. If they are talking excitedly about using the concepts you shared *and* commenting on your oratory skill, you have done an excellent job.

A presentation that we both give and get this response from is the T.E.A.M. Dynamics™ presentation on reading and leading others by virtue of understanding personality DNA. After these presentations, the crowd is carried away with table talk about how this information applies to them and how they can use it to further their career. They see the relevance. In this presentation, we share a parable for the close that wraps up all the principles that have been discussed in the presentation and ties them together in a memorable fashion. This type of close wraps everything they learned in a simple package.

Your close—be it a story, illustration, analogy, or other connection technique—should act as a bonding agent for everything that was taught in the presentation. Never close with facts or statistics. You want your presentation to send off fireworks in both sides of the brain as you reach the mountaintop of your material. The only way fireworks are possible is to end with a story or other tool that is aimed at moving the emotion of the audience. In Chapter 13, "Moving from Agreement to Action," we learned that people don't act until their emotions are engaged. If what you're asking your audience to do is not compelling, your speech should have ended at the introduction.

Work up a close and try it out on friends and associates. Ask those who will give you candid feedback. Keep working on your close until it makes you want to jump out of your chair. We cannot overemphasize the importance of crafting a powerful pinnacle for your ideas. People may not remember everything you say in a speech, but they will remember how people responded at the end. Don't forget this fact when writing the close to your presentation.

You want to deliver inspiration in your speech, but don't forget Edison's maxim regarding inspiration, "Genius is 1 percent inspiration and 99 percent perspiration." You make the choice—do you want to sweat before the speech or during it? We will close this chapter with the same advice the Israeli army gives their soldiers in training: The more you sweat here, the less likely you are to bleed there.

CHAPTER | **17**

Cornerstone #3 of Dynamic Presenting

Having a Flight Plan

Make no little plans, they have no magic to stir men's blood.

—David Burnham

A story is told about a time Einstein was riding a train to New York. When the conductor asked him for his ticket, the absentminded Einstein began looking through his briefcase. The conductor, recognizing him, quickly said, "No problem, Dr. Einstein," and walked on. When he came back, Einstein had the contents of two briefcases unloaded on the seat. The conductor once again assured him that the ticket was no big deal. The scientist responded, "Maybe for you it's not important, but if I don't find that ticket, how will I know where to get off?"

Have you ever listened to speakers who didn't seem to have a clue as to where they were going, and after it was over, you didn't have a clue as to where you had been? A crucial phase of preparation is the development of a flight plan for your speech. Think of the times you have listened to a speaker who bored, confused, or annoyed you. This speaker probably took you on a random journey—a never-ending ride around the ranch—or tried to weave ideas together that had no symmetry. These speakers have not learned the rules of navigating and need to be reminded that they are carrying a ship full of innocent passengers.

Before takeoff, pilots must file a flight plan. This plan gives the final destination and the exact routing that they will use to reach their destination. You won't see any flight plans that state, "We're going to zip around here and there and hopefully work our way over yonder." Flight plans have a stated course and a predetermined finish line. Wouldn't it be a relief if every speaker we ever had to listen to was required to do the same? Think of the times that you sat and listened to a speech or a presentation and kept thinking these thoughts to yourself:

- And your point is . . . ?
- Shouldn't this have ended about 20 minutes ago?
- OK, you made your point, time to move on.
- I'm sure this is all very interesting to you, but . . .

By developing a pattern for your speeches, you breed clarity, eliminate confusion, narrow the focus, and identify the real needs. We have developed some rules of thumb in our training of speakers. Follow this flight plan, and you too will be garnering predictable results and approval at the end of your speeches and client presentations. The three rules are:

1. Establish a destination.
2. Master the takeoff, flight, and landing.
3. Point out what you want your passengers to see.

ESTABLISH A DESTINATION AND KNOW HOW TO GET THERE

It takes about two weeks to prepare a good impromptu speech.

—Mark Twain

The reason many speakers succeed in underwhelming their audience is that they often underestimate the preparation and practice needed to be a good speaker. As we stated in the last chapter, you work to prepare your material and yourself. In the next chapter, "Deliver with Style," we show you how to prepare your voice, appearance, manner, and style as a speaker. In this chapter, we want to guide you on how to take the material you've found and mold it into a cohesive, logical, and emotionally climactic end.

An old rule of thumb for delivering a speech goes this way:

- Tell them what you're going to tell them.
- Tell them.
- Tell them what you told them.

For the speaker, the speech must be predictable. You need to be so well prepared in your ordering of material that you know exactly when your audience will laugh, when sentiment will draw tears, and when they will sit stunned into silence. This process is similar to a pilot methodically going through the checklist for one paramount reason—*they cannot afford to make a mistake.* Remember the adage of the highly trained Israeli army, "The more you sweat before the battle, the less you bleed in the battle."

The approach we take in training financial professionals to improve their speaking skills is to aim for predictability—and practice until they achieve this point of predictability. Once presenters arrive at a place where they control the flow of thought and emotion, their speechmaking ceases to be laborious and actually begins to be fun. There is no excitement quite like taking an audience on a ride from the depths of the problem to the heights of overcoming that problem and receiving their approbation at the end. It's a righteous adrenaline rush to deliver with eloquence a message that can help people's lives—and to see in their eyes that they know it. This rush is a target worth shooting for and worth the pain and price of preparation.

Years ago, Mitch became frustrated with his speaking. He had been speaking professionally for about a decade at the time but was less than satisfied with the way his speeches were ending. Although some of his speeches ended with a standing ovation, most of the time his speeches ended up with warm applause—and occasionally ended with lukewarm applause. Instead of blaming the audience, Mitch sought to find out what the greatest speakers, who were getting red-hot approval at the end of every speech, were doing. Mitch figured that if they could get a predictable response, then he could as well.

His quest for predictability ended upon hearing a gifted Irish speaker. Mitch discovered a number of elements that he has integrated into every speech he delivers. We detail Mitch's discoveries in Chapter 22, "In the Palm of Your Hand." Mitch's most important change in his speaking resulted from his decision to deliver predictable speeches—no more shooting from the hip, and no more impromptu conclusions or introductions. Although straying into a good one-liner or anecdote was all right, staying on the flight plan of the speech was essential. He resolved to develop a route that would deliver each audience to the same awakening—and to stay with that predictable route. The results that came from that decision made a dramatic impact in Mitch's career. We have found through our training sessions that these techniques and methodologies work for any speaker who adopts and practices them.

Another point that is important in determining a destination is deciding exactly what you want your audience to walk away with. Keep it simple and make sure it is anchored to emotion. If it is not anchored to emotion, your audience will lose interest and will not have the incentive needed to act. One of the secrets we share in training financial professionals to be better speakers is to determine ahead of time what the emotional target is with their audience. Is it to raise their confidence? Is it to help them feel hope? Is it to motivate them to take control of their lives? If you do not or cannot articulate this emotional target up front, you will have no chance of hitting it by the end of your speech.

We cannot overemphasize how important it is to simplify and reduce the lessons you want your audience to walk away with. Most speakers we see try to accomplish far too much with too little time in their speeches. Consequently, they end up resorting to presentations that could be characterized as either *info-dumps* or *idea smorgasbords*. Neither of these is enjoyable or helpful to the audience.

Your presentations need to be crystallized to the point where the audience can articulate in a simple sentence what they learned. Your speech should be so crystallized and tight as a flight plan that you can announce to the audience at the beginning, "This is what you are going to learn today," and then be able to follow through on your promise. Do not make the mistake of overestimating how much information your audience wants to hear or is able to retain. It has been estimated that audiences retain as little as 10 percent of what they hear. Also, remember that stories with emotional impact are the most memorable material for your audience.

The first rule for getting to your destination is to choose the shortest route between points A and B. Look at every point you wish to make in your talk or presentation and ask yourself, "Is this information absolutely crucial for making my point?" If it isn't crucial, lose it. Streamline and simplify. Don't try to help your audience memorize the encyclopedia—learning the definition of one word is enough.

Be clear about your destination and be settled on the route you will fly. Take it from a couple of guys who have experienced more than our share of less than stellar performances—predictability is preferable. Build a speech plan that is bulletproof. The only way to do this is to stand up and deliver speeches that aren't bulletproof until you learn where the vulnerable spots are. You will learn quickly once you practice in front of an audience of any size. Embarrassment either motivates us to improve quickly, or to quit. You will make some mistakes as you develop your foolproof flight plan, but you will also build your confidence.

One of the great thrills in our career is watching people improve as presenters and the impact improvement has on their personal confidence and business. If you are faithful to the process, the day will come when you know *before* you stand up exactly what the result will be. You know what to say, you know how to say it—and you don't say any more than is necessary. Your flight plan is predictable, and you end up at the same great destination every time you get behind the controls.

MASTER THE TAKEOFF, FLIGHT, AND LANDING

Every passenger who boards a flight wants to get somewhere. Nothing is quite as exhausting as spending precious time sitting on runways and flying in holding patterns. Remember that all presentations should be about solving problems. Therefore, the destination of every presentation is arriving at a place where a problem has been solved. Don't leave your audience on the runway or in holding patterns.

Many speakers lose the interest of their audience in the first few moments because they don't point to a problem that needs to be solved. If there is no problem, why should anyone listen? There is nothing to engage the listener emotionally. In Chapter 21, "Setting the Hook," we will take you on a crash course in what we call "disturbing the audience." The beginning of a speech is like having a snake loose in the room—if you don't grab the snake by the back of the neck quickly and disturb it, the snake will disturb you throughout the entire presentation.

People generally need to be disturbed into believing that good enough isn't good enough. Your client or audience will more than likely be in a state of lethargy to varying degrees, until you properly disrupt that state. Point out a problem or set of problems that they have or will have if left unattended. Until you do this in your presentation, you give the listener no motivation to listen.

What do you think is the greater motivator—something to be gained, or something to be lost? Time and again, people demonstrate that the threat of loss spurs them to action more than the possibility of gain. If the thought of accruing $2 million was a highly effective motivator, then every American would save every penny to get there—because it is mathematically possible for the majority of people. The fact is, most people aren't saving what they should, because they are not intrinsically motivated by this thought.

If you wish to see higher levels of motivation, you begin talking about the problems that will arise and the freedoms and opportunities that will be lost. Suddenly, this lethargic human species sits up and takes notice. They are sufficiently disturbed to listen to the solution and to take some action. Just recently, we talked to a financial professional who is experiencing tremendous success selling long-term care insurance through his insurance firm. Each day, he runs ads on the radio talking about how to avoid the devastating cost of long-term care—and the phones ring off the hook.

We know one financial professional who asks potential clients how much they love their job. Then he asks them if they had a choice, how much longer they would stay in their line of work. Because many do not want to be stuck in a career, he says two out of three are sufficiently disturbed to take some action.

Mitch has a friend in the insurance industry who built a legendary reputation on his ability to sell life insurance. One of his standard disturber lines to the client is, "I didn't buy life insurance because I like it—I bought it so that Mrs. Johnson, the widow, would be as well dressed as she is today." The client, mortified and shamed by the thought of his widow in rags, usually bought the life insurance. If you don't disturb your audience at the beginning, you're wasting your breath in the middle and at the end.

Now We're Flying

You don't need to invent any new methods of motivating listeners. You point out a problem, share the solution, and facilitate the process of solving the problem. The disturber is your takeoff—nobody is getting off board at this point. You now have a captive audience.

The flight is the information you give that reveals both the ramifications and hazards that people may experience if they do not fix a particular problem, as well as the rewards gained by those who take initiative and address the issue at hand. The drama begins to unfold at this point, and stories will serve you well. Don't make the mistake of letting numbers tell your story exclusively; instead, you tell a number of stories. You need to engage your audience emotionally at this point. In Chapter 14, we shared how to best utilize stories in your presentation to give it the dramatic effect to hold your client's or audience's attention.

In Chapter 12, we discussed how to make the solutions you offer clients relevant to their life. To paraphrase an old saying, you could have the greatest shoe in the world, but if it doesn't fit, the client won't wear it. Presentations that work are the presentations that deal only with issues that are relevant to the listener. Your clients don't want to hear about issues in other people's lives—they want to hear stories and illustrations that act as windows into their own world.

Bringing Them Back to Terra Firma

Finally, you must bring your passengers in for a safe landing. A good landing is one that is smooth and makes passengers feel relaxed at the end of the flight. Remember, never let applause fool you—they may be clapping because you finally quit. We've noticed that the only time passengers clap at the end of a flight is when it has been a white-knuckle experience. In the case of a turbulent flight, it's not the pilot's fault that the conditions were turbulent; however, in piloting a speech, the speaker is at fault if the ride is rough. A safe landing is one where all conflicts are resolved and your audience leaves with a precise plan of action to begin the implementation process. A safe landing in the realm of presentations is judged by the ease of implementing your ideas into the world in which they live. If your ideas aren't usable, then your flight has been locked into an interminable holding pattern and will eventually land—but not so gently.

In the one-on-one sales presentation, the takeoff, flight, and landing are described in slightly different terms. These three stages are:

1. *Takeoff.* The discovery process
2. *Flight.* Presentation of products and services
3. *Landing.* Advancing the sale or the close

We feel that these three stages of the client presentation are important enough that we dedicated a chapter to each stage in the section of this book entitled "Connecting with the Individual." Chapters 11 to 14 illustrated how to master each stage of the client presentation and how to purge your presentations of extraneous material.

POINT OUT WHAT YOU WANT THEM TO SEE

On our flights, we both enjoy when the captain takes the time to point out sights of interest outside our window. If he didn't announce, "Outside the left wing, you can see the Grand Canyon," we more than likely would have missed this spectacular sight. We all get so absorbed in our own thoughts that we miss the obvious. This rule also holds true in speaking and presenting. The audience needs you to point out where you are taking them and what they will see along the way.

You can do this in the front end of your speech by giving two or three objectives you hope to achieve by the end of the speech. You also can achieve this by stopping at various points—after a good story, for example—and asking, "What did we just see?" Playing tour guide as well as pilot when you speak is important. Do not assume that the audience will naturally absorb every lesson you intend for them. Tell your audience what you're going to tell them, tell them, and tell them what you told them. We don't mean to imply that you should be redundant. Instead, restate your points in a number of ways, but continue to reinforce the major points you want to leave embedded in their psyche.

Like a flight, your talk should take people through different altitude levels. According to public-speaking coach Steve Mikez, a well-developed speech needs to address people at three levels, or altitudes:

1. *Logos.* At the level of intellect
2. *Pathos.* At the level of emotion
3. *Ethos.* At the level of principle and integrity

Take a look at the speeches you are giving or desire to give, and see if they pass this acid test. Are they appealing to the intellect, emotion, and spirit of your audience? Are they challenging your audience intellectually, emotionally, and morally? Make sure you take your audience to higher altitudes so they can see your point from ground level and from 30,000 feet.

We feel the ultimate challenge in speech making is to deliver a call to higher ground. Ask people to do something that either will better their own life or something that will better their life by bettering someone else's life. The effective presentation must contain some sort of challenge to action; otherwise, your words are music in the wind. Be the kind of speaker who asks the audience to do something that will make them proud in the doing.

GIVE YOUR LISTENERS HOPE

A small detachment from a Hungarian army unit was once lost during maneuvers in the Swiss Alps. It had snowed for two days, and the lieutenant who had dispatched the unit had all but given them up for dead. But to the lieutenant's surprise and relief, the soldiers turned up at base camp safe and sound. When the lieutenant asked them how they had survived, the soldiers explained that they had despaired initially, but then one of them found a map in his pocket. That map gave them hope. They held camp for two days and when the storm cleared, they figured out their bearings.

The lieutenant asked to see the map. When he inspected the map, he discovered that it was not a map of the Alps but of the Pyrenees. The soldiers had found their way back by following the wrong map! The map had so heartened and inspired them that they made the treacherous trip back to camp. It turned out that the map's most important function was not the directions it gave, but the sense of hope it inspired.

The map to your speech should do the same. It should inspire hope that your listeners are getting somewhere, learning something, and arriving at a better place. Take the time to develop a flight plan that will guarantee an enjoyable voyage for your passengers. After all, most of us have suffered through enough speeches where we were held hostage in a flight going in circles.

To develop a flight plan, complete the following statements:

- The emotional target I want to hit with my audience is . . .
- The way I will disturb my audience from their lethargy is . . .
- The one or two memorable points that I want my audience to take with them are . . .
- The stories I will tell to make a memorable impact emotionally are . . .
- I will impact my audience intellectually by . . .
- I will impact my audience emotionally by . . .
- I will impact my audience morally or ethically by . . .
- To make my presentation bulletproof and predictable, I need to . . .

CHAPTER 18

Cornerstone #4 of Dynamic Presenting

Deliver with Style

Half the world consists of people who have something to say and can't,
and the other half of people who have nothing to say and
keep saying it.

—Robert Frost

The final cornerstone to building a powerful presentation is to decide on and develop your delivery style—your signature upon your ideas. We commonly see two extremes in public presenters:

- The presenter who really has something substantial to say, but who loses it in a lack of charisma and a voice on life support
- The presenter who has some natural dynamics in front of a crowd but has not put any order or orchestration to the delivery

The previous three cornerstones, conviction, preparation, and developing a flight plan, are given respiratory power by developing the final cornerstone, delivering with style. You don't have to look and sound like other speakers. In fact, your chances of building a reputation as an effective presenter increase exponentially if you pursue a unique signature style. Like a basketball player who studies other players' moves, picking up on others' techniques is wise as long as you have the ability to pull off the same moves. Don't attempt any 360-degree dunk shots if you know your vertical leap is 11 inches. In other words, go with the techniques that fit your personality.

Some personalities are adept at facilitating group interactions and discussions. Other personalities can use a commando approach and take a room by storm—by sheer power of personality. Other personalities like to overwhelm their audience with proof, like a well-prepared lawyer before a vacillating jury. Then there are the personalities who are the natural performers or comedians. These individuals stand up in front of a crowd—and radiate with neon light.

ENTERTAINMENT VALUE

When training financial professionals to speak, Gary likes to compare the overly aggressive style of speaking he used when he began with the style he uses today. In Gary's words, "I opened with a knockout punch and kept punching. By the end of the talk, I was worn out and they were punch-drunk." Then Gary discovered what all veteran speakers eventually discover: a successful public presentation needs to be a killer combination of entertainment and education—or what we call *edutainment*. Like it or not, most groups today suffer from as much attention deficit disorder as their Ritalin-addicted kids and complain if presentations do not entertain as well as inform.

Does this mean you have to juggle or dance? Do you have to be a comedian to successfully deliver a speech? No. But you must provide the audience with a little bit of fun while you're trying to administer your frontal lobotomy—or a little anesthetic so the needle of truth doesn't sting so much. This objective can be accomplished in large part by becoming better at telling stories (see Chapter 14) and by simply designing presentations that contain lighter moments.

Your job in delivery is to help your audience feel like they are going to walk away informed, but yet have some fun in the process. You can get this balance across with the style of delivery you choose. Don't pound your audience. Even pigs quit coming to the trough if they get beat over the head every time they come. Also don't overwhelm your audience. You don't have to teach them everything you've learned in the last 20 years in the next 20 minutes. Find a style that relaxes you—and you will relax your audience. Your audience will never be any more comfortable with you than you are with yourself.

No Business Like Show Business

In developing your personal style, mold a delivery manner that is consistent with your personality. Stay within your natural element when developing what is referred to in show business as a *shtick*. Your shtick is the characterization of your style. If you have not given this aspect of delivery any thought, you need to. You can choose from a thousand characterizations to define your manner in front of a crowd.

We've seen speakers who like to play the coach, giving the crowd a game plan as a mixture of Xs and Os and an inspirational halftime speech. We've seen others who like to play the professor. We saw one that was characterized as a mix between a professor and an evangelist. We've seen others who prefer the military style and give marching orders like a commanding officer. Our friend Scott West has mastered the self-deprecating sales professional, and audiences love his delivery. Don Connelly has mastered the wily veteran who has seen it all and can tell you stories about what works and what doesn't. We've seen others play counselor, detective, armchair psychologist, jet fighter, comedian, machine-gun idea guy, grandpa sitting in the rocking chair, and advice from mama. The most memorable presentations come from those people who have crafted a style that is unique to them. All the above characterizations work for the people who use them because they are aligned with their personality and background. Don't try to put on a style that is out of your field of expertise.

Gary and I both have been speaking to professional groups for almost 20 years. We have both experienced success in front of a crowd, and yet have completely different approaches to our audiences. There is no one, good way to present. As you'll see in this chapter, there are elements that must be honed for you to be successful with your style, whatever it is. Gary's approach is like that of a coach, challenging and teaching people how to win with the right game strategies blended with inspirational stories and ideas. While Gary speaks, his audience practically has to absorb his enthusiastic energy. I, on the other hand, use a style that is a cross between philosopher and humorist. I like to dangle my audiences between laughter and soul searching, and open the door to the latter with the former.

Look within your resume of experience, personality, and abilities and try to carve out a picture of the ideal shtick for you. If you skip this particular part of preparation, you run the risk of sounding like every other speaker. Most people don't take the time to develop a signature style and, consequently, sound like a thousand voices that came before them. Many people make the mistake of believing that their content will carry the day—which may well be—but the odds for this are not great. However, you are sure to succeed if you have well-organized, "killer" content and a stage presence that is uniquely you.

How would you characterize your style? If someone were to ask your audience members what your presentation style was like, what would their answer be? Take a moment to think about your personality, skills, experiences, and background, and see if a shtick rises from it.

- My speaking style is like . . .

THE ELEMENTS OF STYLE

Developing a good message is one thing, but bringing it to life is an altogether different matter. Your only tools for bringing a presentation to life are the four basic elements of style—your voice, your eyes, your body, and your speaking props. Gary likes to say that your voice, eyes, and body movements are the engines that drive your delivery. You may have the prettiest vehicle on the block, but it isn't going anywhere until you fully utilize the physical tools that put it into motion.

An often-quoted statistic about communication states that when people listen to a message, they are paying the most attention to body language (45 percent) followed by voice tones (38 percent), and, finally, content (7 percent). Think about it—have you ever been completely distracted regarding the content of what someone was saying because of her nervous body language or unsure tone of voice? The body, the eyes, and the voice should affirm what the words are saying—or the words will vaporize.

The Eyes Have It

"I remember being at a conference recently and, after the morning session, we were standing around drinking coffee and talking about the last speaker. Somebody mentioned that she couldn't concentrate on what the speaker was saying because he kept blinking the whole time he talked. Everybody started laughing and said they were having the same problem. One guy said he and a friend had actually started counting the blinks per minute (BPM) rate on the poor guy. I thought to myself, "If I get up in front of a group, I am going to pay very close attention to the message that my eyes are sending."

—Nicholas E., financial professional

What message are your eyes sending? We see a number of mistakes speakers make with their eyes.

- They look only at one part of the audience.
- They avoid eye contact.
- They hold eye contact too long on one party.
- Their eyes register nervousness.

You want your eyes to make *focused visits* with your audience. As your eyes make visits around the room, you'll see four types of audience members: tourists, terrorists, listeners, and groupies. Tourists are just passing through, and you're simply taking up their time. Terrorists don't believe a word you're saying, and they're telling you so with their facial language. Listeners are paying close attention to your words, and groupies are shouting "Amen" with their body and facial language; they are tuned in to what you are saying.

To gain momentum, make focused visits with the listeners and the groupies. If you are focusing toward the disinterested and the skeptical early on in your presentation, they will zap your energy and enthusiasm. However, when we begin to sense that one of these negative stereotypes is beginning to be engaged we will make a short visit with our eyes. Use eye contact to energize yourself by finding those in the audience who are your friends. Remember, 99.9 percent of people in an audience want you to succeed. Also remember that 99.9 percent of those people would not want to change places with you. Have this attitude going into a presentation and it will get you off to a great start.

Much of what you do with your eyes has to do with your own confidence level. If your confidence is shaky, you'll want to avoid the lethargic and cynical audience members. If your confidence in what you're saying is unshakable, you will have no fear of these individuals and will pay them focused visits with your eyes just to watch them squirm. The chief point of paying attention to your eye language is to make connections with the audience and to communicate the strength of your convictions. If you fail to make eye contact with your audience—even though you may have strong convictions about your topic—your audience will be more likely to have doubts about what you are saying. Look them in the eye in a way that says, "I know what I'm talking about here, and if you listen, I will help you."

Many Voices in the World

"When I was shopping for a business law attorney, I was looking for three things: expertise, experience, and a voice that commanded respect. I have seen too many instances where the wrong tone or pitch of voice failed to command attention and had a negative effect on the negotiation process. I believe the tone of voice can make or break your case—if it is authoritative and believable, you'll get far. I was fortunate enough to find an attorney whose basso profundo voice causes anyone who hears him to sit up and take notice."

—Mitch Anthony

Your voice is your chief tool in public speaking. We wish more speakers would pay as much attention to their voice as they would to their content, because if they did, it would give their content more potency. Gary shares two major rules for voice control in public speaking:

1. Inflect for impact.
2. Pause for power.

Instead of inflecting their voice, many speakers simply raise their volume. We have heard some individuals who think that volume is a replacement for substance or a way to display their conviction to an audience. Loud tones will put the audience into a state of high alert (much like hearing a siren), then into a state of defense, and finally into a state of annoyance. We have seen this audience reaction as speakers have tried to shout their way to persuasiveness—the technique doesn't work.

Raising the volume at scripted points in your presentation is fine for effect—when you want the audience to be in a state of alert. But you must understand that inflection is an art that includes not only volume but rhythm, tone, and cadence of speech as well. Great speakers have learned how to modulate their tones and pace in a way that keeps their audience engaged. The art of powerfully timed inflection comes only from preparation and rehearsal of impact points.

Think of your voice as a musical instrument. You wouldn't play just one chord over and over as some people do when they deliver a monotone presentation (they think they are being *controlled* in their delivery, but they are coming across as *boring*). Neither would you pluck the strings as loud and as hard as you could. You would attempt to establish a rhythm and draw the audience in with it. You would hit highs and lows and change the pace and cadence to continue their engagement and, finally, attempt to end on a high note.

Americans seem to be a bit handicapped in this area because of the breakneck speed at which our society and businesses are running. Consequently, the majority of speakers we hear are in too big a hurry and rush through their material, and the audience doesn't get the opportunity to absorb the tune being played. Mitch has made the observation that the Irish are the most naturally gifted talkers in the world and that the average Irishman on the street is twice as engaging to listen to as most speaking professionals in America. There are two reasons for this: first, the Irish brogue has a musical timing; and second, the Irish share a great appreciation for the art of storytelling. We will help you further develop this skill in Chapter 22, "In the Palm of Your Hand."

Give Your Audience Pause

It would be a poor song, that had no rests in it.

—Anonymous

We have had audience members come up after a speech and say, "The most powerful moment in your speech was that moment where you said nothing. It made us all stop and examine ourselves in light of what you were saying."

The dramatic pause is probably the most powerful yet underutilized tool that speakers have at their disposal. Yet, because of the aforementioned American pace and because most speakers believe they should say all they can in the allotted time, most speakers don't give their audience time to absorb fully the ideas they are sharing.

If your purpose in speaking is to get people to change or adjust some behavior or attitude, then the best weapon you can use is a well-placed dramatic pause. When you come to that place in your speech where you are sharing a grave reality or a powerful truth, *shut up* and just give that thought time to sink in. You'll be amazed at the impact that moment of pause can have. We suspect that many speakers fail to utilize this technique because they are not comfortable enough with themselves to stand there and stare the audience down in a moment that calls for introspection. Remember, what you don't say at given moments in your speech can have far greater impact than anything you could say.

Body, Props, and Tools

People ask all the time what the rules are when it comes to body movement. Rather than focus on what not to do, we have one simple guideline—move with a purpose. There is nothing more. Move in a way that shows your audience you are enthused about your topic—and also move enough to allow the audience to keep track of you.

The props and tools you choose will affect your physical movements in a presentation. This area of preparation should not be ignored. Ask yourself the following:

- What kind of props best fit my message?
- What kind of props best fit my personality?
- What kind of props best fit my speaking style?

"I once saw a speaker who was so bad with his props that it almost became a comedy. He had a projector showing PowerPoint slides. The first thing I noticed was that he would talk right past his PowerPoint slides and then have to jump ahead to try to find the one he wanted. But the most distracting thing was that the speaker would walk out toward his audience as he talked and then start backing up toward his projector—and as he backed up, he would trip over the leg of the projector stand. This happened *nine* times! I have never seen anything like it. This was one speaker who should not be using PowerPoint and projectors until he first learns how to walk. Oh, by the way, the speaker was my coauthor, Mitch Anthony."

—Gary DeMoss

"OK, mea culpa, Gary. Truth be told, I hate PowerPoint with a passion. I suffer a condition known as *speakus interruptus* every time I am forced to use Power-Point. My favorite props are a flip chart and a high stool. Every time I tell a story, I sit on a stool (á la Bill Cosby). Before long, the audience begins to anticipate a story as soon as they see me heading toward the stool. I can tell when I sit down that the audience begins to relax and anticipation begins to build. I like to use the flip chart to draw illustrations and simple numbers or facts. PowerPoint is "Power-Point less" to me. With my style of presentation, that sort of technology is distracting to both me and to my audience because the pictures are drawing their attention away from the stories I'm telling.

I would also like to weigh in with the fact that I've seen far too many speakers use PowerPoint as a speaking crutch. They would be better off to develop their own storytelling ability and speaking skills than to try to wow the crowd with fancy graphics and images. I'm often told that the justification for using this technology is that audiences need visuals in a speech. My answer to that is that the greatest visual you can give an audience is to paint a picture in their imagination by being an engaging storyteller. Let them see in their imagination the people, places, and incidents you are describing—now that is visual impact!"

—Mitch Anthony

What works for Gary may not work for Mitch. What works for us may not work for you. You have to assess your content, your personality, and your speaking style and determine if and what props are best suited to you. Everything you do in a public presentation should be an expression of who you are. You want your material, your props, and your style to flow together in one rushing current that sweeps up the listeners and keeps them engaged until the final word drops.

Don't assume that you need any props. Use props for illustrative purposes. If you feel that you would be naked without a bunch of props, then you probably need to develop your performance skills. When a prop, a tool, or a technology will enhance the dynamics of your presentation, then plug it in.

Gary likes to remind people that their greatest tools for presentation are not electronic—they are physical. Learn to fully utilize the power of your voice. Use your eyes to engage your audience and to drive points home. Use your body to create an atmosphere of positive energy and excitement. Develop a style that is uniquely you, and people will remember you. Deliver your message fully utilizing your physical dynamics, and people will remember the essence of your message. If the audience remembers you and your message, then you know you are *delivering with style.*

PART V

Connecting with the Crowd

CHAPTER 19

Know Thy Audience

This part of the book will focus specifically on the skills necessary to connect with your audience. Group presentations offer unique challenges and require a unique preparation process. In the next four chapters, we will help you to prepare and to stand confidently before any group. Most important, this section will conclude by showing you how to avoid the mistakes that cause people to fall flat in front of an audience.

"An apocryphal story tells of a speaker who was asked to address the handicapped bowlers' league. He never called his host to check on the audience because he assumed that the name said it all. He carefully prepared his remarks to focus on issues related to disabled athletes. He was prepared to commend them on their tenacity and courage in pursuing athletic activities in the face of physical disabilities. As he stood at the lectern and looked across the audience, he suddenly noticed that not a wheelchair was in the house. *Handicapped* referred to their bowling scores. The only thing disabled was his speech."

—Michael M. Klepper (Michael M. Klepper, *I'd Rather Die Than Give a Speech,* 1993, p. 81)

Some of the greatest speakers in history have looked foolish because they did not perform the proper recognizance on their audience. Mark Twain, in his official biography, tells the story of his most shaming moment as a speaker. In his day, Twain was very likely the most-sought-after speaker in America. He wrote one best-seller after another and gained a wide and robust reputation as a humorous after-dinner speaker. Because he bored easily with the repetition of giving the same talk, Twain would sometimes work up more risky material.

This particular event that Mark Twain was asked to speak at was a dignified dinner honoring the renowned poet, Dr. John G. Whittier. For this occasion, Twain decided to write what in his day was called a *burlesque* and would be comparable to a parody, satire, or lampoon. The burlesque presented the repartee of three disreputable tramps, who just happened to be named Longfellow, Emerson, and Holmes.

During his preparation, Twain was taken up with the humor of the material and was convinced that the crowd would howl with delight. They may well have if Twain had not neglected one minor item before deciding to deliver the speech—checking to see who would be in attendance at the event. As it turned out, Twain ascended to the podium and became utterly mortified to see no less than Longfellow, Emerson, and Holmes sitting at the front with the honorary guest, Dr. Whittier. For a fleeting moment, Twain flirted with scrapping the burlesque speech and giving an impromptu address. But for some strange reason, that later even he could not articulate, he forged on ahead.

The biggest problem wasn't so much that the subjects being parodied would take great offense, it was that the audience was paralyzed with shock and apprehension. This was to be an occasion of honoring a great man, and men of equal stature had turned out to pay their respects. Later, through apologetic correspondence with the three great poets, he learned that although they were surprised by Twain's speech, they all received it with the same humorous spirit in which it was given. The observers and organizers of the event, however, were a different story. The gathering went into a collective gasp that lasted through the entire speech. They dared not laugh in the presence of these immortal men. Their mouths sat agape and their brows were raised in astonishment through the whole talk. Imagine what was going on inside of Mark Twain as he choked out word after word of this oratorical embarrassment.

Newspapers widely distributed the accounts of Twain's faux pas. It caused him great embarrassment and took him over a year to get over the emotional self-flagellation he put himself through. Even the great ones can be brought low if they fail to obey this cardinal rule of presenting: know thy audience. A hundred good speeches can barely remove the blighting souvenir of an incident like this. As important as it is to prepare your material and yourself, it is equally important to prepare yourself for the audience you will deliver to.

WHAT YOU NEED TO KNOW

An anxious executive once told his company's spokesperson, "We're not paying you to make us look like a bunch of idiots. We're paying you so they won't know we're a bunch of idiots." You need to go through the process of *audience analysis* to ensure that your speech hits its intended mark. In fact, we could say that you have no chance of knowing what the intended mark is until you complete the process of audience analysis. Why would anyone want to take the risk of offering subject material that an audience has either heard before or doesn't want to hear?

Before we address an audience, we need to discover the following pieces of intelligence and do the necessary recognizance to gather them:

- Their attitudes and interests
- Their current needs and wants
- Their lexicon of language

Attitudes and Interests

How would you know whether or not the group you are presenting to has a built-in bias toward the ideas you plan on sharing? You wouldn't have any way of knowing unless you asked someone within the group to advise you on their attitudes and interests. Walking blindly into a public presentation with the assumption that people will be warm to your ideas is never safe. For example, your audience may have already heard these ideas from someone else (a competitor), and your presentation will be redundant.

We recently heard an analyst stand up and present to a group brought in by a sales team for a fund family. The analyst stood up and gave a talk regarding a certain type of investment discipline used in a fund he managed. After his presentation, a member of the audience said, "Everything you said sounds exactly the same as one of your competitors whom we heard just a couple of days ago. What do you do that they don't do? What makes you different?" The analyst was thrown off his linear game plan by the question and hemmed and hawed his way through this blushing predicament. Not only had he failed to find out that his audience had listened to a talk just like his two days before, he didn't have an answer that could help differentiate his product from his competitor's. A little bit of audience recognizance could have solved both of these problems. If he had taken 20 minutes to talk to the meeting organizer and asked, "What is your people's attitude toward this idea?" and "Have you or will you be hearing any similar talks from anyone else?" his embarrassing situation would have been obviated.

Some predicaments, however, simply cannot be avoided. At times, all speakers are caught by surprise and have to adjust on the fly. In these types of scenarios, one does best by using improvisational ability and agility. Our point with the analyst story, however, is that most people fail to recognize the importance of taking their audience's temperature regarding possible biases. This checkpoint can save you considerable discomfiture.

Their Needs and Wants

Todd Taskey learned that you can build not only a good presentation but a very good business by taking the time to understand the needs and wants of your potential clients (Karen Hansen Weese, *Investment Advisor,* October 2000, p. 72). For years, he was running all over the place trying to meet the needs of a spread-out client base. He looked out his window and saw the headquarters for a national company with over 4,000 employees and decided to find out their financial needs and wants.

A bit of sleuthing among executives revealed that many of them needed help understanding their company's benefits such as profit sharing, stock options, deferred compensation, and other programs. Taskey made it his job to become an expert on these issues to better present to and troubleshoot for this company's employees. He said, "Many planners gloss over the company portion of clients' financial plans because there's nothing there that they can be compensated for. Yet for a lot of clients, it's the biggest part of their financial future. We help employees not only wade through the benefits information, but also answer the question, 'How should I integrate this with the rest of my financial life?'"

Having the foresight to investigate this large corporation's needs and wants has led to his firm now having hundreds of clients from this company. He built a prospering companycentric business with all his clients right across the street—simply because he decided to do his homework before he presented his ideas to their executives. That bit of homework paid off handsomely.

Do your homework. Every company or group has specific needs that are not being met or are not being met adequately. If you ask, someone will tell. The opportunity comes to those who ask. Start asking someone who knows your audience preparatory questions like:

- What are the most glaring needs these people are facing?
- What would be the most valuable piece of information I could bring to this group?

- How can I best help these people reach their goals?
- Are there some specific issues people are confused or frustrated with?

People will want to listen to you when they get the sense that you are in touch with them and their goals. Investigating your audience's needs and wants will help to position you as an invaluable resource. You'll find that not many competitors out there are doing this kind of homework, and the fact that you have done your homework will help to position you as *the* resource in the mind of your audience.

Their Lexicon of Language

Some years ago Mitch was asked to speak at a national convention for a financial services company. When asked what topic he thought might be most appropriate, Mitch asked some questions about the company's culture, needs, and goals. He then asked if he could ride along with one of the company's employees in order to get a feel for the business. Although it was an unusual request, the executive liked the idea and arranged for Mitch to accompany one of their representatives. That one-day ride turned into years of work for Mitch with this particular company. When it came time to present at the company's national conference, Mitch lucidly integrated language from the company's lexicon regarding clients, products, and the selling challenges they faced on a daily basis into his speaking topic. This audience was accustomed to hearing speakers come in and download broad and basic ideas that had little chance of taking root in their culture. They marveled that anyone would take the time to understand their world and the language they spoke daily.

The decision to spend time with someone on the front lines has become standard preparation for developing presentations in Mitch's business. A complaint that he often heard about other speakers was that they always seemed to come with generic ideas that the audience was supposed to somehow plug into their highly specialized world. Consequently, their attentiveness was outweighed by their cynicism. However, when these same people heard ideas framed in the scenarios they faced on a daily basis, they suddenly saw the relevance and began paying closer attention.

Every industry, group, and company has its own preferred lexicon. The insiders are the people who know what those positional acronyms stand for and what the responsibilities of each acronym are. Each group faces unique challenges with their clients and their business and personal lives. Understanding and being fluent in their specialized language communicates that you have more than a passing interest in working with them and that you are not the average presenter. The company that first called

Mitch years ago still calls him to speak today for one simple reason—he speaks their language.

For you to connect with your audience, you need to connect on the language level, and if you fail to prepare for your audience, you are facing a serious handicap. When you take the time to learn the attitudes and interests, the needs and wants, and the preferred language of your audience, you are a success before you ever open your mouth.

CHAPTER 20

Mistakes Speakers Make and How to Avoid Them

"William Henry Harrison's inaugural address in 1841 was 9,000 words long. It took two full hours to deliver, and it was a freezing day. Harrison came down with pneumonia and died a month later."

—Charles Osgood (*Osgood on Speaking,* 1988)

The moral of this story? A bad speech can kill your career. It may not literally kill you like it did Mr. Harrison, but it certainly can contribute to shortening your career. Since both Gary and I exercise a majority of our human connection opportunities in the public-speaking mode, we are including a special chapter dedicated to the biggest mistakes presenters can make in this arena. Because of the frequency with which we speak, we have the opportunity to see hundreds of presentations made to financial professionals each year. These observations and our own personal snafus provide the text for this chapter.

As we stated in the beginning of this book, polished oratory skills can greatly enhance opportunities for advancement in your career and industry—but the opposite holds true as well. If you believe you have the gift of public gab and venture into public speaking waters without the safety check that this chapter offers, you may find yourself far from shore and fighting the current. This chapter will discuss the classic mistakes speakers make and how you can avoid following their poor examples.

What most orators want in depth they make up for in length.

—Montesquieu

Talk: To commit an indiscretion without temptation, from an impulse
    without purpose.

—Ambrose Bierce

SPEAKING MISTAKE #1—SPEAKING AD INFINITUM

Speakers hold forth longer than they should for many reasons, but none that are acceptable to the audience. The reasons for speaking past the bell are listed below, along with common excuses a speaker might give to explain long-windedness.

Reason for rambling: Trying to accomplish too much in too little time.

Excuse: I don't get many opportunities to address these people and I need to get a lot done.

We've got news for you. You did get a lot done. You annoyed your audience. You've prepared them for your next speech so they can bring a crossword puzzle, and you gave some of your audience the slumber they needed because of your filibustering. We see this classic mistake constantly, speakers trying to accomplish too much in too little time. We have seen speakers' notes piled six inches high with notations as dense as the great northern pine forests, and they were planning on delivering all this in 45 minutes.

One executive, who was given 30 minutes to address a group, had notes that summarized just about everything written by Peter Drucker, Tom Peters, Steven Covey, and Dale Carnegie. This sort of overpreparation somehow makes speakers feel obligated to tell all they can, which, in turn, leads to public displays of *logorrhea*. A common error is to overestimate how much can actually get accomplished in a 30- to 60-minute time frame. To avoid going on too long, one must face the following realities:

- The audience will only retain one or two good ideas at best.
- As you go past an hour, your audience turns sour.

Prune your notes to the highlights, the best stories, and the most compelling features. Remember the old proverb, "Blessed are the short-winded for they shall be heard again." However, if you think *everything* you have written down is deeply compelling and you just can't get yourself to trim it, go present in a graveyard—you'll have a large audience and run no risk of putting them to sleep.

Reason for rambling: In love with the sound of your own voice.

Excuse: I think I have some extremely important things to say and want to get them said.

Don't ever lose touch with the fact that what is important to you is not necessarily important to your audience. Very few things are as important to your audience as their time. Don't lose sight of this fact. Don't let your ego cloud you in this matter. Face it—some folks just love to hear themselves talk and have a hard time turning themselves off once they get wound up. Check out your own pattern. Can a lot of excess fat be trimmed from your comments? Are you stretching your stories out longer than is necessary? Are you holding forth longer than needed simply because you love being up in front of people? These are tough questions, but we can guarantee that if you don't ask these questions about yourself, your audience members will be asking them about you.

Reason for rambling: Lack of discipline in preparation and presentation.

Excuse: A lot of ideas came to me while I was up there talking.

Have you ever sat through the acronym talk where the speaker used every letter of a word to develop a particular theme? "Ladies and gentlemen, I've chosen a word that describes the kind of service we need to bring to our clients today—*supercalifragilisticexpealadocious.* Now the *S* stands for sincere desire. We have to really want to . . ."

Every eyeball in the audience rolls back. The dread is almost palpable. Now maybe you haven't heard an acronym talk that is quite that bad, but chances are that you have heard one that is close. We personally do not advise the use of such a technique because this approach causes the audience to feel antsy when you're not making quick enough progress toward the end of the word you plan to spell out in your presentation.

Discipline yourself in both the preparation and presentation of your ideas. Some insightful thoughts may come to you while you are in front of your audience—and it's OK to include those inspired thoughts. However, you may have to drop some of the items you had scripted for time's sake. Don't stand up to talk without knowing how long this speech material will last. If your presentation times out to 45 minutes, allow for a margin of error of 5 to 15 minutes when you actually get to the event, depending on your delivery, audience response, etc. Don't even think of speaking at an event without rehearsing the timing of your comments.

You want to overprepare but not overdeliver. As one preacher put it, "I like to overprepare so I'm preaching out of the overflow. Nobody wants to come and hear me deliver instant oatmeal. But no matter how much I've prepared, I still give them 30 minutes' worth and leave them wanting more. It fills the pews the next week." This sort of discipline is what we advise—overdo it on the preparation side and leave them wanting more in the presentation.

SPEAKING MISTAKE #2—DRIVING OVER THE LIMIT AND RUNNING STOP SIGNS AT THE END

How many times have you seen these two mistakes? First, the speaker suddenly realizes that time is running short and crams a half-hour's material into the last five minutes. Second, the speaker comes to a climactic point in the speech, the audience senses that this is the end, and the speaker keeps rambling on another 15 to 20 minutes past the climax. These mistakes are often repeated, and we would like to address them here lest you be tempted into repeating them yourself.

Driving over the Limit at the End

Let's get realistic here. Whose purposes are being served by a speaker trying to cram in material during the last few moments of a talk? The audience certainly isn't being edified. Ask an audience what they remember about a speedy conclusion to a talk, and they will tell you they remember that the speaker was hurrying at the end. They will remember none of the content that you were so harried to deliver because they were distracted by your reckless driving. The purpose of the talk is to leave something memorable and useful with them. To keep yourself from breaking this traffic law of public speaking, make sure you discipline your pace and material to fit your time frame. If you find yourself running short of time, have a story ready that capsulizes what you want to say, and use that story to pull everything together. People will remember a good story, but will struggle to recall material delivered in a heated rush.

Driving through the Stop Sign

The speaker's speech is building up. The high point is just around the corner. The speaker delivers the punch line, the revelation, and the great truth he or she has come to share. The audience relaxes. They have gotten the point. They are ready to move on. The speaker then speaks the fatal words, "And my next point is . . ."

How can you avoid such a violation in your own talk? The best antidote we can give is to rehearse your material in front of knowledgeable and candid critics—and allow them to do surgery on both you and your script. Every speech can and should end on a high point. Every anticlimactic word you speak subtracts from your reputation as a speaker. Present the conflicts, resolve the conflicts, and then sit down! It's that simple. In a good movie, after the denouement, the credits roll. Your speech can be the same. The credits will roll for you—if you stop when you should.

SPEAKING MISTAKE #3—BAD LANGUAGE, BAD JOKES, POOR JUDGMENT

There is a story about somebody complaining to Bess Truman because her husband, Harry Truman, used the word *manure* to describe some politician's position on an issue. "My dear," said Mrs. Truman, "you have no idea how long it took me to get him to use the word *manure*."

Is the joke you're thinking of telling just a little in the gray area? Is it a little racy or heavy on the innuendo? Don't touch it. You will regret it if you do. If you can't bring laughter to your audience with real-life scenarios and observations, then forget about using humor at all. Unless your speech is at a nightclub, then the audience isn't expecting to hear a comedian. We've seen many speakers cheapen what they had to say with slightly blue material and crusty old jokes that wouldn't get a laugh even if the jokes were well told.

We can talk about having been on both ends of the poor judgment issue in public speaking. We have sat and observed the audience as it happened, and, unfortunately, we have stood and watched the audience as we caused it to happen. Mitch tells the story of doing a joke that was a little sensitive on the political correctness scale. It was original material, and he had tried it out on a couple of people to see if it would get a laugh. He stood in front of 400 teachers and opened with his new joke. When he delivered his punch line, some people laughed but one teacher gasped. Yes, *gasped*. It was not a moan or a groan, it was a gasp. Mitch will never forget how hard he had to work to get his audience back into a speech that was normally foolproof. He decided he never wanted to work that hard in a speech again and now stays away from any material that smells the least bit iffy.

SPEAKING MISTAKE #4—HACKNEYED AND PLAGIARIZED MATERIAL

Borrow from one and it is plagiarism, borrow from many and it is research.

—Wilson Mizner

Research or Thievery

The three greatest authors in the world are *Copied, Anonymous,* and
        Selected.

—Anonymous

Have you ever listened to a talk that sounded like one you had heard before or maybe even sounded *exactly* like a talk you had heard before? Chances are you did hear that talk before, either by the original artist or another imitator. Borrowing material and the occasional sound bite that fits your talk is fine as long as you tell where you got it, but to borrow the majority of another person's structure and content may just be illegal. You take an unnecessary risk when you claim an idea as your own that has been published elsewhere. Some learned member of your audience will have heard or read the material in its original form and will suspect your credibility. There is no shame or embarrassment in making a presentation of previously published or delivered ideas. In fact, all good talks borrow from the works of others. However, some folks reveal their sources, while others are inclined to act as if they thought it all up themselves. The way you join, couple, build brick upon brick, and rationalize these ideas may be original, and you can claim intellectual ownership in such a case. Just be honest about it. "I took these ideas from —————— and joined them with these ideas from ——————, and the unique chemistry we get from that combination are the ideas I'm going to present here today." Now you're being big enough to recognize the work of others before and to build upon it and present it in a new light.

New ideas are the result of two old ideas on a blind date.

—Mitch Anthony

Older than Dirt

Some stories have been around so long that as soon as you try to tell them the audience is finishing the telling for you. If you attempt to tell a hackneyed old joke, fable, or tale, you had better be a master of delivery. You would have to be able to give it a Garrison Keillor–like dramatic touch to pull it off, and even then, moth-eaten material is risky business. More work on the front end of preparation can keep you out of this trap. We've heard far too many speakers tell the same Ben Franklin or Abraham Lincoln stories to try to make a motivational point, probably because they all read the same book of illustrations and quotes.

Expand your research library, or spend more time digging at the library to come up with material that hasn't been widely circulated. People enjoy learning facts and illustrations that are out of the ordinary. Also, don't underestimate the most potent resource for illustrations that you own—your own memory bank of stories and experiences. Your experiences and those of your peers can be just as powerful for illustrative purposes as any you would find in a book of illustrations.

Originality should be the highest aspiration of every public presenter, because uniqueness gives the speaker unyielding confidence that her message will be fresh to the listener. Originality is attained both by inspiration and perspiration. Run your ideas by an intelligent critic whose instincts you trust on the basis of what material is likely to move an audience. Gary and I always do this because we have found how unpredictable an audience's reaction can be. The more experience we get, the more inclined we are to pass our ideas by seasoned speakers or critics. If your idea has the necessary impact, they will tell you. If your speech lacks the necessary punch, they can help you by editing it or convincing you to abandon it. Either way, this sort of preparatory accountability will make you a better speaker.

SPEAKING MISTAKE #5—SPEAKING OUT OF YOUR WHEELHOUSE

When asked why he never painted angels, renowned artist Gustave
Courbet replied, "Because I have never seen one."

In baseball, the skilled batter is trained to swing only at pitches in a specific hitting zone. The opposing pitcher will try to tempt him to chase balls outside that zone, but the veteran will avoid the temptation to go outside his "wheelhouse," or the hitting area where his percentages for getting on base are the best. A major-league player, considered a good hitter but a poor fielder, strangely possessed an above-average fielding record. He explained, "Don't touch it if you can't handle it. They don't call it an error if it's beyond your reach." The veteran speaker follows the same rule for public presentations—never go outside of the zone of your greatest expertise. You never want to stand up in public and make a speech on a topic where someone in the audience may know more about the topic than you do. The mere suspicion of such a possibility would undermine your confidence.

It has been estimated that if you were to spend 15 minutes a day studying a given topic for two years, you would know more than 99 percent of the population on that particular area of expertise. When determining whether or not you want to stand up and speak on a given topic, ask yourself the following:

- Do I feel as if I can speak authoritatively on this topic?
- Do I have third-party sources I can quote to validate my points?
- Do I have experiences I can tell to affirm these points?
- Do my ideas make sense on both a rational and an intuitive level?
- If questioned, do I have a storehouse of background and additional material I can cite to validate my case?

MISTAKE #6—FAILING TO PREPARE

We would be remiss to talk about public-speaking preparation without addressing the environment and circumstances in which you will deliver. Here is the STOP acronym that Gary uses in speaker training. He says this acronym reminds financial professionals to stop and thoroughly think through these practical preparations for a talk.

- *Situation.* The physical setting of the presentation: room setup, the audience, LCD projector, flip charts, seating arrangements, refreshments, etc.
- *Time.* No one wants a speaker to go too long!
- *Objections.* Anticipate any possible objections an audience may have.
- *Presentation materials.* Plan and prepare for needed materials. Make sure you have an ample supply—running out of materials is very embarrassing.

As you prepare your speech and for the event you will deliver it in, keep in mind the STOP sign; it could save you from a head-on collision in the middle of your presentation.

We may seem to be incessantly beating the drum of preparation, but here again, we face another challenge in public speaking that is rooted in research and groundwork. We have witnessed many financial professionals who have tried to stand up and deliver a message on a topic where you could sense the uncertainty while they delivered. Either they weren't familiar enough with the material so that it flowed naturally, or they lacked practical experience with the ideas they were speaking on.

No audience member coming to a finance-related speech wants to hear theories. They want to hear about ideas that have strong evidence from both a factual and an empirical basis. They want to hear about ideas that have instant application in their lives. They want relevance. If you know an idea so well that you can immediately establish relevance and talk for an hour about that topic without ever having to read a note, then you are ready to stand up and deliver.

The ability to connect with your audience boils down to believability. People are not just hearing what you say, but how you say it. A certain swagger comes with knowing a topic well, and when the audience sees the swagger, they know they are going to learn something from you. Your preparedness breeds confidence, which is instantly transferred to your listeners. No shortcuts to this brand of connective prowess exist. Prepare yourself to the point that when you pick up the microphone and begin to talk, the audience knows instantly that you are in your zone.

Setting the Hook

If you don't strike oil in the first ten minutes, stop boring.

—George Jessel

What you say at the beginning of your speech will make or break you. It's terribly difficult to start bad and finish strong. Those first remarks are critical especially when viewed through the lens of personal relevance. Research (Wanda Vassallo, *Speaking with Confidence*, 1990) has shown that you only have four minutes to prove yourself as a speaker. In those opening moments, the audience decides whether or not you are worth the time they spent.

While you can gather momentary attention from an audience either by being a dynamic personality but lacking content or by possessing relevant content but lacking speaking dynamics, neither attention span will last long. It has been said that grabbing an audience is kind of like catching snakes. If you grab them by the back of the neck, you have them free and clear, but if you miss that first lunge, you might end up dead. If you manage to grab the audience from the outset, you have a good chance of holding onto them throughout the speech. But if you lose them at the outset, you're better off sitting down.

The audience has given you their time, but their attention is something you'll have to earn.

—Michael Klepper

The beginning of your speech must act as a lightning rod for their attention and interest. You establish a lightning rod by showing your audience how your talk will *specifically* help them—for a speech about everything is a talk about nothing. Author Peggy Noonan compared such a talk to a miner's packhorse that is so loaded down with supplies that it collapses before it can reach the gold mine. Your first objective in every speech is to set the hook with an irresistible lure that has great bearing in the life of the listener. You don't need many lures—you just need one good one.

WHY THE FISH DON'T BITE

The best method for setting the hook we know of is to lead with a "disturber," a thought or an idea that knocks the listeners off their center of gravity. The disturber is the lure. Human nature is to disregard what we are hearing until we understand the relevance to our own lives. One of the most common errors we see with speakers is the failure to properly disturb their audience. If the members of your audience were not made acutely aware that they have a problem, why would they bother to listen to your answers? Create or animate the problem before you attempt to fix it.

Your speech should solve a big problem, not a little one. As a matter of opinion, we would advise that if you do not have a problem to solve, then you should not give a speech. You may have clever and even interesting material. You may be a gregarious and engaging presenter. But if you do not solve a palpable problem for your audience, your words have little contextual ground to take root in. Your speech becomes clouds without rain. The occasional thunderclap and flash happens, but the listener receives no nourishment.

Your first and foremost responsibility is to establish clearly how the listener will lack, suffer, or be taking a gamble if they do not listen to what you are about to say. This disturber does not have to take place in an ominous tone. In fact, the disturber is probably most effective if delivered in a matter-of-fact fashion. For example, you could say something like, "Here is a problem we all face. Do this and you will save yourself trouble and regret. Ignore it, and you will multiply your troubles." If you can make this characterization with your speech material and then present a convincing argument with your content, you will win over your audience.

We have met many sales professionals who erroneously believe that all you have to provide for the listener is the WIIFM (What's in it for me?) factor. Speakers who follow this strategy preach benefits to their audience and expect that the audience will respond to the benefit possibilities laid before them. We have found that the majority will not. This can be explained with one simple psychological rule: people are more motivated by consequence than they are by benefit. You can lead with benefits if you wish, but we will show you a better way to motivate your audience—lead with consequences.

For example, take the man who is watching the infomercial on TV that shows the slim and trim physique, the improved attitude, and the bountiful babes that will pursue him if he buys this particular piece of exercise equipment. He picks up the phone, rattles off his Visa number, and begins to envision the benefits of burning those 35 pounds of excess baggage. Six months later his exercise machine is for sale, and he's now 45 pounds overweight.

Now, picture this same man going to the doctor who tells him his weight has become a serious health risk, especially given his genetic predisposition to heart trouble. Now, he's thinking of his widow and fatherless child. Six months later, he is 45 pounds lighter.

Glen, a financial professional, tells the story of how he used to try to cajole undisciplined clients with visions of easy retirement living—only to watch them perpetuate their spend-first-and-invest-later manner of living. Glen decided he needed to rock their thinking. He began to show his clients scenarios of people in retirement years, short on income and long on stress, who had put off investing. These people have to work long, hard hours in retirement, can't afford the best health care, and do not get any help from their children because they'd neglected to save for their children's education as well. Glen said that when he started showing real-life consequences, he started getting better responses from these procrastinating souls. Why? Because consequence is a superior motivator to benefit. Blissful infomercial images could not accomplish what a doctor's warning could. Like it or not, the Homo sapiens psyche is such that fear of consequences is what gets most people to act. Most of us don't often do what we should, but we will do what we must. On the financial side, many of our clients' patterns of procrastination are repeated until they fully realize the consequences of their inaction. Your job is to make it painfully clear as to what the consequences are—and then how to avoid them. If you don't paint a vivid enough picture of the consequences, the fish simply won't bite and all the reeling you do in your talk is futile.

Fear, Uncertainty, and Doubt

When electronic locks were first introduced in automobiles, some car salespeople had trouble selling them to customers who couldn't, in their mind, justify spending a couple of hundred extra dollars for such a "luxury." Conversely, other salespeople sold them without any trouble to every customer they talked with. When the sales tactics of these two groups were compared, the only difference found was that the unsuccessful group sold benefit, while the successful group sold consequence. The benefits promoters talked about the convenience and the glamour of all-electronic security in the automobile. The customers quickly ran a cost versus benefit analysis, and in their minds, frequently decided against this luxury. However, the consequence crowd used this approach:

> "If you've ever taken a ride in a not-so-desirable neighborhood, come to a stop sign, and felt the anxiety of strange eyes staring down you and your family, you'll understand why people opt for electronic locks. In a moment like that, you don't want to be trying to reach into the back seat, fumbling around with manual locks."

When Disney resorts advertise, they could choose to promote exclusively the fun and frolicking benefits of their theme parks or cruise ships. But if you pay close attention, you will see Disney advertising that talks about consequences. "Those kids are growing up awfully fast. Where is the time going? Before you know it, they'll be grown up and gone." The parent feels the emotional pang of the fleeting years of youth and the irretrievability of the same and is motivated to book that Disney vacation.

The top financial professionals in the financial services world are those who understand this basic piece of sales psychology. When they talk about consequences, they do not use a foreboding, ominous tone. They talk about consequences calmly, almost expectantly, as their experience has shown them what will happen if people do not act. A friend of Mitch's was a master of selling life insurance policies to people who had always turned them down before. He was fond of matter-of-factly stating to the resistant male client, "I just want to make sure that Mrs. Jones is as well dressed when you're gone, as she is today." He would take the discussion no further and let the client think about it for a week or so. Inevitably, when he called the client back and brought up the life insurance issue, the client would say, "I suppose we'd better look at it."

This insurance rep was wise enough to sow the emotional seed of consequence and to let the client water it with imagination and emotion. What man wants to be accused of leaving his wife and family in worse shape when he is dead than when he is alive? None, but millions do it every year. Why? Because the people selling the product that could prevent this punishment have not done a good job of illustrating and animating consequence.

The Inconsequential Speech

Twelve years ago, Mitch heard an interesting program on personality styles. After the program he walked around and talked to participants to see what they had retained from the presentation and how they would use it. He was surprised at the low level of retention for what he thought was highly applicable material. Why had the audience not seen instant applications for what they had learned? They found the material interesting but not critical to their success. Mitch thought the material to be highly critical to success in building relationships and set about discerning where and how the presenter had failed to communicate this fact.

When Mitch thought about the introduction to the workshop, the coin dropped. The facilitator had only preached benefit. He had failed to address the consequences of not understanding why certain personalities have trouble connecting and the ultimate cost in business of a failure to connect. Mitch took the information and developed a way of presenting it that immediately alerts the business professional to the price of not being aware of personality-based conflict and the role it plays in client attraction and retention. The result has been the T.E.A.M. Dynamics presentation that we both present and that is very popular with financial professionals. Audiences love the presentation because they immediately see how this knowledge can help them in their business.

Here is how we set the hook for this presentation.

- First, we talk about a study that shows that 87 percent of the people who leave their financial professionals do so because of the relationship, and over 90 percent of those who left said they were happy with the returns.
- Next, we talk about how brain science has demonstrated that people have an emotional reaction before they have a rational reaction when we are speaking to them, which makes creating a positive first emotional impression all the more important.
- Next, we show the research on personality style. We reveal that we have about a 50 percent chance of achieving a favorable impression because of the preferences and biases of the four basic personality styles.
- We then talk about how interviews with each personality group revealed that each group had a preferred approach in selling situations and that failure to approach them in this manner acted as an impediment in the process.
- Next, we give a couple of quick examples of this personality clash we often face with clients.

All this material is covered in the first ten minutes of our presentation. By the time we reach this point, the hook is well set in the audience psyche. The listeners are now anxious to learn specifically what their personality persuasion is, which groups find their particular style to be annoying, and how they can build relational bridges with those styles that they struggle with. The consequences of not understanding this material are clear, and the audience is fully tuned to the rest of the presentation.

Most successful presentations follow this formula. Without fully realizing the consequences of *not* following your advice, the audience will find your material inconsequential.

WHAT'S MINE IS MINE

Michael Kaselnak, a financial services professional, has learned to put this principle to great gain for both his clients and his advisory business by offering a program for seniors titled, "Take Your Hands Off My Piece of the Pie." Michael saw an emotional trend with his senior clients—age and the accumulation of assets had put their psyche in a highly protectionist mode. They were not as interested in growth and accumulation as his younger clients were. They just wanted to ensure that they could keep what they had worked so hard and long to gain. Michael looked at all the threats to their wealth:

- Abundant taxation because of poor financial planning
- Overzealous, misguided, and sometimes incompetent vendors of insurance and investment products
- Imposing children who thought their parents had swallowed a stupid pill when they turned 65
- Probate courts that swallowed their fortunes because of a lack of preparation

Sensing the threat these seniors felt, Michael decided to offer the "Take Your Hands Off My Piece of the Pie" seminar. He sent out a mailer to residents over the age of 55. His first seminar had an impressive turnout, and 15 members of the original audience became clients. He now repeats this process four times a year and has seen his business grow tenfold in less than three years. He now works *only* with clients in this age group, because he has formed an expertise in communicating with them.

His idea works for two simple reasons that are highly pertinent to making client connections. One, he has identified a genuine emotional motivator for a demographic that controls the majority of wealth in this nation, and second, his message centers on consequences. No one wants to lose what they worked so hard to earn. No one wants to pay income taxes unnecessarily. No one wants to see his or her estate plundered. No one wants others meddling in their financial affairs. No one wants to be taken advantage of. Michael Kaselnak has helped clients avoid these consequences. The hook is set by the time they read his mailing.

FROM THE HEART

Years ago a journalist saw the late mayor of New York, Jimmy Walker, dazzle an audience by saying, "Ladies and gentleman, I arrived here this evening with some written remarks, but I've decided to discard my prepared speech and speak to you from the heart." With that, Walker balled up the paper he had been holding and tossed it aside. He went on to deliver an electrifying speech. After Walker and his entourage left, the journalist picked up the discarded "speech" and looked at it. The paper was nothing more than an advertisement. Walker had spoken from memorized remarks freshened with observations he had made about the people, theme, and event.

—Laurie E. Rosakis (*The Complete Idiot's Guide to Speaking in Public with Confidence,* 1995)

Although we have mentioned the topic of passion and enthusiasm in previous chapters, we would be loath not to bring it up in this discussion of capturing an audience's interest and attention. Assuming you have developed a presentation that meets a real need, fixes a real problem, and properly disturbs your audience, the chief intangible you must now address is how heartfelt your presentation is. This intangible factor plays a major role in setting the hook in the attention center of the brain. What is your audience looking for? Can they see that you are a person on a mission? Does your material seem to flow from the center of your being? Does your audience get the impression that you are deriving satisfaction from helping them to address their problems? These intuitive questions are being processed somewhere in the limbic portion of your listeners' brain. Passion about your material sets off a flare in their brain and stirs the desire to know what you are so excited or intensely concerned about.

People cry during inspirational moments in a movie because they love to see someone express noble sentiment. They like to see people become passionate about the things that are worth being passionate about. Do your opening remarks make people want to follow you like a fire truck, or do your words make them want you to get out of the way like a sluggish snowplow? You will not receive a second chance to make this first emotional impression. Your opening comments need to indicate to your audience that you have skin in the game—that this is not just a nice little talk that you're giving. Before developing a talk that you will give publicly, ask yourself these questions:

- What issues or ideas do I feel passionate about?
- Have I gathered sufficient expertise regarding these topics?
- Do I convey the enthusiasm I feel when talking about these ideas, or do I squelch it?

People are more engaged to listen to a person who feels passionate about a topic, even if they are not rationally inclined to agree with the speaker's ideas or opinions. When you give your audience the impression that this is more than just a talk, you have created a magnetic emotional field between you and your listeners—and the hook is set. Capture their attention by disturbing their lethargy regarding financial well-being, and capture their emotion by being passionate and purposeful. You've got 4 minutes to get this done. If you don't accomplish it in those 4 minutes, you can't say much in the next 56 minutes that will make up for it.

CHAPTER 22

In the Palm of Your Hand

The Dynamics of Connecting with the Masses and Moving Past Fear

The teenage crowd sat momentarily in what seemed to be a stunned silence. The crowd of nearly 1,000 teenagers—a mixed canvas of black, brown, and white faces—were all staring at me. Every eye seemed to be telling me they heard and understood every word.

Somewhere in the crowd, one set of hands began a slow, pensive clap as if pulling out of a hypnotic trance. Another set of hands joined in, and another, and another. Suddenly all 2,000 hands were united in a melodic storm of applause. It was a slow, methodical sound. It wasn't a "Way to go Joe—we're fired up" kind of applause. It was an affirmation saying, "I feel it—you found me where I live." It kept building until it rang like thunder in my ears. Somebody shouted out "Yes!" and suddenly, there was yelling, stomping, and clapping until the walls of the gymnasium reverberated.

I was flushed with a blend of embarrassment and gratitude. For years, I had been speaking in public but had never experienced this kind of unanimous connection. I was feeling self-conscious so I turned to the dean of students. Just an hour earlier, she had been having an anxiety attack about how these students would respond. The school had never assembled this group in one place before, for fear of losing control. But now she had tears streaming down her cheeks, and she was shaking her head incredulously at the students' response. She looked at me and gently turned her palms up toward the crowd as if to say, "Yield to them—this is their message to you."

It went on for four of the longest minutes of my life.

—Mitch Anthony

As Mitch drove home that day, he began to see how this magical process of mass audience connection really worked. The speech he had given that day was a big risk. The first time he had ever given it, he was delivering under highly tempestuous circumstances. Mitch had become highly dissatisfied with the unpredictable results he had been getting from his speeches for the last eight years. Sometimes he received hearty applause, and other times he received lukewarm approval. He grew restless and dissatisfied knowing there was higher ground, but not knowing how to get there. He had spent several months studying the greatest public speakers he could find in a quest to try to unlock the specific elements or dynamics that could place a crowd in the palm of a speaker's hand.

Mitch's search for the right pieces had taken him to the other side of the world where he heard an Irishman, who was living in Australia, give a speech that offered everything he was looking for in one, moving speech. In two short hours, every element Mitch had been missing in his own speaking career crystallized in his mind.

In an article on right-brain persuasion techniques, Mitch wrote:

> I sat transfixed as the Irishman took the crowd through a journey of the joys and sorrows of his life. His stories painted emotional details that made my heart race at times and ache at others. When he drew to a close I looked at my watch—two and a half hours had passed! It had seemed as if 30 minutes had gone by. No one had moved, and no one wanted to move now. How had he done it? This is what I wanted—this magic of making a tangible connection with the audience. It came to me in a flash. I knew what my biggest problems were. The first was that I was an American.
>
> Not my nationality, but rather the manner of speech that I possessed as an American, handicapped me as a speaker. The Irishman, as all Irish do, had a beautiful, lilting, melodic brogue. Listening to him was like listening to a concert that built to a crescendo. Not a single note was wasted. With the melody and rhythm of his natural brogue, this speaker had literally hypnotized my attention. As I listened to him talk, I could literally count out 4/4 time in his speech. This rhythm explains why the Irish are so renowned for their ability to capture imagination and emotion with their stories. I had seen firsthand how the average Irishman in a pub is a better communicator than most paid professional speakers in America, present company included. And now I knew exactly why.
>
> We Americans are generally in a hurry—and the machine-gun delivery of our speech reflects this fact. With few exceptions, such as the Dixie brogue, very little rhythm is to be found in American speech. Rather than being musical in quality, it sounds industrial, like a machine pounding out components. I decided I would take

the Irish rhythm, incorporate it into my Midwestern accent, and observe the effect it had on the crowds I spoke to.

I learned and borrowed a second element from the Irishman. He had completely won over his audience. He had drawn us in with his rhythm, but he had kept us in the palm of his hand with his humanness. He told stories that showed his imperfections, his vulnerability, and even his insecurity. Even his humor, which was plentiful, was at his own expense. He gave us all permission to laugh with him at the sometimes ridiculous portrait he painted of himself. We could identify with his humanness, for we have the same feelings lurking just below our skin. An emotional partnership was formed and we were with him, identifying with every experience he shared. We had shared both in his victories and his defeats because of the way he chose to share them.

Those two keys—a mesmerizing rhythm of speech and the stories that make us human—are the elements of connecting with an audience that will take a speaker to a place that few orators experience. It is a place of total and complete connection with the emotions, imaginations, hopes, and failings of the audience. As soon as I returned to America, I designed and delivered a speech around these two elements. I laughed at myself. I told stories that exposed my sense of inferiority and fear of failure. I stopped trying to make myself look good in front of the audience and decided to look human. My first words were spoken in purposeful 4/4 time and I continued the rhythm in a subtle fashion throughout the speech. I decided to test the method in the most threatening speaking circumstances I could find—a notoriously unruly group of 1,000 teenagers. If it would work with this audience, it would work with anyone. I was stunned at how quickly and effectively these two dynamics went to work.

As a speaker I had unwittingly made the classic misassumption that they were here to hear about me. They were not. They were there to hear about themselves. I had to start where they were and take them where I wanted them to go. The day I heard that Irishman was one of the luckiest days of my life.

No doubt the Irish have a distinct jump on speaking skills with their melodic rhythm. But you can build a better sense of rhythm into your speeches too. Approach the art of achieving effective rhythm with your audience the way a rider develops rhythm on a horse. A skilled rider understands that, though the pace may change, he must maintain a sense of rhythm while he progresses from the walk to the trot to the canter and on to the full gallop. What your rhythm does is to set a pace for the ears and heart of the audience. When your talk is in a "canter" and you suddenly say, "And what we really need to do to secure our future is . . .", you bring that horse to a sudden stop. You have achieved the dramatic pause, and the audience is hanging on with all their might.

Good speakers pay attention to content and articulation. Great speakers pay attention to those elements but add the dynamics of musical, hypnotic rhythm, as well as self-revelation to reach a rare level of power.

FROM GOOD TO GREAT

If you are serious about going from the place where you can give a pretty good talk to the place where you make a vital connection and lasting impression with your audience, you will want to pay close attention to the observations we share here about highly effective presenters. Those who have mastered the art of capturing and holding the crowd's full attention are more than students of speaking—they are students of the human condition.

Speakers who are willing to stand up and tell you how much they know, how great they are, and how much they can help you are a dime a dozen. The speaker, however, who can readily identify with the daily dilemmas of the audience and do it from a lateral rather than superior stature is harder to find. This ability is the hallmark we have observed in all master persuaders.

The true story or the truth in your story moves the audience. You may not be telling your story, but if the story has the ring of truth and identity to it, the audience members latch on to it and hang on for hope's sake. Precisely the lack of this ability keeps many a speaker from connecting with their audience the way they could and should.

A cardinal rule that most speakers ignore is, "Speak unto others as you would have them speak unto you." We've seen many people who literally become somebody else when they step up to a microphone. It's a Jekyll and Hyde kind of thing where they lose touch with who they are in a vain attempt to impress or control an audience. In the process, they lose their relating ability, which is the only real reason anyone would want to listen to them in the first place.

Following are some tips we offer for those who wish to retain as high a degree of relatability as possible when addressing a group. By meeting with an audience beforehand, a speaker can ensure success by staying in the audience's shoes at all times. Most speakers want to cloister themselves away behind the curtain until it's show time. They are making a mistake by passing up an opportunity to grow comfortable with the audience and to let some members of their audience grow comfortable with them. Meeting your audience can help you in a number of ways.

- The people you meet will feed you material and insight for your opening comments, which can lead to an instant connection with the culture and goals of your audience.
- You will establish rapport with some friendly faces that you can seek eye contact with as you are delivering your speech.
- You will effectively break the ice with your audience so that you are no longer a stranger or an unknown to them—much like what would happen if you had attended a cocktail party with them the night before your presentation. You are, in effect, creating your own cocktail party by engaging members of the audience in conversation beforehand. These conversations tend to be more grounded and human and help to break the ice, especially for the speaker.

The audience most appreciates the speech and the speaker with whom they can identify in some way. We remember hearing Colonel Hubbard, who was in solitary confinement for years as a POW in Vietnam, tell about the fears, struggles, and survival tactics of being in a confined, claustrophobic, hopeless experience. We watched him tell his story to a large group of financial services professionals—and we watched the audience get swept away with his story. They were swept away in part because they were fascinated with the amazing test of courage he faced, but they were also swept away because they could identify with the emotional story he told. None of the financial professionals present, that we knew of, had ever been in solitary confinement (if you don't count cubicles), but they were identifying with the emotional traumas of that experience and how they confronted such emotions in their daily experience.

The key is telling a story to which the audience can emotionally relate in a manner that the audience can identify with. The more you give your audience to identify with, the greater impact your message will have. Mitch was once taken aside by a meeting organizer after addressing 3,000 teenagers and told the following, "Three months ago we brought in an Olympic champion to talk to these kids, and they hated him. He tried to make himself sound extraordinary. The kids couldn't connect emotionally and completely tuned him out. Today they connected because you talked about life right where they live. You didn't make yourself out to be something special." If the audience cannot relate to you as a human being, they will have no desire to hear your story.

LUCKY ME

Retired Lt. Col. Oliver North was heard to say at the start of a speech,
"It's nice to be invited somewhere without a subpoena."

—Joan Detz *(How to Write and Give a Speech,* 1992)

The more you try to make yourself out to be successful, the more ground you will lose with your audience. Scott West, a well-known speaker in the financial services world, argues that the greatest key to connecting with an audience is self-deprecation. Anyone who has heard Scott speak would have a hard time arguing with him, as he is a master of the self-deprecating art. He lifts up his theme by good-naturedly pounding down his persona. He often opens with comments like, "I started my career selling soap with Procter & Gamble, and if things don't pick up soon, I'll be back at it."
West states:

"The higher you make yourself appear, the lower the regard they'll have for you. The fact that you hold the microphone speaks volumes. The audience knows that whoever organized this meeting had enough faith in your ability to hand over the control of the meeting for the next hour or so. They know this was not 'open mike' night. That in itself is a notable endorsement. There really is no need for you to build yourself up. There is no need to tell the group how qualified you are. There is no need to tell stories that paint you out to be a hero. The more you try to elevate yourself in front of the audience, the farther you move from a connection with them."

One speaker stands up and justifies his presence by reading off a list of credentials and accomplishments and establishes a rational connection at the expense of an emotional connection. Another speaker gets up and says, "I may not be the sharpest saw in the shed, but I've been hanging around a long time and have made a few observations." Now the audience is emotionally and rationally connected because they too have been hanging around for a while and have made a few observations of their own.

Be it for good or evil, part of human nature is to want to bring people who begin to think too highly of themselves down to size. In Australia, they call it the *tall poppy syndrome,* where mates feel obliged to chop each other back down to the planet when they start to feel like maybe they have risen above the crowd. This instinct seems to manifest itself with audiences when speakers start to sound like they are breathing rarified air. Every speaker would serve themselves well to ask the following questions regarding their presence and presentation style:

- Are you comfortable laughing at yourself?
- Do you have a problem telling stories about mistakes you have made?
- Do you feel the need to justify your time and presence in front of the group?
- Do you feel insecure and, consequently, take yourself too seriously?
- When things go wrong in front of the group, do you take it all in stride?
- Does your intensity mask your humanity?

PERSON TO PERSON

We have heard many a speaker err on the side of intensity. They were so intent on getting their material across, or they took themselves and their mission so seriously, that their intensity caused discomfort to enter the audience. We remember specifically one student who was driving through his material with the force and speed of a freight train. He seemed like he was trying to change the world with one speech. He rattled off answers for everything with a machine-gun patter. He never smiled even when trying to be clever. All his speech seemed to reveal was his type A personality. Unwittingly, he had disengaged his audience, who gave up on even feigning interest and waited for the time to expire. In his conclusion, he told a story about how he had struggled early in his career and how a person who had become a close personal friend had come to his rescue with a great opportunity. In his entire hour of speaking, this moment was the first where this speaker had uncloaked his humanity. We noticed many people leaning forward to get the story. Their posture and attitude had turned toward the speaker in a moment—the moment that he showed he was like them. The problem was that it was too little too late. He had already alienated most of the audience because of his robotic method to public presentation.

No matter what a man's vocation or avocation may be, the nature of his
progress through life is largely dependent upon his ability to
sell. And the most important things he has to sell are himself
and his good qualities.

—Frederick W. Nichol *(The Forbes' Book
of Quotations)*

People don't come to speeches to hear laundry lists of suggestions and impersonal dos and don'ts. People come to hear stories from those who have answers to the problems that they face. They want to hear those stories from people who appear to be, in many ways, just like they are. People connect best with your ideas when they can easily connect with you as a person. Great public speaking is accomplished by bringing together both internal and external dynamics. Getting an audience into the palm of your hand is a matter of first revealing yourself to create receptivity to your ideas, and secondly delivering those ideas in a rhythm of speech that creates a unified pulse for your audience. When you come to the place where you, your material, and your rhythm are in sync, your speech will truly be music to your audience's ears.

Bibliography

Anthony, Mitch. *The New Retirementality: Planning Your Life and Living Your Dreams . . . At Any Age You Want.* Dearborn Trade, 2001.

Anthony, Mitch, and Scott West. *Storyselling for Financial Advisors: How Top Producers Sell.* Dearborn Trade, 2000.

Anthony, Mitch. *ARROW*™ Program. 2001.

Anthony, Mitch. *T.E.A.M Dynamics.* 1991.

Bierce, Ambrose. *The Devil's Dictionary.* Dover Thrift Edition, 1993.

Detz, Joan. *How to Write and Give a Speech: A Practical Guide for Executives, PR People, Managers, Fund-Raisers, Politicians, Educators, and Anyone Who Has to Make Every Word Count.* St. Martin's Press, 1992.

Forbes, Inc. *The Forbes' Book of Quotations.* Black Dog & Leventhal Publishers, 1997.

Freedman, Joshua (Illustrator), Patricia E. Freedman, and Anabel L. Jensen. *Handle with Care: Emotional Intelligence Activity Book.* Six Seconds, 1998.

Goleman, Daniel. *Emotional Intelligence.* Bloomsbury, 1995.

Hansen Weese, Karen. "In Good Company," *Investment Advisor,* October 2000, 72–78.

Klepper, Michael M. *I'd Rather Die Than Give a Speech.* Irwin Professional Publishing, 1993.

Lewis, Allyson. *The Million Dollar Car and $250,000 Pizza.* Dearborn Trade, 2000.

McKenzie, E. C. *Mac's Giant Book of Quips & Quotes.* Harvest House Publishers, 1980.

Noonan, Peggy. *Simply Speaking: How to Communicate Your Ideas, Style, Substance, & Clarity.* DIANE Publishing, 1999.

Osgood, Charles. *Osgood on Speaking—How to Think on Your Feet without Falling on Your Face.* William Morrow, 1988.

Oxford Dictionary of Quotations, The, 3rd edition. Oxford University Press, 1979.

"Pat Croce's Top Ten Business Rules," as quoted in *American Way,* 1 November 2000, 162.

Seligman, Martin. *Learned Optimism.* Random House, 1995.

Sternberg, R. *Successful Intelligence: How Practical and Creative Intelligence Determine Success in Life.* Plume, 1997.

Index

A

Abruptness, 98
Accuracy, 88–89
Acronym talk, 219
Adversity, 30
Alexander the Great, 105
Amygdala hijack, 29
Analogies, 162–64
Analyzer personality, 59–61, 68,
    100–101
    axis, 40
    common conflict responses, 107
    core-personality compromises,
        104, 105
    critical selling adjustments,
        86–89
    liabilities, 117
    signals, 74–75
Anecdotes, 88, 90, 161–62
Anthony, Mitch, 13, 18, 128, 135,
    164, 172, 191, 203, 206, 215–16,
    222, 235–37
Armstrong, Louis, 181
Arrogance, 32–33
ARROW Program™, 24–27
Assumptions, 134–36
Attitude, 19
Audience
    attitudes/interests of, 213–14
    connecting with, 233–42
    "disturbing," 193, 228
    knowledge of, 211–16
    lexicon of language, 215–16
    needs/wants of, 214–15
Awareness, 25, 28–29, 53–54

B

Bach, David, 169, 182
Bierce, Ambrose, 127, 218

BIT test, 184
Blanchard, Ken, 182
Body language, 34, 75
Body movement, 205
Borg, Bjorn, 115
Brain
    design of, 147
    research, 151–52
Buffett, Warren, 158, 160

C

Candor, 96
Charisma, 13–21
    hope and, 20–21
    impressions, 15–17
    passion and youthfulness, 18–19
    positive energy, 19–20
    reality and, 17
    respect for others, 17–18
Client(s)
    see also Client connections;
        Critical selling adjustments;
        Personality
    clarifying interests of, 136
    client/financial professional
        conversations, 127–28
    conversation profile, 69, 70
    focus on, 145
    goals of, 139–40
    identifying personality style of,
        68–71
    meeting and greeting, 13–21
    personality profile of, 38, 39
    perspective of, 79
    relationships, 6
    senior, 18, 232
Client connections, 5–7
    calculating potential, 9
    conversation skills, 8–9
    dynamic, 8, 10–11

emotional intelligence and. See
    Emotional intelligence
    opportunities for, 8–10
Close, of presentation, 186–87
Coachability, 32–33
Comfort zones, 94–95, 102, 108,
    145, 148
    vernacular and, 82, 83, 86, 89,
        92
Communication/communication skills
    see also Critical selling
        adjustments
    challenges and obstacles, 80
    client/financial professional
        conversations, 127–28
    communicating value, 5
    empathy and, 33–34
    eyes and, 19
    opportunities, 8–10
    personality-based, 99–108
    storytelling and, 157–64
Competency, 14, 84
Competition, 91
*Complete Idiot's Guide to Speaking
    in Public with Confidence, The*
    (Rosakis), 233
Compliments, 16
Compromise, 103–5
Confidence, 84–86, 203
Conflict management/resolution,
    99–108, 143–50
    connecting in conflict, 109–19
    empathy and, 33, 99–102
    intuitive leap, 148–50
    linear logic-jam, 146–48
    negotiation and, 35
    personality-based tendencies,
        105–8
    polar opposites as origin of,
        50–51
    recognition of motivators and, 35
    stress in the workplace, 102–8

Confrontational rules of thumb,
110–19
determining an "I" or "we"
problem, 112–13
give credit/take blame, 111–12
humble approach, 114–19
self-deprecating humor, 113–14
transparency, 110
Connections. *See* Client connections
Connelly, Don, 201
Consequences, as motivators, 229,
231–32
Consistency, 89
Control, 85
Controversy, 83
Conversation profile, 69, 70–71
Conviction, 167–75
Critical selling adjustments, 79–92
Analyzer personality, 86–89
Enterpriser personality, 83–86
Motivator personality, 89–92
Togetherness personality, 80–83
Croce, Pat, 15–16
Curiosity, 32, 126–27
Customization, 86
Cynicism, 32

D

Deadlines, 96
Decision making
emotions and, 33, 144–46, 150
intuitive leap and, 148–50
Delivery (presentations), 199–207
entertainment value, 200–201
style elements, 202–7
DeMoss, Gary, 4, 153–54, 174, 206,
224
Demotivators, awareness of, 35
Dent, Harry, 182
Detail, attention to, 97
Diplomacy, 105
Disappointment, 30
Discipline, 219
Discouragement, 30
Disney resorts, 230
"Disturbing" the audience, 193, 228
Domini Social Equity Fund, 129
Douglas, Stephen, 177–78
Dramatic pause, 205
Dynamic telling, 6

E

Education, presentations and, 200
Einstein, Albert, 189

Elderly clients, 18, 232
Emotion(s), 29, 87
anchoring presentations to,
191–92
decision making and, 33,
144–46, 150
discussing, 17
emotional agenda, 145
money and, 130
Emotional intelligence, 23–35
awareness, 28–29
communication and. *See*
Critical selling adjustments
competencies, 24–28
empathy and, 33–34
increasing, 35
principles of, 23
profile (ARROW), 27
recognition and restraint, 29–30
resilience and, 30–33
social skills and, 34–35
success and, 28–35
Emotional Intelligence (Goleman),
23
Empathy, 23, 25, 28, 33–34,
99–102
Energy, positive, 19–20
Enterpriser personality, 56–59, 68
axis, 40
common conflict responses,
106–7
core-personality compromises,
103, 104
critical selling adjustments,
83–86
liabilities, 116–17
signals, 73–74, 100–101
Enthusiasm, 171–72, 233–34
Ethos, 196
Exaggeration, 87
Expectations, 105
Eyes
communication and, 19
effect of, on audience, 202–3
eye contact, personalities and,
72, 73, 74, 75

F

Facts, 87
Failure, 30
Financial professionals, client
expectations of, 131
First impressions, 15–17
Flattery, 73
Franklin, Benjamin, 118, 146, 160
Fun, 16

G

Gold mines, 128
Goleman, Daniel, 23, 29, 99
Graham, Benjamin, 160
Great Boom Ahead, The (Dent), 182

H

Hackneyed material, 222–23
Harrison, William Henry, 217
Honesty, 110
Hope, 20–21, 196–97
Hornung, Paul, 138
Human brain, 147
Human drama, the, 8
Humility, 114–19
Humor, 19, 83, 91, 161–62
self-deprecation, 113–14, 240–41
Hyperbole, 86, 88

I

I'd Rather Die Than Give a Speech
(Klepper), 179
Impatience, 58
Imposter syndrome, 114
Impressions, 15–17
Improvisation, 214
Impulsiveness, 62
Innovation, 57
Inquiry skills, 34
Intelligence Quotient, 23–24
Intensity, 241
Introspection, 205
Intuitive leap, 148–50
Investing, personal guidelines and, 129
IQ, 23–24
Irish speakers, 204, 236–37

J–K

Jesus, 160
Jones, Edward D., 170
Kaselnak, Michael, 232
King, Martin Luther Jr., 160
Kissinger, Henry, 179–80
Klepper, Michael, 179, 211, 227

L

Land mines, 128, 157
Language
lexicon of, 35

poor judgment with, 221
recognition skills, 34
Laughter, 17, 33, 113
Learned Optimism (Seligman), 30
Lewis, Allyson, 158
Lexicon, 215–16
LIFE Inventory, 131
Likability, 13–14
Lincoln, Abraham, 3, 19, 168,
177–78
Linear sales process, 146–48
Listening skills, 34
Logos, 196
Lombardi, Vince, 138
Longest yard, the, 6
Longfellow, Henry Wadsworth,
137
Long-winded speeches, 218–20

M

Mastering the Short Game (Pelz),
182
Metaphors, 90, 158–61
Mikez, Steve, 177, 180, 182–83,
184, 195
*Million Dollar Car and $250,000
Pizza, The* (Lewis), 158
Mining your life, 154–55, 184–85
Mishel, Walter, 24
Mistakes, admitting, 17
Mohammed, Gary, 32
Money, 20–21
Monotony, 98
Motivation
awareness of motivators, 35
consequence over benefit, 229,
231
extrinsic *vs.* intrinsic, 32
motivational triggers, 93–98
moving toward action,
143–50
recognition and, 111
Motivator personality, 61–63, 68,
100–101
axis, 40
common conflict responses,
108
core-personality compromises,
104, 105
critical selling adjustments,
89–92
liabilities, 117
signals, 75–77
Mr. Market metaphor, 160–61
Multitasking, 57, 94
MVP Approach, 67–68, 125–26

N

Narcissism, 33, 98, 127
Negative situations, 32
Negativity, 90
Negotiation
conflict resolution and, 35
voice quality and, 203
New Retirementality, The (Anthony),
183
Noonan, Peggy, 228
North, Oliver, 240
NYSE Rule 405, 38

O

Observational skills, 33–34, 68–71
One-Minute Manager, The
(Blanchard), 182
Opportunity, 8–10
Optimism, 30, 92
Overpreparation, 218
Oversimplification, 97

P

Palmer, Bethany, 20
Palmer, Scott, 20
Paralysis by analysis, 60
Passion, 18–19, 233–34
Pathos, 196
Pauses, dramatic, 205
Pelz, Dave, 182
Performance standards, 97
Perseverance, 175
Personality
Analyzer personality, 38,
59–61, 74–75, 104, 105, 107,
117
balance grids, 46–49
comfort zones of, 102
connecting ours with others,
37–51
critical selling adjustments. *See*
Critical selling adjustments
Enterpriser personality, 40,
56–59, 73–74, 103, 104,
106–7, 116–17
leading/supporting/villain roles,
41–43
Motivator personality, 40,
61–63, 75–77, 104, 105, 108,
117
personality axis, 38, 40
personality DNA, 53–54, 68
polar opposites, 50–51

relational results profile, 45, 50
signals, 67–77
stressors/motivators of, 93–98
styles, 231
Togetherness personality, 38,
54–56, 71–72, 103, 104, 106,
116
Personal style, 202–7
Perspective, 34
Persuasion, 4, 7–8, 119
personal conviction and,
167–75
right brain persuasion
techniques, 236–37
Pessimism, 30
Plagiarism, 221–22
Planning a presentation, 189–97
establishing a destination,
190–92
giving listeners hope, 196–97
mastering the presentation,
193–95
points of interest, 195–96
Playfulness, 98
Polar opposites, 50–51
Positive energy, 16, 19–20
PowerPoint, 205–6
Predictability, 43–44, 88–89, 96, 191
Preparation, 175, 177–87, 224–25
material, studying, 179–81
steps, 178–87
theme, building, 182–83
Presentation(s)
see also Speeches/speaking
anchoring to emotion, 191–92
animating, 158–64
assuming nothing, 134–36
body of, 183–84
bridging gaps, 138–41
close, 186–87
delivery style, 199–207
dynamic, 11
enthusiasm and, 171–72
knowledge of target, 133–34
levels of address, 195–96
life simplification, 136–38
materials for, 224
mining your life, 184–85
MVP Approach, 125–26
opener, 183
personal conviction and,
167–75
planning, 189–97
preparation and, 177–87,
219–20, 224–25
problem-solving and, 172–73
revealing characters and
dramas, 124–32
stages of one-on-one, 195

summarizing, 87
theme, 182–83
Pressure, 57–58, 96
Problem solving, 172–73
Procrastination, 152
Professionalism, 16, 85
Promptness, 16
Props, 205–7
Public-speaking skills, 8, 10–11
Purpose, 169

Q–R

Quality control, 60
Quality of life, 4
Rapport, 23, 33
Rationality, 144–45, 147–48, 150, 152
Recognition, 25, 29–30, 32, 111–12
Red tape, 96
Rehearsal, 220–21
Relationship building, 6, 67
Relevance, 224–25, 228
Resilience, 23, 25, 31–33
Respect, 14, 18, 80, 83, 94
Response skills, 34
Restraint, 25, 29–30, 105
Results, 86
Retention, 230–32
Rhythm, of speech, 236–37
Right brain persuasion techniques, 236–37
Rigidity, 60
Risk tolerance, 80, 85
Roaring 2000s, The (Dent), 182
Rogers, Will, 17, 161
Roles, 41–43
Roosevelt, Theodore, 5, 156
Rosakis, Laurie E., 233
Rules, 97

S

Sales process, linear, 146–48
Sales psychology, 230
Seale, Lamar III, 170
Securities and Exchange Commission (SEC), 153
Self-absorption, 33
Self-assessment (ARROW), 26
Self-confidence, 161–62
Self-deprecation, 113–14, 240–41
Self-esteem, 4
Self-knowledge, 173–74
Self-mastery, 29–30

Seligman, Martin, 30
Sensitivity, 38
Sestina, John, 131
Shtick, 200–201
Simplification, 136–38
Sincerity, 80, 83
Skepticism, 60
Smart Women Finish Rich (Bach), 169, 182
Smiling, 19–20, 90
Social aspect, of business, 91
Socially Responsible Investing, 129
Social skills, 25, 34–35
Speak Performance, 8, 11, 145–46
Speeches/speaking
    see also Presentation(s)
    mistakes, 217–25
    opening comments, 233
    retention of material, 230–32
    rhythm and, 236–37
    setting the hook, 227–34
    style elements, 202–7
Sperry, Roger, 151
Sternberg, R., 23
STOP acronym, 224
Stores, 90
Storyselling for Financial Advisors (West and Anthony), 128, 135, 164
Storytelling, 151–64, 204, 206
    analogies, 162–64
    anecdotes, 161–62
    communication and, 157–64
    drawing out client's story, 157
    humanizing effect of, 237
    illustration, 158
    life questionnaire, 155
    metaphors, 158–61
Stress, 20, 102–8
Style elements, 202–7
    body/props/tools, 205–7
    dramatic pause, 205
    eyes, 202–3
    voice, 203–4
Success, EQ and IQ factors of, 23–24
Successful Intelligence (Sternberg), 23
Suspicion, of motives, 110

T

Tall poppy syndrome, 240–41
Taskey, Todd, 214
T.E.A.M. Dynamics, 43–44, 79, 115, 186

10 (movie), 18
Theme, building, 182–83
Togetherness personality, 54–56, 68, 100–101
    axis, 38, 40
    common conflict responses, 106
    core-personality compromises, 103, 104
    critical selling adjustments, 80–83
    liabilities, 116
    risk tolerance of, 80
    signals, 71–72
    stressors and motivators of, 94–95
    word choice and, 82–83
"Top Ten Business Rules" (Croce), 16
Transparency, 110
Truman, Bess, 221
Truman, Harry, 221
Trust, 23, 80
Twain, Mark, 73, 190, 211–12

V

Values, 5, 67, 125, 127–31
Van Kampen, Bob, 170–71
Van Kampen Investments, 8, 170
Vasallo, Wanda, 227
Vernacular
    Analyzer personality and, 89
    Enterpriser personality and, 86
    Motivator personality and, 92
    Togetherness personality and, 82, 83
Villain role, 43
Visualization, 152
Voice quality/patterns, 72, 73, 75, 76, 203–4

W–Z

Walker, Jimmy, 233
Weese, Karen Hansen, 214
West, Scott, 127, 135, 164, 201, 240
What's in It for Me principle, 134
Wisdom, 155–57
Wit, 33
Women, wealth and, 169
Word choice, 35
Youthfulness, 18–19
Zealousness, 88

Share the message!

Bulk discounts
Discounts start at only 10 copies. Save up to 55% off retail price.

Custom publishing
Private label a cover with your organization's name and logo.
Or, tailor information to your needs with a custom pamphlet
that highlights specific chapters.

Ancillaries
Workshop outlines, videos, and other products are available on
select titles.

Dynamic speakers
Engaging authors are available to share their expertise and insight
at your event.

Call Dearborn Trade Special Sales at
1-800-245-BOOK (2665)
or e-mail trade@dearborn.com

Dearborn™
Trade Publishing
A **Kaplan Professional** Company

DATE DUE

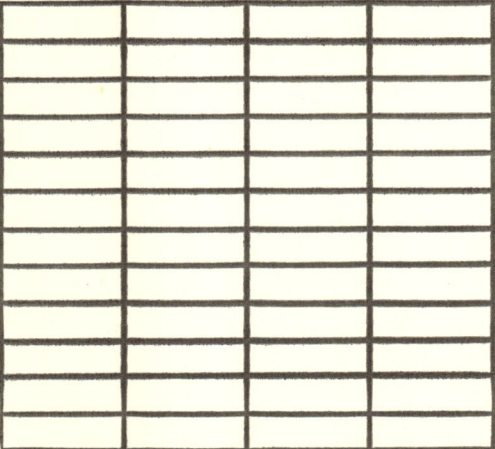

Florida Metropolitan University

Pinellas Campus

2471 McMullen Booth Rd.

Clearwater, FL 33759

DEMCO